The Life of Kings

The Life of Kings

The *Baltimore Sun* and the Golden
Age of the American Newspaper

Edited by Frederic B. Hill
and Stephens Broening

ROWMAN & LITTLEFIELD
Lanham · Boulder · New York · London

Published by Rowman & Littlefield
A wholly owned subsidiary of The Rowman & Littlefield Publishing Group, Inc.
4501 Forbes Boulevard, Suite 200, Lanham, Maryland 20706
www.rowman.com

Unit A, Whitacre Mews, 26-34 Stannary Street, London SE11 4AB

British Library Cataloguing in Publication Information Available

Library of Congress Cataloging-in-Publication Data

Names: Hill, Frederic B., editor. | Broening, Stephens, editor.
Title: The life of kings : the Baltimore sun and the golden age of the American
  newspaper / Frederic B. Hill and Stephens Broening [editors]
Description: Lanham, Maryland : Rowman & Littlefield, 2016. | Includes index.
Identifiers: LCCN 2016004838 (print) | LCCN 2016006823 (ebook) | ISBN
  9781442262560 (cloth : alk. paper) | ISBN 9781442268784 (Electronic) | ISBN
  9781538122167 (paper : alk. paper)
Subjects: LCSH: Baltimore sun—History—20th century. | Journalists—Maryland—
  Baltimore—Biography.
Classification: LCC PN4899.B3 S765 2016 (print) | LCC PN4899.B3 (ebook) | DDC
  071.526—dc23
LC record available at http://lccn.loc.gov/2016004838

♾™ The paper used in this publication meets the minimum requirements of American National Standard for Information Sciences—Permanence of Paper for Printed Library Materials, ANSI/NISO Z39.48-1992.

Printed in the United States of America

As I look back over a misspent life, I find myself more and more convinced that I had more fun doing news reporting than in any other enterprise. It is really the life of kings.

—H. L. Mencken

Contents

Preface

Good ideas come along in unexpected ways. The spark for this book occurred one day in May 2012, when a close friend and former colleague at the *Baltimore Sun*, Jeff Price, and I were reminiscing about good old days at the paper.

It was just before the 2012 Preakness Stakes, the second leg of horse racing's Triple Crown. We talked about poker games and characters at the *Sun*. We talked about travels together in Spain, Portugal, and then the Middle East where Jeff was the resident *Sun* correspondent and I was visiting with Senator Charles "Mac" Mathias Jr. after I'd left the *Sun* in 1985. We laughed about the Preakness in 1972, when we forgot to follow up on a tip to bet on a longshot named Bee Bee Bee, a little-known Maryland horse who bested the Kentucky Derby winner, Riva Ridge.

Recalling those heady days in 2012, as we handicapped the upcoming Preakness, I told Jeff that he really should write a book on his numerous and amusing exploits.

Jeff, or G. Jefferson Price III as his distinctive byline appeared, demurred that day—and once or twice more in e-mail exchanges. But after his second rebuff, I began thinking of the many interesting experiences that so many of our colleagues had had—and that it was too bad so few of them would ever be shared with the public. My muse was aided by the fact that the *Baltimore Sun* had become a pale shadow of the outstanding paper it used to be after several purchases by more bottom-line oriented corporations. By 2012, the *Sun* had no foreign correspondents when it once had as many as nine foreign bureaus strung across the world, no one in Washington where it once had a staff of fifteen, and a once huge local staff that had been decimated.

Soon, I began plotting to put together a collection of essays that would reflect the better days of the newspaper—which I had joined in 1965 and worked for until 1985—as a reporter, foreign correspondent, and editorial writer. Joining forces with Stephens Broening, the first Op-Ed page editor at the *Sun* and later its diplomatic correspondent, we launched plans for a full-fledged compendium of essays by twenty-five leading journalists at the *Sun*. We had two rules. We would recruit only those who had spent a substantial portion of their careers at the *Sun*, and we would ask each person to write interesting stories about a telltale slice of their experiences which would reflect the paper's remarkable commitment to first-rate journalism. This volume is the result of an enthusiastic response from virtually everyone we invited to participate.

* * *

The advent of the Internet and 24/7 cable television has transformed the appeal and financial base of the newspaper industry—with mostly negative consequences. Not just millennials, but the majority of the population of the United States does not sit down with a broad-sheet newspaper anymore. The Internet, the digital age, television, and handheld devices reign.

Yet these developments have underlined the importance of serious, in-depth reporting and a need to share good journalism practices and habits with future reporters and editors. As the late John Carroll, a former colleague at the *Baltimore Sun* and editor of both the *Sun* and the *Los Angeles Times*, asked in a 2006 speech that serves as the conclusion to this book: "Who will make the checks at City Hall? Who—among America's great din of flackery and cant—will tell us in plain language what's actually going on?"

The *Sun* enjoyed many outstanding periods since its origin in 1837, all explored thoroughly by my coeditor in his lively introduction to this volume and in several chapters. We both feel that in the last half of the twentieth century that the paper was the best newspaper for an American city the size of Baltimore.

The freedom allowed to *Sun* reporters in that time—and before—was extraordinary, inspiring, and generally led to outstanding journalism. Reporters were given a long leash, trusted to do their job and more, with watchful but infrequent supervision. It was fun to go to work. A British transplant, Patrick Skene Catling, a reporter and foreign correspondent at the *Sun* in the 1950s, put it best in a charming book titled *Better Than Working*.

That rare blend of outright pleasure and serious commitment is evident in the personal stories highlighted in this book. Take in David Simon's encounters with the police, which explain the street smarts and ear for dialogue he developed and turned into acclaimed television series like *Homicide* and

The Wire. Or Tony Barbieri's account of the colorful characters and idiosyncrasies of the *Sun*, the state of Maryland, the former Soviet Union, and across the globe as he moved in his amazing career from copy boy to managing editor.

Most importantly, the work at the *Sun* (and the Sunpapers) offered an opportunity to make a difference; to make a difference in people's lives, in the conduct of public affairs, in the vital issues of the times—whether it involved the abuse of power, the impact of segregation, an emerging concern for the environment, far-off war zones—by looking behind the superficial flow of events and digging to find deeper realities and disturbing conditions. The chapter by Antero Pietila unveiled the injustice and terrible social dislocation caused by blockbusting and redlining; Tom Horton's pathbreaking reporting focused public attention on the deteriorating condition of Chesapeake Bay; and Scott Shane's investigative series on the National Security Agency came long before the dramatic disclosures after 9/11.

Other chapters demonstrate the value of rigorous investigative efforts to uncover brazen political corruption at top levels of government, even religious institutions, and inhumane industrial practices such as in the breaking up of ships. From abroad, *Sun* correspondents offered exemplary reporting on coups, earthquakes, and the diverse lives of distant and very different civilizations. Read Arnold Isaacs's *Time Travel* or Dan Fesperman's reports from the Balkan wars.

A word to explain the term Sunpapers: The A. S. Abell Company expanded in 1910 to publish an afternoon edition, the *Evening Sun*, and also included a Sunday *Sun* staff, mainly for features. The *Evening Sun* focused on local and state affairs for eighty-five years delivering a vibrant, intensely competitive mix of solid reporting and incisive commentary. Most *Sun* men and women were aware that their main competition locally was not Hearst's *News-American* or the *Washington Post*, but their colleagues one hundred feet away in another city room. H. L. Mencken wrote his acerbic columns for the *Evening Sun*. Several contributors to this book, Dan Fesperman, Laura Lippman, and Bob Timberg, earned their early journalistic stripes reporting for the afternoon paper.

Today, more than a decade into a new century, the outlook for daily newspapers, even first-rate daily newspapers, remains troubled as technology evolves in unpredictable directions and as younger generations change how they receive news and information.

Our personal hopes, our main reason for organizing this book, revolve around two important goals. The first goal is that these chapters offer compelling evidence of a golden age of newspaper reporting, editing, and cartooning—its excitement, its excellence, and its impact on a great American city and an important state. The second is that they will encourage current and future journalists to draw inspiration and some practical lessons from the hard work, spirit, and dedication of their predecessors at an outstanding newspaper.

Frederic B. Hill
Arrowsic, Maine
November 2015

Acknowledgments

This book is a product of collaboration among men and women who worked for the *Baltimore Sun* in a period that many consider to be the last golden age of newspaper journalism. We are grateful for the willingness of so many accomplished reporters, editors, and cartoonists to contribute to our project, which has been a labor of love. They have not only produced fine chapters, but they have also gracefully offered editorial counsel where it was needed and, when asked, critically read the work of others in this volume.

Several colleagues deserve special mention. The guidance of Joseph R. L. Sterne was important in getting the project off the ground. G. Jefferson Price III—reporter, editor, and editorial writer during his long career at the paper—applied the wealth of his unmatched institutional memory to reviewing our chapters. William F. Schmick III, former city editor with a long family connection to the paper, provided valuable counsel.

We are grateful for the indispensable assistance of librarians at the University of Maryland Baltimore County, the Milton S. Eisenhower Library at Johns Hopkins University, the Peabody Library, the Enoch Pratt Free Library, and the Albert S. Cook Library at Towson University. Of particular importance were Thomas Beck, curator of special collections at the University of Maryland, Baltimore County, who made available the unpublished financial ledgers of the *Baltimore Sun* from 1837 to 1979; James Stimpert, research librarian at Johns Hopkins special collections, who provided access to more than a thousand editorial cartoons by Edmund Duffy and Tom Flannery; and finally Vincent Fitzpatrick, curator of the Mencken Collection at the Enoch Pratt Free Library, whose cooperation was important. At the *Sun* we relied heavily on Paul McCardell, the chief librarian, and Anne Lepore, director of the Baltimore Sun Media Group.

We have benefited from the patient guidance of Rowman & Littlefield's editors in American government, American history, and public policy, especially Jon Sisk, executive editor.

Introduction

Of all the things written about newspapers, a favorite of many reporters is Thomas Jefferson's remark that if he had to choose between having newspapers or government, one or the other, he'd take the press. We are professionally inclined to overlook Jefferson's complete change of mind once he became president. But let's take him at his earlier word and suppose he had had the chance to follow the long history of the *Baltimore Sun* as an independent newspaper. May we further suppose he might have been pleased with its generally vigorous, wide-reaching, thorough, and often intelligent operation? We think so—up to a point.

There were lapses, the worst during the Civil War when the paper's ink-stained founder sympathized with the rebellion, privately. Otherwise, he might have ended up in a lockup at Fort McHenry. In later years the paper was slow to get on the right side of civil rights.

But whatever its occasional shortcomings, the *Sun* had persistent strengths, and overall it did pretty well. It was diligent in covering Baltimore and the state of Maryland. For that reason, and because it was seen systematically to hold public officials accountable, its influence in those precincts remained consistently strong over time. In fact, as Sandy Banisky observes in her chapter, the *Sun* "guided the community conversation."

The Life of Kings is not a history of the *Sun*, but a little of its storied past is worth recalling here to frame the accounts of the reporters and editors in this volume about a recent time when newspapers were still thriving as agents of civic virtue and sources of wealth.

From the outset, the *Sun* had large ambitions: it wanted a voice in the national conversation.

Arunah S. Abell, the printer who launched the *Sun* in 1837, saw the possibilities of a presence in Washington, only thirty-eight miles away, an hour or so by the newly built railroad. (Chicago, a village at the time, was weeks away from Washington by Conestoga wagon. Los Angeles was still part of Mexico.) Abell almost immediately hired a Washington correspondent, whose first dispatch, it must be said, was a little soft on news. He reported on the postponement of a court case and expressed satisfaction that the new president (van Buren) was buying American-made furniture for "the palace" (the White House), a welcome change from "the late Mr. Monroe [who] raised a breeze by importing his chairs from England." As for the chief executive, "The President is well, and, for aught I know, is happy. Yours truly."

Things got better. The paper's biggest coup in the early years sealed a connection with the White House. In 1847, thanks to a pony express courier system that Abell set up to bring news of the Mexican War quickly from the U.S. Gulf Coast, President Polk was first informed by the *Sun* of the decisive American victory at Vera Cruz. The *Sun* not only beat other papers; it was ahead of the War Department with the information. Polk expressed his gratitude in a letter to Abell. Not bad for a paper that sold for a penny.

Before long the *Sun* was a factor in Washington, whose own papers were weak or far too partisan. It could be delivered to homes and government offices in the capital with a fairly complete Washington news report at the same time as it was circulated in Baltimore—and hours ahead of the big New York papers. Sometime in the 1850s, Joseph Gales Jr., publisher of the *National Intelligencer*, Washington's oldest newspaper, was asked by someone he passed on the street, "What's the news?" "I don't know," Gales replied. "I haven't yet seen the *Sun*."

Later, Grover Cleveland as president would have a special affection for the *Sun*. As would Woodrow Wilson, whose nomination in 1912 at the Democratic Convention in Baltimore had a good deal to do with the *Sun's* exertions on his behalf. The president's inner circle chose the paper's chief Washington correspondent, J. Fred Essary, to tell the world that Wilson had had a stroke. In his diary on April 27, 1920, Navy Secretary Josephus Daniels noted of Wilson, "Only reads the Balti. Sun in the morning & rarely sees other papers."

The *Sun* was one of three out-of-town papers Franklin D. Roosevelt read every day when he had breakfast in bed at 8:30. Harry Truman made it a habitual morning read along with the *New York Times* and the *Post*. Lyndon B. Johnson was a close reader of the *Sun*, especially where it concerned *him*. Jimmy Carter wrote an essay for the inauguration of the *Sun's* Op-Ed page in 1977. With its large Washington bureau, the *Sun* was a serious player. More important, the paper's readers were favored with a full report of reliable news from the capital.

Through the 1920s and 1930s, the *Sun* was a force in the national culture wars. A good example was the Monkey Trial in the summer of 1925. At H. L. Mencken's initiative, the *Sun* loudly took up the cause of John Scopes, the Tennessee high school teacher who defied a state ban on teaching evolution in the classroom (figure I.1). Mencken recruited Clarence Darrow, the country's leading trial lawyer, to defend Scopes. To cover the trial, the *Sun* sent Mencken, two reporters, and the editorial cartoonist Edmund Duffy. When Scopes was convicted, the *Evening Sun* paid his fine.

During World War II, the *Sun* fielded an impressive team of war correspondents whose work was revived in the 2009 book by Joseph R. L. Sterne, *Combat Correspondents: The* Baltimore Sun *in World War II.* In the postwar period, as the United States deepened its involvement overseas, the *Sun* expanded its foreign operation to as many as nine bureaus at one time. No American newspaper of comparable size had such a long foreign reach.

Baltimore and its surroundings retained most of the *Sun's* interest and resources. The paper's coverage of the city and state was dense, from the proceedings of the state legislature in Annapolis down to regular meetings of the city liquor board in Baltimore, where a politician's fingerprints might be found on the transfer of a liquor license.

The *Sun* newsroom typically had beat reporters covering the State House, City Hall, Baltimore County, Anne Arundel County, Howard County, Harford County, the Eastern Shore, city courts, state courts, federal court, labor, poverty/social services, state politics, housing, transportation, aviation, the police districts, zoning/planning, regulatory agencies, the environment, medicine, science, education (lower), education (higher), investigative, the black community, religion, and obituaries. Moreover (not counting the sports, business, and features sections), there were several general assignment reporters and rewrite men (and eventually women). Most reporters (except the investigative team, or anybody on a project) filed daily. It didn't always make for a very lively read, but it sure was thorough. The *Sun* was the paper of record.

The strength of the *Sun* was organically connected to the way it trained its reporters. New hires, no matter what their previous experience, were required to go through what amounted to an apprenticeship in the police districts. The period covering cops could be a matter of months, or a couple of years. (By the time the reporters in this volume began at the *Sun,* these routines had long been in place.)

The immediate advantage of this arrangement was that the new reporter learned the city in its grim and sometimes comical particulars. For the longer term, the reporter was expected to form good habits under the close supervision of the city desk: an appetite for news, eye for detail, ear for patterns of

Figure I.1. When science teacher John Scopes went on trial in Tennessee in 1925 for teaching evolution, the *Sun* sent H. L. Mencken and cartoonist Edmund Duffy to cover the proceedings.

speech (easy in Baltimore), and strict attention to accuracy. (For more on how the system worked, see Russell Baker's chapter, "Getting Started.") The intention was to produce not just a good reporter, but a good *Sun* reporter.

The foundation of everything was trust.

As the reporter demonstrated that he was getting things right without too much prodding, he would be brought inside periodically for general assignment, doing small-bore stories such as a dinner meeting of the Eastern Shore Society with its exotic fare of Maryland beaten biscuits and muskrat (or "marsh rabbit," as the more fastidious called it). Then after a couple of weeks back out to the districts.

At some point, when the districts reporter had won the absolute confidence of the desk, he (or she) was brought inside for good, at the start to do obits or a low-pressure beat pretty far down the hierarchy—and hope, eventually, for City Hall, Annapolis, Washington, or London with the confidence that nobody would be brought in from outside to jump the queue.

It depended on the work. The more the reporter showed he could do it, the more independence he accumulated until, at some undefined point, he was practically a free agent on his beat. For good reason, the *Sun* was widely known in the trade as a reporter's newspaper.

Mencken got it right. The paper opened up a domain no other enterprise could match, and gave reporters the authority to explore its subjects. We were able to visit fabulous or dangerous places on somebody else's dollar and write about it. We could ask questions of anybody. With a little digging, we might find out things nobody had known before, even important things. We could go places no civilian could go. For the energetically curious, there was no better realm.

Along with the freedom, so rare in the universe of work, now and then there was the perfect enjoyment of what we got to do. Some of us have had assignments—I know I have—that we would have paid to do, in theory, at least. And in the lore, there was much talk about long dinners at grand watering holes at the end of the day. (As a friend of mine, the AP correspondent Hugh Mulligan, was fond of saying, "There's only two things you need to be able to say in any foreign language: 'What's the best restaurant in town?' and 'My friend will pay.'") There was also a lot of standing around in the rain waiting for something to happen, or weeks going through dusty records—not such heroic memories.

This collection is by men and women who worked at the *Sun* before it became the kind of corporate newspaper where the overriding aim is profit. Their stories combine for a picture of what it was like to write and report in what may have been the last golden age of American newspapers—when journalism sometimes seemed like "the life of kings." The moment may never come again. The newspaper industry has been shaken by disruptive technologies and stifled by the rule of accountants. More and more independent dailies are being driven into the corporate fold; at latest count, about 80 percent of daily newspapers in the United States were owned by corporate chains. We can't do much against the powerful economic forces at work. But we can recall the standards that made the *Sun* and other fine independent newspapers a bulwark of civic life for so long. Our hope is that what comes through in our work here is a realization that the core principles guiding us then are no less valid for the new forms of journalism that are replacing the ones we practiced. While most of us may have operated a little short of chivalry, we still kept close a strong sense of the public interest in whose name we were acting, a reverence for accuracy, and an obligation to keep faith with the reader.

This book is not a lament. Yet it is hard to forget what has been lost.

The *Sun* was a paper controlled for most of its history by a few families who valued their property as an indispensable tool of citizenship no less than as a source of sometimes modest profits. The proprietors did not bend to the vicissitudes of the economic cycle by ordering staff cuts in bad times to maintain income. They took the long view, knowing that the basis of financial success was the maintenance of public trust that came from consistently good journalism.

The owners hired the publisher who hired the news executives, giving them liberty to run things. Shortly after he was named publisher in 1951, William F. Schmick Sr. told his top men: "You're the editors. I want you to keep running the paper as you have been." His son, William F. Schmick Jr., who succeeded him, had the same attitude (adding to a strong protective barrier between the newsroom and advertisers). And so on down the line. When Charles H. Dorsey Jr., the managing editor, sent Peter Kumpa out on his first foreign assignment, Kumpa asked Dorsey what stories he should go for first. The managing editor replied, "If I didn't think you were a good reporter, I wouldn't send you abroad. I'm the editor, you're the reporter. . . . You find out where the news is." So, too, it went in the city room.

The owners didn't scrimp. To make sure their readers got a first-rate daily report on the national government, they underwrote a staff of up to fifteen full-time reporters in Washington, as large as the bureau of the *Chicago Tribune,* which had a circulation four times as great, and double the *Boston Globe's,* whose circulation was two and a half times as large. The same held true for foreign reporting, which gave *Sun* readers a unique account of the world outside the United States.

For local coverage, the heart of the operation, the outlays were much greater. At one point the *Sun's* news staff totaled 423 people, according to Michael E. Waller, who was publisher from 1997 to 2002. The *Sun* created a community, connecting a couple hundred thousand people a day with a sense of shared experience.

One measure used by journalism academics is capacity, a metric that is supposed to predict the quality of newspapers based on the resources the paper devotes to newsgathering. Capacity is the ratio of staff to circulation. The rule of thumb is that a good newspaper employs one staffer for each thousand of circulation. The average for good papers comes in at about 0.98. The *Sun's* average capacity in the decades before the *Chicago Tribune* conglomerate bought the newspaper in 2000 was about 1.6—far higher than the industry standard.

Here's what has changed under Tribune ownership. From nine foreign bureaus, today there are none. The *Sun's* Washington bureau, one of the oldest continuous news outposts in the capital, was shut down. The newspaper's circulation, which stood at 314,819 in 1999, on the eve of Tribune's purchase, shrank to less than half that in the intervening years—to 247,193 in 2005, 186,639 in 2009, 170,510 in 2011, 152,397 in 2012, 139,094 in 2013, and average weekly circulation of 99,765 in 2014. The newsroom staff was cut to about eighty people, one-fifth of its previous peak, reducing the *Sun's* capacity number to 0.52. On a typical weekday in the late 1970s, the morning *Sun* published sixty-four pages with about sixty articles, most of them staff written. These days, the paper has maybe thirty-six pages with about twenty news spreads. These are the results of a deliberate corporate policy to protect the balance sheet by cutting expenses. There is no longer any pretense of national prominence.

The first important break with the past, the preliminary cause of the present circumstances, was the decision in 1986 by the *Sun's* owners to sell to Times Mirror, the rich and highly regarded group of papers with the *Los Angeles Times* at its center. Times Mirror was an indulgent patron, with respect for the *Sun* and for good journalism. Things held steady for a while as Baltimore retained a great deal of autonomy and made, as it turned out, a nice profit. Times Mirror's touch was so light that editors and reporters operated pretty much as they had before. The calculus changed altogether when Times Mirror sold itself to Tribune and the *Sun* became what Chicago primarily saw as a profit center. Basically unprepared for the Internet, Tribune was blindsided by it, as were many others who mistook it for a mere appliance. The present-day paper is trying to recover.

It has a lively local news report, limited by the budget restrictions Chicago imposes. The *Sun* has shown a strong pulse, especially evident during the Baltimore race riots of 2015, when editors and reporters worked practically without rest and produced excellent reporting on the disturbances and their causes. Parallel to the print coverage, reporters filed online around the clock, resulting in awards for breaking news and explanatory reporting from the Online News Association.

As the Internet upended the old newspaper culture, so the Tribune over-ran the old *Sun's* with barely a backward glance. An unfortunate example of this led to James Bready's accidental discovery in the spring of 2002.

Retired from a long career as an editorial writer, Bready still wrote a books column, which allowed him regular visits to the paper. On one of these visits, he noticed something unusual near the back door in the basement: stacks of what looked like old ledgers on two pallets that were headed for the dumpster. Bready investigated and found in the stacks the original cash ledger of Arunah S. Abell from the *Sun's* first day of publication on May 17, 1837, along with all the other handwritten financial registers of the paper through 1979.

Here, in one place, was the secret financial story of one of the country's oldest and most venerable newspapers, whose owners never, ever disclosed the details of their operation.

What did Abell pay his printers? 0.02 cents an em. Who were Abell's biggest advertisers in those early days? Dr. Benjamin Brandreth for his Bran-dreth Vegetable Pills Good for Asthma, Costiveness, Dyspepsia, Bile &c., and Dr. William Evans for his Evans's Camomile Tonic Pills for Ladies Especially Who Suffer from Nausea and Lassitude Incidental to Interesting Changes of Health.

What was Abell's cash take on the first day? $149.16. How many extra papers did Abell print on April 10, 1847, the day of his Vera Cruz exclusive? 5,458. What was the Sunpapers' net profit in 1951? $1,430,686.58. What was the dividend paid on July 31, 1974? $3 a share. What did the morning *Sun* spend on news gathering and editorial in 1979? $7,920,701. How much cash was on hand going into 1980? $47,731,326 in bank deposits, stocks, and bonds.

Contained in the ledgers was a case history of an important newspa-per's finances growing in parallel with the expanding republic. A historian's dream—headed for the trash heap.

I can quote from the ledgers only because Jim Bready rescued them. He arranged for their safekeeping with Thomas Beck, the chief curator of Special Collections at the University of Maryland, Baltimore County, where they reside today.

Stephens Broening
November 2015

Sellout at the *Sun*

Joseph R. L. Sterne

At four o'clock on the Wednesday afternoon of May 28, 1986, members of the operations committee of the *Baltimore Sun,* an esteemed newspaper one year short of its 150th birthday, drifted into a sixth floor conference room in a mood of suppressed excitement. Just the day before, the Hearst Corporation's *Baltimore News American*, which fancifully traced its origins to the Revolution, had gone out of business, sadly. For months, it had offered itself to anyone willing to take on the Baltimore Sunpapers, a morning-evening-Sunday combination lush in advertisements appealing to a middle class readership. There were no takers. All that Hearst had left was a dilapidated building on a choice Inner Harbor waterfront site destined to be a parking lot for at least a quarter century.

While pre-meeting talk that afternoon speculated on how much *Sun* circulation would grow or which of the opposition's star writers should be brought into the *Sun's* orbit, the *News American* chatter suddenly ceased when John R. (Reg) Murphy, the *Sun's* publisher, marched into the room. For with him came W. Thomas Johnson, Robert Erburu, and David Laventhol, top officials of the Times Mirror Company, owner of the *Los Angeles Times* and other media properties. They knew hardly anyone in the room except Murphy and a *Sun* editor who had sat next to Laventhol at a Florida poolside a few months earlier. On that occasion, a meeting of the American Society of Newspaper Editors, Laventhol in a gossipy manner had asked how Murphy was getting along. The reply: Reg was doing just fine, raising doldrum profit margins, and installing business practices that a beginning MBA student would consider rudimentary—but which were stunning developments in the red-brick *Sun* citadel.

In his slow, soft Georgia accent, Murphy announced to his appalled colleagues that the A. S. Abell Company, owner of the Sunpapers, had been sold to Times Mirror (figure 1.1). Just like that, a century and a half of home-town Baltimore ownership came to an end. Dutifully, Murphy and the *Sun* editorial page assured readers that their newspaper's high standards would be maintained. They could not foresee that within less than fifteen years the *Sun* would be torn from the warm embrace of Times Mirror into the clutches of a dysfunctional *Chicago Tribune* and then into a multibillion dollar bankruptcy with Baltimore interests treated as an asterisk.

The figures and the calendar are crucial to the evolution of this mess. Let's put it briefly. Times Mirror paid $600 million for the *Sun* in 1986 (more of this later.) Fourteen years later, in 2000, Times Mirror sold itself to the *Chicago Tribune* for an astounding $8.3 billion, the largest newspaper deal in US history. Wall Street analysts, with their customary acuity, hailed a deal creating the nation's third largest newspaper conglomerate. Seven years after that, in 2007, the floundering Tribune Company sold itself to Sam Zell, a billionaire Chicago real estate wizard, and to some hedge funds and

Figure 1.1.   The sale of the *Baltimore Sun* to Times Mirror was announced by *Sun* publisher Reg Murphy on May 28, 1986. To Murphy's left, Times Mirror executives W. Thomas Johnson, publisher and CEO of the *Los Angeles Times*, and David Laventhol, a senior Times Mirror executive.

too-big-to-fail super-banks. It was a deal financed by a $13 billion debt and shiny new tax-avoidance gimmicks. Then, in 2008, the whole tangle wound up in a Delaware bankruptcy court and there it stayed while squadrons of lawyers ran up bills totaling more than half a billion dollars. Tribune's various assets, separately or as the whole kit-and-caboodle, were on the auction block. While the Internal Revenue Service went on the hunt for questionable tax dodges, Sam Zell lamented his "deal from hell." Outside observers and victims saw him and many others as its devils.

All this occurred as the Internet Revolution, eviscerating print journalism, wrought the greatest change in human communication since Gutenberg's press in the fifteenth century. The *Sun*, like many big city papers, emerged from the ordeal vastly trimmed down and focused on local coverage that constituted, in fact, a return to its roots.

Despite its tawdry southern California past, the *Los Angeles Times*, under the leadership of Otis Chandler, had improved in quality to a point where it was preferable in *Sun* circles to any other would-be buyer. Just two weeks before the *Sun* was sold, the *Louisville Courier Journal* had been acquired by the Gannett Company, a huge chain made up mostly of money-making smaller papers, alongside *USA Today*. Neither *Sun* management nor reporters in the newsroom, all proud of their paper's reputation, wanted anything to do with Gannett.

Behind the scenes, the owners and top managers of the Baltimore Sunpapers had been discussing their future for a decade. Their collective DNA mandated a reverence for a mission in which the *Sun* would set a standard of excellence comparable to that of the *Manchester Guardian* in Great Britain. Keepers of the *Sun* exchequer continued to spend huge sums of money to maintain a large Washington bureau and as many as nine news offices abroad at the same time—a network easily outshining that of any other American newspaper of comparable size.

Its writers, once led by the irrepressible H. L. Mencken, had long made the *Sun* an important voice in the country's intellectual conversation. While most newspapers were reveling in high profits in that pre-digital age, the *Sun's* finances were disappointing. Lavish spending on news coverage was a reason. Lackluster circulation efforts and a smug insularity were others. Leading members of the *Sun* hierarchy resisted advice to begin acquiring other papers or to syndicate their own exclusive (and expensive) national and foreign news reporting. On that score, the *Washington Post*, the *New York Times*, and the Gannett organization would have no competition from the *Sun*. No wonder Baltimore stockholders were getting restless. The big ones got a lot of psychic income from the international prestige of their property. Community leadership came with their mother's milk. The *Sun's* prestige was

Figure 1.2. President John F. Kennedy greets Soviet leader Nikita S. Khrushchev at the Vienna summit, June 4, 1961. To Kennedy's left stands *Sun* correspondent Joseph R. L. Sterne.
Courtesy of Joseph R. L. Sterne.

as much a part of the land of pleasant living as manorial estates large enough for horse races. Some of those comfortable with their current level of inherited wealth or the sheer joy of newspapering may have been willing to settle for their modest dividends (on the order of 5 percent of the nominal share price). Others were not.

Like dynastic newspaper families in many other cities, younger generations with distant connections to the paper longed for the big payout. Pressure to sell rose during a period of high profits and newspaper consolidation in many other parts of the country. Optimists in charge of some papers tried to acquire enough property to make them hard to digest in the open market. Others, including most in *Sun* management, chose to capitulate.

In fact, Murphy's arrival in Baltimore in 1981 was a key part of that narrative. His task was to raise anemic *Sun* profit margins so the papers could stabilize and/or attract higher purchase prices. His natural ally was William E. McGuirk Jr., a powerful Baltimore bank president who had joined the Abell Company board of directors and became its first non-family chairman. A strong businessman with a canny feel for finances, he was the real overseer of the Sunpapers sale. As a banker and trustee, McGuirk was duty bound to fulfill his fiduciary responsibility for major owners and other stockholders. Fulfill it he did.

Times Mirror paid $600 million for the A. S. Abell Company, which included the Sunpapers, some suburban papers, and two TV stations that had to be offloaded quickly under federal law. Overnight, the value of A. S. Abell stock jumped more than seven-fold (from $803.21 book value, to $5,741.18 actual value as priced in the sale). The endowment of the Abell Foundation, established by the legendary chairman Harry C. Black, grew to more than $112 million in one day—making it, for a time, the largest foundation in Maryland. Similar benefits added to huge family fortunes and turned middle-sized stockholders into millionaires. W. Shepherdson Abell, the great-great grandson and namesake of the *Sun's* founder, said he was not happy to see the paper lose its independence but called the Times Mirror offer "a preemptive bid." It was certainly so in retrospect. Thirty years later, the *Sun's* estimated value was $50 million and falling.

Murphy, over the course of his nine years in Baltimore, had proved he had the authority to shake up the company by discarding even high-rankers whose jobs were supposedly secured by the divine right of nepotism. At one time in the 1950s, the publisher and the general manager of the paper were sons of fathers who held the same positions. For middle managers who stayed on, some changes were welcome. For years, they had been informed only about the operational goals of their separate departments. The company's performance had been a tightly held secret. One day, Murphy distributed to his department heads documents revealing overall company performance. He watched the astonished faces around the table with undisguised amusement as, for the first time, they contemplated their roles in determining the bottom-line of the whole company.

A career newspaperman who started as a reporter in Macon, Georgia, and went on to become editorial page editor of the *Atlanta Constitution* and publisher of the *San Francisco Examiner*, Murphy had a historical understanding in 1986 of what he was doing by selling one of the most prestigious newspapers in America. The *Sun* had been founded in 1837 by Arunah S. Abell, a printer out of Rhode Island who, with two partners, set out to establish "penny papers" in New York, Philadelphia, and Baltimore. Only the *Sun* survived past the middle of the twentieth century. Its economic goal in the beginning was to compete with six-cent papers that were primarily propaganda sheets for political special interests. The *Sun's* journalistic mission, stated at the outset, was to be "free, firm, and temperate" and pursue "the common good without regard to that of sects, factions, or parties." Its logo promised "Light for All." The *Sun's* approach ensured its survival while scores of would-be rivals disappeared. (It is quaint to note in the foreground of the

Sun's colossal sale price in 1986 that the paper, on its first day of publication, May 17, 1837, took in a total of $149.16, as recorded in Abell's original accounts ledger.)

As a young entrepreneur, Abell was an innovator. Only weeks on the job, he beat every newspaper in the country by printing, in full, a presidential speech on the intense financial crisis gripping the country in 1837. The B&O Railroad rushed him copies of the speech which he had turned into type by enlisting just about every job printing outfit in town. He resorted to a pony express to carry news on the Mexican War that the White House itself had not yet received. He arranged coverage of a New England trial that had the British muttering war over the Oregon Territory. And always, he wisely concentrated on local news, on local crime, on local government, on local, local, local.

The Civil War and the wounds it inflicted on the South, Baltimore's natural market, was a trying period for the *Sun*. When Confederate sympathizers stoned Massachusetts infantrymen as they crossed the city on the way to the Virginia battlefields, the first blood in the long conflict was shed. Some hotheaded Baltimore editors wound up jailed under federal martial law. But Abell kept his head down, concentrating on securing scarce newsprint supplies. The Civil War and its early aftermath were a near thing for the *Sun* and for Baltimore's economy. But as the years went by, the paper prospered and Arunah S. Abell became a very rich man, purchasing a large tract of land that, in time, became the elegant neighborhood of Guilford.

As Abell's early energy faded—he died in 1887, fifty years after starting the paper—the founder's three sons and a couple of his grandsons formed troubled partnerships. While the *Sun*, true to its original mission, took on political bosses, corrupt judges, and the general malaise in the city, it did so in pedestrian fashion. The real Baltimore ginger paper in the 1890s was the *Baltimore Evening News* under the control of Charles H. Grasty, a newspaper wonder boy who sometimes mocked the *Sun* for its stodginess. Two decades later, Grasty had become the boss of his old competitor. In doing so, he smashed the dreaded Gorman-Rasin political machine, the longtime nemesis of civic-minded citizens. It was Grasty, too, who influenced American history by flooding the 1912 Democratic National Convention in Baltimore's Fifth Regiment Armory with special Sunpapers editions as he worked behind the scenes to swing the tide to Woodrow Wilson. The *Sun's* alliance with Wilson, a reformer, was quite a switch from the longtime friendship of the Abells with a far more conservative Democratic president, Grover Cleveland.

Disputes and irritations within the Abell family were factors in the *Sun's* economic performance during the early years of the new twentieth century. A crisis was in the making. When it came in 1910, Abell suzerainty dissolved,

never to be seen again. Abell heirs sold 80 percent of their stock to other af-
fluent Baltimore families represented by H. Crawford Black, Robert Garrett,
R. Brent Keyser, and John Campbell White. They were successful Maryland
businessmen but had no experience in newspapering. Quickly, they cut
Grasty into the deal, selling a special class of stock which put him in essential
control of the operation of the paper—but not the ownership. This remained
in hometown hands, and when the arrangement with Grasty blew up five
years later, a lasting pattern was firmly set. Ownership was one thing. Being
publisher was another. Hometown ownership was preserved and it would
remain for another seventy-six years (half the then lifetime of the paper) until
the sale to Times Mirror.

If the Abells were dominant in the first great chapter of *Sun* history,
that mantle shifted dramatically to the Black family and, more specifically, to
three men important to this tale. The first was Van-Lear Black, a man who
fit comfortably into the golden realm of industrial giants who made immense
amounts of money and knew how to spend it. What John D. Rockefeller
was to oil, Van-Lear Black was to coal. Following the financial career of his
banker father, Black, at age thirty-one, was handed the board chairmanship
of the *Sun* after the sale of 1910. "Handsome, athletic and gregarious," as the
Sun historian Harold A. Williams described him, Black arrived and told those
in charge that they had one year "to show a black line on the ledger."

Black was no curmudgeon. He loved circuses, fireworks, and the horses a
lot more than business meetings, and was one of the most flamboyant airplane
adventurers of the pre-Lindbergh era. He befriended Franklin D. Roosevelt,
gave him a finance job on Wall Street, and took the future president aboard
his yacht, the *Sabalo*, on a trip from New York to Campobello Island. While
there, FDR came down with polio that left him crippled for life. Black disappeared from his yacht off the New Jersey coast in 1930 and was never seen
again (unless you believe a *Sun* sports reporter who claimed he saw his old boss
on a Hartford street before he vanished with a wink).

Van-Lear Black, later to be succeeded by his brother, Harry, and then
by his own son, Gary, had an enormous impact on what became known as
Sun tradition—a tradition that for most of the twentieth century made the
Baltimore newspaper one of the most respected in the nation. Owners relied
on publishers, publishers on editors, and editors on reporters in a system of
personal trust. Black did not keep an office in the *Sun* building. He did not
try to influence editorial decisions or the operation of the news staff. His job
was to put the the *Sun* in a sound, solvent position while professional editors
and reporters, often grossly underpaid, practiced their craft with unparalleled
freedom. A smart businessman with a flair for customer-catching promo-
tions, Van-Lear Black left unfilled Grasty's old jobs as company president

and editorial director. He went about his task of making sure the morning *Sun* and the upstart *Evening Sun*, launched in 1910, could flourish.

Of equal importance, Black vested enormous power over both *Sun* newspapers in John Haslip Adams, as editor of the editorial pages, and Frank R. Kent, as news editor of both newsrooms. After Adams died in 1927, H. L. Mencken described him as the only journalist he ever knew "who never made a visible compromise with his convictions. . . . He saw a great modern newspaper largely, if not mainly, as an engine for rectifying injustice . . . [with a duty] to get behind the news to find out whence the news had come and by whom it had been set afloat, to detect any falsity that was in it, or any self-interest."

Perhaps Mencken, the best-known of all *Sun* writers, had been thinking about his colleague, Frank R. Kent, who had exposed the machinations of the great powers in drafting the Versailles Treaty at the end of the First World War. Taking leave of the Sunpapers newsrooms, Kent had gone to Paris and found himself free of the strict censorship imposed on reporters accredited to cover the negotiations. He returned to the United States to tell all. "For weeks past, under the surface," he informed the world, "Paris has been simply seething with international jealousies, friction and feeling, and between us and our noble allies there is a tension and a strain that does not appear at the top." The Kent scoop, in twenty-one long articles, fulfilled Mencken's prescription for great news enterprise. It revealed much that was wrong in the carving up of Europe that was to lead to World War II.

The *Sun* was fortunate to have Mencken not only on its staff but also in a position to influence the top officers of the newspapers. He was heard and hated or lionized—not only because of his writing on the *Evening Sun* editorial page but also in the national magazines he launched and in literary circles of which he was a valued and often-feared member. He enjoyed mocking the booboisie and the blue-noses, the pious and the pulpiteers, and the creationists and other caretakers of American morality. In both world wars, even at the cost of abandoning his newspaper column, he dared to maintain his reverence for things German. Such was the power of his brand that the *Evening Sun* was known as "Mencken's paper."

While Van-Lear Black would remain as chairman of the board of *Sun* directors until his disappearance in 1930, his brother and successor, Harry C. Black, was in the process of becoming a newspaper enthusiast, a believer in a lofty mission for the Sunpapers he would later lead until his death in 1956. He loved to stroll through the newsrooms, talking with reporters, but was careful never to impose his views.

During his early tours of duty, Harry Black had two men who were his nominal employees and also his mentors. One was the redoubtable Mencken.

The other was Paul Patterson, a Midwesterner who worked for papers in Chicago and Washington before Grasty brought him to Baltimore as first managing editor of the new *Evening Sun* in 1911. From there, he made a long ascent on the business side of the company until he was appointed president and publisher in 1919, thus filling the slots left vacant after Grasty's abrupt departure.

Like Grasty before him, Patterson was first and foremost a newsman. The gathering and presentation of news was not only an occupation but a preoccupation, a passion that dropped editorial opinions to second place. Even as his leadership thrust him into the business and operational duties of a publisher, Patterson recognized that news excellence was preeminent. He cleared advertisements from the front pages. He opened the *Sun's* first foreign bureaus. He took high positions in the governance of the Associated Press and United Press. In 1948, he was instrumental in building what is still the *Sun's* headquarters on Calvert Street. He remained active and exacting and dominant until 1951, a man respected by both the paper's proprietors and its workforce. Patterson stands out as the man who guided the institution during some of its greatest years.

Patterson and his onetime deskmate, Mencken, found in Harry Black an owner who was attracted to newspapers with a zeal that could inflame an idealistic cub reporter. A triumvirate formed. Patterson, Mencken, and Black would gather frequently at Black's home to talk about a future in which the *Sun* would rank with the *Times* of London, the once "Great Thunderer" of the British Empire.

One evening in 1920, Harry Black handed his two collaborators the beginnings of an "Editorial Memorandum" that became known ever after as the *Sun's* White Paper. When it was completed, it bore the stamp of H. L. Mencken, who later claimed to have written nearly all of it. Like the pro-nouncements of the founder Abell eighty-three years earlier, the White Paper enunciated ethical newspaper doctrines still heard in schools of journalism throughout the United States. A "great newspaper" should be grounded on "absolute independence of judgment and a persistent and intelligent concern for the national welfare," it said.

In charting a course for the future, the authors envisaged a newspaper that would "lead rather than follow," "find news sources of its own," and present issues "in dramatic form to show the people what is going on and not infrequently what is going on in secret." The object was to "lift the *Sun* above the average of other newspapers." This anticipated the *Sun's* efforts in the 1920s to establish a network of stringers to report from foreign capitals and in the 1940s onward to build on its masterful coverage of World War II by establishing expensive news bureaus of its own all over the world.

Figure 1.3.   Gary Black, chairman of the board of the A. S. Abell Company, and William F. Schmick Sr., president, 1957.

"The *Sun* is a good newspaper and is an honest newspaper," the White Paper declared. With sound finances and "a peculiarly favorable position editorially," it is well placed "to increase its importance and influence . . . out of all proportion to its size and the nature of its principal circulation."

In becoming a "newspaper of national distinction," the *Sun* "must be free from any suspicion of loyalty to private interest or to rigid formulae. The *Sun* must convince by means of sound information, unquestionable honesty, and unshakable common sense."

The White Paper provided inspiration for generations of *Sun* reporters.

But in some lamentable respects, it was a document that reflected attitudes of time and place: "As between the black man and the white man, [the *Sun*] must be in favor of the white man." It aligned the paper squarely with the Democratic Party in local and state affairs—this at a time of strict segregation in Baltimore and the Democratic South.

Despite these flaws, the White Paper signaled the determination of *Sun* owners and managers to create newspapers that would become standouts. It ushered in a period of financial stability, news-gathering innovation, editorial leadership, and a well-earned reputation that was to last for decades. The *Sun* was regularly listed among the nation's top papers, won a respectable share of Pulitzers and other prizes, and offered a great nesting place for reporters who would become well-known writers.

The genial leadership style of Harry Black that coincided with the issuance of the White Paper continued when his nephew, Gary Black, succeeded him in 1956 (figure 1.3). There remained an abiding reverence at the top of the Abell Company for the creative freedom of its editors and reporters.

This was seen during what could be called the Schmick era, from 1951 to 1978. Two conscientious publishers, William F. Schmick Sr. and Jr., did not have the news-side experience of Charles Grasty or Paul Patterson, but they showed they had learned what a great newspaper required. Their editors were granted the wherewithal to pursue lofty ambitions. Foreign bureaus were to open at one time or another in Bonn (later Berlin), Moscow, Rome, New Delhi, Rio de Janeiro (later Mexico City), Hong Kong (later Beijing), Paris, Beirut (later Jerusalem), Johannesburg, and Tokyo, in addition to the London office. A *Sun* correspondent spent sixteen months in sub-Saharan Africa in the 1960s, working out of a suitcase. It was not the practice of the Schmicks to summon editors to their office. Instead, they ended their working days by visiting with news and editorial editors in their lairs, mostly to keep in touch. William Schmick Sr. memorably said, "You're the editors. I want you to keep running the paper as you have been." William Schmick Jr., having spent his whole career on the business side, displayed a genuine commitment to the newspaper's independence. Though it cost the *Sun* revenue, he gave advertisers no special favors, however loud their demands.

The younger Schmick served in tandem with Gary Black, the last of the hometown owners, whose efforts to avoid interference with the news side of his paper became the stuff of legend. When he died the year after the *Sun* was sold, an editorial described him as a man "utterly lacking in pomposity. To his employees, he was almost always 'Gary,' a term of friendship, not condescension." That it was Gary Black's destiny to play a part in the sale of the *Sun* added poignancy to all that happened later.

While the White Paper seemed to assume that the *Sun* would have no difficulty fulfilling its recipe for greatness, this was not to be. The definition of the "national welfare," by its very nature, is a matter of individual choice and inclination and events. The top journalists on the *Sun* were tough-minded men who had their own opinions. When Patterson led a large delegation to the 1920 Democratic Convention, Mencken had just enraged colleagues by calling that longtime *Sun* favorite Woodrow Wilson a "congenital liar." When two of his editors threatened revolt, Patterson brought out a soothing case of Prohibition whiskey, which, in turn, led to comradely

Figure 1.4. *Maryland, My Maryland.* Edmund Duffy's 1931 cartoon following the lynching in Salisbury, Maryland, of Matthew Williams, accused of killing his white employer. Following publication of this cartoon and scalding denunciation of the lynching by Mencken, *Sun* newspaper trucks on the Eastern Shore were set afire, their drivers beaten.

singing. When the editorial board in 1936 decided to abandon support for Franklin D. Roosevelt as he sought a second term, Gerald Johnson quit. He was the *Sun's* liberal alternative to conservative Frank Kent, who, in turn, was an interventionist Anglophile at odds with isolationist Mencken as World War II approached. In presidential endorsements, the *Sun* switched back and forth from Democratic to Republican or non-declared.

During the 1920s, 1930s, 1940s, 1950s, 1960s, and 1970s—in other words for more than half a century—there wasn't a lot of turnover among the top editors: J. Edwin Murphy served as managing editor of the *Evening Sun* from 1920 to 1939; William E. Moore was morning managing editor, 1929 to 1941; Philip S. Heisler, evening managing editor, 1949 to 1979; and Charles H. (Buck) Dorsey Jr., morning managing editor, 1947 to 1966. Neil H. Swanson, the only man to serve as executive editor over both papers, 1941 to 1954, ruled with flamboyance in updating the look of the papers and in going after Pulitzers that enhanced the Sunpapers' national reputation. In temperament and inventiveness, he resembled Charles Grasty.

The *Sun* was widely and enviously known throughout the newspaper industry as the ultimate reporters' paper. Ambitious newspapermen throughout the country saw in it a rare open door to assignments abroad and in Washington. Paul Patterson, the trendsetter, did not mind if his reporters left for other papers, as they often did, particularly for the *New York Times*. In fact, three former *Sun* men—Carr V. Van Anda, Edwin L. James, and Turner Catledge—held the managing editorship of the *Times* consecutively for sixty years, from 1904 to 1964.

Normal discipline kept local staffs somewhat in line. But when reporters were sent overseas or on out of town assignment, discretion or indiscretion, good judgment or bad, rested in their hands. Foreign bureau chiefs often went months without instructions from Baltimore. Russell Baker famously covered a Beatles concert in London (and covered it memorably) while ignoring a foreign ministers' summit. A roving correspondent in sub-Saharan Africa wrote Buck Dorsey from Mali asking if his stuff was all right. It was "satisfactory," Dorsey curtly replied, adding, "Stop asking me to write you letters." Then, characteristically, he signed it, "Love. Buck." The Washington bureau, though only a telephone call away, enjoyed almost as much autonomy. Its diplomatic correspondent, Paul W. Ward, covered the early doings of the United Nations in such length that historians would be in jeopardy if they were to ignore his reports. How many readers followed his multiple columns of copy to the exhaustive end remained a matter of conjecture. When Dorsey felt in need of a front-page exclusive, he was known to call reporters and ask if they had anything in their back pockets.

A good, hard look at the morning newsroom in the 1950s would have told a management expert what was going on. Dorsey had a tiny corner office overlooking the Maryland Penitentiary; no glass-enclosed central throne room for him. Outside his office were standard impersonal desks for his secretary, his assistant editor, and a single news editor occupying open space. Then came the copy desk, with a slot for its chief and seats in a tight semicircle. Green eyeshades abounded. A bit off to the left of the vast room was a nerve center—the city desk for an editor, assistants, and rewrite men taking phoned-in reports from police and general assignment reporters. Farther away were banks of desks for beat reporters. No cubicles; conversations could be overheard, especially with the added accommodation of screaming invective. It was all great fun, right out of "Front Page," with the daily miracle of a published newspaper the result.

But in the 1960s, the limited hierarchy of the newsroom gave way to more discipline—and more bureaucracy. The number of junior editors and sub-junior editors proliferated in papers all over the country. And in the 1970s came far more important developments. Bulky electronic writing machines replaced manual typewriters, typesetting machines in the composing room downstairs turned linotype operators (a revered craft) into paper cutters and pasters. Cold type replaced hot type. Carbon paper disappeared. The Internet Revolution was about to begin. And the newspaper industry, as it had developed over the centuries, would find itself swept by enormous tides at the very same time the *Sun* plunged into the uncertain waters of conglomerate journalism.

For months and even several years after May 28, 1986, when hometown ownership disappeared in Baltimore, the Sunpapers fit in fairly comfortably with Times Mirror big shots in Los Angeles. They figured the Baltimore paper was about as close as they could get to the influential Washington market if their East Coast edition proved unprofitable—which it did. They also took pride in the *Sun* as a publication associated with ethical journalism long before Otis Chandler injected it into his family's newspaper.

(Two *Sun* alumni—Michael Parks and John S. Carroll—served as top editors of the *Los Angeles Times* [*LAT*]. Mark Willis, the first non-family publisher of the *LAT*, chose Parks, a former *Sun* war correspondent in Vietnam, as his editor. Once Tribune took over Times Mirror, its managers asked Carroll, then editor of the *Sun*, to move to Los Angeles. Under his leadership, the *Times* won thirteen Pulitzer Prizes in five years. Carroll resigned in 2005 rather than carry out deep staff reductions ordered by Tribune.)

In Baltimore, Times Mirror executives tried to show they could be benign bosses. Improvements went ahead in the Calvert Street building, a vast new printing plant was built in South Baltimore and Reg Murphy, despite

The "Outstretched Hand"

The Sun's cartoonist, Mr. Edmund Duffy, yesterday was awarded the Pulitzer prize for 1939. The committee based its judgment largely upon the above drawing, which appeared in this paper on October 7, 1939, just after the Germans had successfully completed the conquest of Poland. Mr. Duffy has now received the Pulitzer prize award three times, in the years 1931, 1934 and 1939.

Figure 1.5. This 1939 cartoon by Edmund Duffy won the Pulitzer Prize.

Figure 1.6. The front page of the *Baltimore Sun*, on May 9, 1945, announces the surrender of Germany in Reims, France. As the article below the headline notes, *Sun* war correspondent Price Day was the only reporter for an individual newspaper present.
Courtesy of Baltimore Sun Media Group, all rights reserved.

skepticism in the ranks, said he had not taken his job to shut down the still feisty *Evening Sun.* He did not. Times Mirror did in September 1995.

Changes were bound to come, and Murphy had already started. Dissatisfied with some of the executives he had inherited, he shocked the whole company one day in 1982 when he removed the much-liked Paul Banker as managing editor of the morning *Sun* and brought in James Houck, who had worked for Murphy as news editor of the *San Francisco Examiner.* On the same day, he shook up the business side by replacing several high-level executives who had been regarded as immovable. He was, in effect, consolidating his power. Eventually, after the sale of the paper, he would encounter increasing difficulties with the top management of Times Mirror. And there came a day in 1990 when Murphy himself quit. To be publisher of the *Sun* became a short-term honor rather than a lifetime job.

In the turbulent seventeen years that followed, six publishers, all Times Mirror or *Chicago Tribune* appointees, moved in and out of the top jobs in Baltimore. Editors came and went as well. Indeed, there was one publisher who lasted less than a year, hardly enough to find her way around Baltimore. And another, following orders from Los Angeles, wasted a lot of money on county-based editorial writers who had no discernible effect on circulation. Still another, Timothy E. Ryan, apparently under orders from Chicago, fired more than sixty newsroom people in April 2009, and had some of them escorted from the building under guard. In late 2015, Ryan was named publisher of the *Los Angeles Times,* succeeding Austin Beutner, who was fired by Tribune after only thirteen months on the job.

Deprived of resources, the *Sun* radically slimmed down and concentrated its assets on covering local news, which was the meat and potatoes of Arunah Abell's early days.

Permit me to end this story with a personal reminiscence. In 1957, three years after I joined the *Sun,* I was talked into the presidency of the Baltimore Newspaper Guild, in those days a pathetically weak outfit (and not exactly a career booster). During negotiations, I sat across the table from Donald Patterson, the son of a publisher and a future publisher himself. Don was a self-effacing, modest, straight-arrow kind of guy. No reason for a young reporter to be intimidated.

So I said, "Mr. Patterson, I own this paper as much as Gary Black does." With a wry smile, Don replied, "You do?" "Yes, sir," I pontificated. "Because the *Sun* is as much a part of my life as of Gary Black's life."

A young reporter's passion? Sure. Yet, I still believe that.

Getting Started

Russell Baker

"**S**o you think you can be a newsman," were Mr. Dorsey's first words.

We were in an office with a wide picture window overlooking the newsroom. I sat in the rigor mortis posture of the eager-to-please job hunter. Mr. Dorsey leaned back in a swivel chair behind his desk, smug as a hanging judge, and stared at me without a trace of a smile. He was Hollywood's dream of a managing editor: tall and lean, iron-gray hair closely cropped, with chilly gray eyes, infinitely wise to the world (figure 2.1). His imperious manner, and a way of holding his head suggested arrogance, impatience, and maybe danger. A dangerous man, I thought. Not a man to trifle with. Not a man to tolerate fools. Though we were both seated, he managed to make me feel that he was looking down from great height.

Still, when he said, "So you think you can be a newsman," it didn't sound like a sneer. Yet, it wasn't a question either, so for a long pause I didn't know whether he expected an answer. While I hesitated about what to say to this awesome man, his phone rang.

"I've got to talk to the Washington bureau," he said to me. "It'll only take a minute."

Those words, "the Washington bureau," had an intoxicating effect on me. This was the big time, and for a brief instant at least, I was part of it.

"What the hell is Truman up to now?" Mr. Dorsey was saying to the Washington bureau man on the telephone.

My God! He was talking about the president of the United States, and the Washington bureau at the other end of the line was actually telling him what the president was up to. I was among people who really knew what the president was up to. In the *News-Letter* office we often talked about what Truman was up to, but it was silly, of course, because none of us had the slightest idea of what he was really doing.

"What's your experience?" Mr. Dorsey was asking.

"I've worked on the Johns Hopkins *News-Letter*."

How ridiculous that sounded when spoken to a man who had just talked to the Washington bureau.

"I'm the managing editor," I blurted.

Mr. Dorsey snorted noisily.

Very close to panic, I almost said, "My mother's cousin is managing editor of the *New York Times*," but stifled the impulse. Managing editors probably all knew each other; suppose Mr. Dorsey telephoned Cousin Edwin and asked what he knew about me and found out Cousin Edwin knew nothing about me. I'd better leave him out of it.

"You realize you can never get rich in the newspaper business," Mr. Dorsey said.

I scoffed at the idea that I might dream of wealth. "Rich?" I tried to smile the smile of a man calmly resigned to a life of penury. "I never expect to make a lot of money."

"If you want money, the news business is the wrong line of work to get into," Mr. Dorsey said, and sent me away with a handshake and a loud snort.

A week later the phone rang while I was eating supper at Marydell Road, where I lived with my mother.

"This is Dorsey. If you still want to work for me, you can start Sunday at thirty dollars a week."

I was flabbergasted. Thirty dollars a week. That was Depression pay. This was 1947. The price of coffee was up to fifty cents a pound and milk to twenty cents a quart. A pair of shoes cost $9. I'd been to New York a few weeks earlier, and the prices there were incredible. A theater ticket cost me $1.50, the hotel was $4.50 a night, a sirloin steak dinner, $3.25. Thirty dollars a week was an insult to a college man.

"Well?" Mr. Dorsey asked.

"I'll take it," I replied.

I knew almost nothing about my new employer except that it also published an afternoon paper, the *Evening Sun*, and that the *Sun* and *Evening Sun* collectively were called the "Sunpapers." I was surprised to learn they had separate staffs, separate newsrooms, and separate editors.

I was surprised to learn that the awesome Mr. Dorsey, though managing editor of the *Sun*, was not the supreme law of the Sunpapers, but that the *Evening Sun* had an equally powerful managing editor.

I was also surprised to learn that above these two giants towered an even more magnificent figure, a widely dreaded tyrant named Neil H. Swanson. Swanson held the grandiose title of "executive editor of the Sunpapers" and justified it by behaving sometimes like Louis the Sun King and others like Cecil B. De Mille directing a Hollywood epic for the silver screen.

Figure 2.1. Charles H. (Buck) Dorsey Jr., managing editor of the *Sun* (1947–1966).

Another thing I didn't know was that a police reporter was the lowest form of life in the *Sun's* universe. Titans like Swanson and Mr. Dorsey had no time for police reporters. Theirs was the world of foreign correspondents, war, diplomacy, global catastrophe, national politics, and presidents. They dealt with the great reporters, men who could tell them what the hell Truman was up to now. What police reporters dealt with, I soon learned, were purse snatches, liquor store holdups, traffic accidents, six-alarm fires, and lost pets. On rare occasions when our paths crossed, Mr. Dorsey looked through me as though I were invisible. The dreaded Swanson was so remote that our paths simply never crossed.

My main contact with power was Clarence Caulfield. He was day city editor, which was not as important as being city editor. "Cauley," as everyone called him, came to work in the late morning, made early assignments, and left at six o'clock when the night city editor arrived to take charge of the city room through the busy night hours. It was Cauley I reported to on my first day at work. He was a red-haired, blue-eyed, freckled, genial, nervous wreck.

He wore steel-rimmed glasses and scratched constantly at imaginary itches around his rib cage.

It was midafternoon on a quiet summer Sunday, and the newsroom was quiet and uncluttered. A couple of older gents of the green-eyeshade variety were seated at the copy desk smoking philosophically and brooding silently about whiskey, racehorses, and commas. Two or three men who looked like they might be reporters chatted quietly on the far side of the room. The silence of it was surprising. Movie newsrooms had shaped my vision of the business, and I had expected uproar.

Caulfield seemed all right, though. He got up and shook my hand and smiled a shy, boyish smile when I introduced myself, then absently scratched the side of his ribcage. We exchanged small talk, and I waited for him to assign me to a desk.

"I'm going to send you out to the west side tonight with Hunter," he finally said. "It'll give you a chance to learn where the police stations are, and Hunter will show you what the go-around is."

After a little more talk about nothing much, I asked, "Where will I be sitting?"

"Sitting?"

"My desk, I mean. When I come in to write, where do you want me to sit?"

For the first time, Caulfield looked a little uneasy about me, gave his ribcage a good scratching, and said, "You don't come in to write."

"I see. You mean I'll have to write in the police station."

"You don't do any writing," said Caulfield.

This was astounding news. No writing? One of the reasons for taking this job was the opportunity to get some writing experience.

"The rewrite men do the writing," Caulfield said. "When you get a story, you ask for the desk and give it to a rewrite man."

"Police reporters don't do any writing?"

That was the way the job worked, Caulfield said.

"You mean I won't really need a desk in the office?"

"Police reporters don't come into the office," said Caulfield.

"Never?"

"Well, they can come in if they want to visit now and then."

"I see."

"Of course, you come in every Friday to pick up your pay down at the cashier's window, but you don't have to come up to the office."

I was first amazed, then disappointed. Amazed because I hadn't known all along that police reporters didn't do any writing. Disappointed because writing was the one side of newspaper work I had looked forward to. Reporting had never much interested me, and now I had stumbled into a job that was all reporting and no writing.

Caulfield saw I had lost some of my fizz. Later I learned he had been a schoolteacher, which probably accounted for his sensitivity toward the young. "Do you like to write?" he asked.

"A little," I said. I didn't want to let on that I wasn't crazy in love with reporting.

"If you do all right in the police districts," he said, "you'll get a chance to come inside and show what you can do on general assignments."

That would mean a desk of my own, writing my own stories, he said.

How much police reporting would I have to do to earn a prize like that? Caulfield, who wasn't authorized to discuss the future, scratched noncommittally, and said, "Oh, you never know. A year or two, maybe, if you're still here. Sometimes faster."

A year or two, and I was already almost twenty-two years old, and not getting any younger. A year or two would be forever.

As it turned out, I was a misfit at police reporting. After a year on the job I was going nowhere in my fantasy of catching up with Cousin Edwin. Worse, I was falling behind at the *Sun*. While I rode trolleys month after month from police station to police station, new people were being hired, assigned to police coverage for a month or two, and then moved inside.

"Moved inside." On the *Sun* those words were the stuff of dreams. They meant getting a chance to write and never having to humor a policeman again.

As I passed through my second year without relief, it sometimes seemed I was destined to grow old and die among the cops. Gradually, I adapted to the squalor of the life, began finding it easier to talk with policemen, began liking a lot of them, and began understanding that the good ones were just as appalled as I was about the wretched underside of Baltimore that was their place of business. Gradually, I became skillful at collecting the sad details of the city's misery and started accumulating a pile of newspaper clippings whose headlines recorded the progress of my education:

MAN, 30, WAKES TO FIND ROOM IN FLAMES, DIES OF BURNS
MAN, 39, KILLED WHEN CAR ROLLS INTO STREAM
WIFE BEATER FINED $25
HOLDUP MAN GETS $25 FROM BARBER SHOP
BOILERMAKER BURGLAR GETS $29 FROM MUSIC STORE
BOY, 17, SHOPLIFTS PANTS, GETS 90 DAYS
TWO MEN JAILED FOR STEALING HAM IN LEXINGTON MARKET

MAN, 42, PLEADS GUILTY TO THEFT OF CAR HE HAD
"AN URGE TO DRIVE"

Week after week, month after month, this tale of humanity's sorrow
unfolded ceaselessly, filling the wads of copy paper I stuffed into my pockets
for note-taking.

I studied newspaper writing under Paul Banker and Jay Spry, the regular
rewrite men who took the material I phoned from the police stations and
turned it into news stories. By reading the paper the next day to see how they
turned facts into stories, I slowly learned the tricks of news writing: how to
compress a complicated story into a few paragraphs if space was tight, how
to expand a flimsy story into an entertaining tale when the city editor needed
something to brighten the back page, how to write hard news leads and feature leads, how to use the short, telling quotation for maximum effect, and a
hundred other small skills.

Banker was the finest writer on the local staff. Spry was the most careful. They embodied what Mr. Dorsey meant when he told newcomers that
learning the business on the *Sun* would qualify them for a welcome at any
paper in the country. Banker and Spry were as different as the *New York Herald Tribune* and the *New York Times*. Their difference extended even to their
dress and physical appearance.

Banker, a Yale graduate only four years older than I, was as Ivy League as
the *Herald Tribune* in his Oxford shirts with button-down collars, soft tweed
jackets, natty bow ties, loafers, and gray flannel slacks. He was tall and trim,
broad-shouldered, with wide cheekbones and wide jaw, broad pleasant smile,
voice low and pleasant, the picture of easy relaxation in a job that kept him
constantly under deadline pressure. He wore his hair in the fashionable close-
cropped military style of the era, and, except for a cigarette habit, seemed as
unflappable as it was possible to get in the newsroom of a big metropolitan
daily during the pandemonium of an approaching deadline.

When I phoned with a story that was slight and unimportant, but funny
and offbeat, I prayed to get Banker, whose wit and natural talent for writing
might turn it into a small gem.

Jay Spry, though only thirty years old, had the old-timer's weary, seen-
it-all look about him. His wardrobe was like mine: basic country-boy un-
distinguished. Baggy slacks, mismated shirt and necktie, and neither much
to look at. He had the kind of hair that won't stay combed. This, combined
with a slight puffiness around the eyes, made him look as though he'd just
got out of bed.

Banker and Spry worked at facing desks pushed up flush against the city
editors' desks. They consulted constantly throughout the night with the city
editor and with each other. Rewrite at the *Sun* was a position of power, and

both could handle the city editor's job when he was absent, and sometimes did.

On rewrite, Jay was the man for eight-alarm fires, and you had better come to the phone with the correct identification of every fire company on the scene; the name of every fire chief, including middle initial; the identity, address, and job of the person who turned in the first alarm; what he was doing when he first noticed the fire; how many people he was doing it with; what part of the structure was burning when he noted it; and the time and method of sounding the alarm.

It wasn't enough to tell Spry that blazing shingles had fallen on a parked car. He would send you back to the scene to get the correct color of the car, its make, its model year, its owner's name, its price at the time of purchase, how much the owner still owed on it, why it was parked at that particular location, whether blazing shingles had ever fallen on it in the past, whether it had previously suffered any similar battering whatsoever, be it from hail-stones, lightning strikes, or flowerpots accidentally pushed from third-floor windows . . .

Whining, as I sometimes did after being sent back for the fourth time with orders to find out if the car had white sidewall tires, was a grave error. Immediately, Spry launched into an endless lecture on the urgency of thorough-ness in journalism. It was garnished with long-winded anecdotes about famous news stories in which white sidewall tires played vital roles. You couldn't understand what the sidewalls of the tires had to do with the eight-alarm fire that was consuming the pants factory? Well, when you had a little experience of newspaper business you would know that writing a fire story requires a great many precise details. A reporter wasn't much good, was he, if he was sent to an eight-alarm fire and stood there gazing at the spectacle for an hour, and then went to the phone with nothing to say except, "It was a big, spectacular, beau-tiful fire with lots of flames." A reporter had to get into the habit of noticing details, just like a good detective. And incidentally, while checking on those tires, find out if the car's front end is out of alignment, and . . .

That was Spry, a one-man school of journalism preaching the vacuum-cleaner philosophy of reporting then practiced by the *New York Times,* though not with the demanding exactitude he brought to it. His passion for thoroughness made him study every page of every paper published every day in Baltimore and vicinity. Since he was usually a week or two behind in this labor of Hercules, he always traveled to and from the office with twenty-five pounds of old newspapers under one arm, hoping to catch up on his reading on the streetcar.

When he left the paper in 1952 for a public relations job, a mock edition of the *Sun* mourned his departure and suggested perpetuating his memory with "a mound of aged newspapers garlanded with wreathes woven from clippings of the 32,959 purse snatches he wrote during his long tenure on the city desk."

By 1948 it looked as if I would stay in the police districts long enough to cover 32,959 purse snatches.

Then, one afternoon Cauley got me on the phone at the Western Police Station and said, "When you report to work tomorrow, come into the office."

"Is there something wrong?"

"You'll be working inside for a while."

He'd said the magic word: inside. I was finally being moved inside. After almost two years of my life out there in the lower depths, I was finally going to work inside. It was like the end of a long sentence to hard labor. Inside. I was being moved inside. I felt as Edmond Dantès must have felt when he finally escaped the Château d'If. Caulfield was moving me inside. Caulfield was a wonderful editor.

• 3 •

Here's to You, Mr. Dorsey!

Muriel Dobbin

We used to chat, very politely, in the elevator from the fifth floor in the red brick building on North Calvert Street to the lobby.

He was the unflappable Buck Dorsey, managing editor of the *Sun* at a time when it still raised its collective eyebrows over the idea of a woman reporter in the newsroom. I was a *Sunday Sun* feature writer, newly arrived from Scotland, where I launched my career in journalism at the age of seventeen on a weekly newspaper, covering everything from rabbit shows to murders.

The tall, lean, sober-faced man in well-cut tweeds was always courteous and even smiled on the occasions when I would bring up the the *Sun's* Washington bureau—an elite group of male reporters with a number of Pulitzer prizes to their credit.

He even nodded once when, in the space of a few minutes, I managed to mention that President Kennedy was reigning over the New Frontier and that Jacqueline Kennedy was really a good story. And I quickly added that the *Sun* had no woman reporter in the bureau! He nodded and made a humming sound, and I looked at him hopefully because he was the only person in the building who could do anything about moving me from the *Sunday Sun*, where I was bored to death writing stories about ladies painting flowers on eggshells and listening to the four women in the Society Section solemnly discussing which weddings should be on page one, two, or three. I didn't fit well in the Sunday section.

I missed covering criminal courts. And although it appealed to the Sunday editor, Hal Williams, that I could write at high speed, it did not appeal to him that, in a nine to five section where you were allotted thirty minutes for lunch and could have your salary docked for being late, I had been known to take three hours to eat. Worse still, I made friends with the police reporters

27

on the morning *Sun* who hung out at a shabby bar called the Calvert House, which sported a tattered sign suggesting, "Let us cater your next affair."

One day, I received a telephone call from Mr. Dorsey's secretary, an imposing woman with a deep voice. I arrived in Mr. Dorsey's office at the speed of light. He looked at me solemnly, and I looked at him anxiously. He said he had decided to use me for an experiment—though he really didn't think it would work.

I was too scared to say anything since it didn't sound like a promising start. He then revealed that he had decided to send me to the Washington bureau to cover Jackie Kennedy. I wasn't sure whether to nod or curtsy, so I said, "Yes sir," and didn't tell him that there was little I would not do to get away from the *Sunday Sun*.

In a melancholy tone, he said he hoped I wouldn't get in any trouble with all those men, and I shook my head vigorously and said, "No, sir." He then hesitated and said he supposed he shouldn't say this, but he hoped I was not planning to get married any time soon.

I shook my head even more vigorously, probably keeping in mind the totally inappropriate man I was currently interested in, and he nodded approvingly. Almost as an afterthought, he said I should go to Washington the next week and, by the way, what was I earning at the *Sunday Sun*? My response sent his eyebrows up, and he told me I would receive a substantial raise. Since the *Sun* had a reputation for being exceedingly parsimonious about salaries, I realized at that point just how little I was being paid. What I didn't realize was that I was not only entering the world of the expense account, but I was also part of the beginning of a small revolution.

I am reminded of the great Russell Baker's portrayal of a similar encounter with Mr. Dorsey's deadpan directness in his delightful book, *The Good Times*. Baker recalled his own experience as a frustrated police reporter who was suddenly invited to have lunch with Dorsey at one of the most expensive restaurants in Baltimore. Mr. Dorsey—only a few veterans called him "Buck"—was drinking martinis. Baker, who was not accustomed to drinking at lunch, was determined to match the managing editor's intake. He didn't know what the lunch was about until after the third round of martinis. Once he sobered up, he staggered home to inform his wife they were moving to London, where he was to be the London correspondent of the *Baltimore Sun*. I can understand how amazed he felt.

There was indeed a revolution in the world of journalism—especially after World War II, when women proved themselves in some very challenging jobs. I was no revolutionary, God knows. I simply wanted to cover more interesting stories and not starve. But I watched women move from an entrenched masculine belief that the female sex had no role in the newspaper world except writing about weddings and food to becoming a real force in reporting and editing the news.

What they had to prove was that they could write as well or better than men, so that they could move into the real world and write about that.

Oddly enough, the British, who formed the most rigidly class-conscious society in the world, allowed women to transgress social boundaries in journalism long before the United States did. I was lucky that I emerged from high school to work for a Scottish weekly paper where nothing was forbidden. I was assigned to police courts, sheriff courts, high courts, crime, local politics, and dog shows, and was expected to write about them in concise English. My gender had nothing to do with it. To increase my meager salary, which began at two guineas a week—about ten dollars at the time—I wrote as a stringer from southwest Scotland for daily newspapers in Glasgow and London.

The *Sun* was an Anglophile newspaper, and had already hired the daughter of the lord lieutenant of an English county and made her an editorial writer—but not a reporter. Being on a less exalted social level, I was ahead of my time at the *Sun*, but in Washington there was enough eccentricity in the bureau that they not only put up with what I didn't know, but welcomed me—especially when I proved I could drink. The bureau was then run by a quiet and gentle man named Gerald Griffin—who might have been taken aback by the fact I barely knew where Capitol Hill was, let alone how bills were passed.

Griffin was succeeded by the formidable Philip Potter. He taught me American politics and treated me very much like an egg he was determined to hatch. A tall, lean man, Potter resembled a superannuated Gandhi except for his height and pointed white head of hair. He yelled at me and was delighted when I yelled back—although I could not match the volume of his voice. And he taught me a great deal because he had a great deal to teach. He was a veteran war correspondent who was also one of the few reporters who went after the witch-hunting senator Joseph McCarthy. Potter not only taught me what the McCarthy hearings were about, he taught me how to drink martinis in the National Press Club, which at that time permitted only men in the bar. Women were confined to what was dubbed "the passion pit," a room adorned by a painting of a Rubenesque woman in flowing draperies who looked to me like a Victorian postcard.

When I reached Washington, there were very few women reporters except for those assigned to cover social events like state dinners. Their numbers were meager in the White House press corps. There was Marianne Means of Hearst Newspapers who was assigned to the president, Helen Thomas of United Press International, and Frances Lewine of the Associated Press.

Being assigned to the president was traumatic for me because I grew up in a monarchy and Lyndon Johnson was culture shock. I was supposed to be covering Jackie Kennedy but had arrived in Washington in 1963 at the time of the assassination and the dramatic funeral that followed.

In fact, I never covered Jackie Kennedy except at the time of the funeral, but I admired her. There was a woman who went through hell and was tough enough to turn around and help plan the kind of funeral the British do so well, using Abraham Lincoln's as her model. I was at Andrews Air Force Base with the press when Air Force One arrived bearing the corpse of John F. Kennedy, and I saw her in that blood-encrusted pink Chanel suit, impassive of face and betraying not emotion but anger when she was asked if she wanted to change her clothes. She refused, saying, "Let them see what they've done to him."

I would have loved to cover Jackie Kennedy because she was interesting, but as far as I know, she wasn't fond of women reporters, and she liked her privacy. Suddenly I was covering Lyndon Baines Johnson (figure 3.1), who required a lot of work, which meant the *Sun* sent a highly experienced political reporter, Pat Furgurson, to cover the political Johnson and added me to write about how colorful he was. And he was.

Lyndon Johnson may be the only president who led the press on walks around the White House grounds with his dog in ninety-five-degree heat while Mrs. Johnson called plaintively that lunch was ready. I distinguished myself by breaking the heel on my shoe and being asked by a photographer to do it again.

There was also the time I witnessed LBJ picking up his beagles by the ears, insisting they liked it and enraging the SPCA. But there were other problems. I couldn't understand Johnson's accent and he couldn't understand mine. So any conversations we had usually began with him saying, "Talk up, honey."

And there was the awful moment when I complained to the rest of the press corps about his driving. I didn't drive, and LBJ liked to show off what his white Lincoln could do on Texas roads. So there I was on my first White House press corps trip, sitting in Johnson's huge Lincoln while he showed off and sipped beer from a paper cup. Marianne Means was in the middle seat beside me. Our recollections vary, but I still maintain she expressed some concern about the speed at which he was driving—I think it was eighty-nine miles an hour. Johnson assured Marianne that she hadn't seen the power that car had. I believed him. I had visions of winding up paragraph eighty-nine in a presidential obituary—and later in an Austin bar I referred to the president as "an adolescent idiot."

Johnson never forgave or forgot. A few days later, he tracked me down in the middle of a ceremony in the Rose Garden and accused me of betraying

Figure 3.1. President Lyndon Johnson tempts Republican legislators.

him. When I denied it, he bent over me in that vulture posture he assumed to browbeat inferiors and said, "Yes, you did." I quailed. As the possessor of a green card and no American passport, I had visions of being deported.

Johnson was the most fascinating politician I ever covered—and he had some reason to think me peculiar. Once when I interviewed him in the White

House, I rose to leave and opened the door to a closet. I never had any sense of direction.

Even when I covered his departure from office, he walked down the line of reporters and when he reached me he kissed me on the forehead and said, "Come to the ranch, Muriel, and I'll give you a ride."

But what mattered were the dramatic changes I witnessed and experienced in both American history and the culture of journalism. After the turbulent Johnson presidency, I covered Richard Nixon and the Watergate scandal. I spent almost two years covering criminal trials and hearings during Watergate, and I was very happy. It was an amazing and always unpredictable story, one I'll never forget, where the crumbs of political corruption led straight to the White House.

There were a few women reporters on Watergate: Lesley Stahl of CBS and Connie Chung of NBC. Women were trickling in, but it took a few more years before the *Washington Post* and the *New York Times* assigned a female to cover a president full-time.

After Watergate, I went back to the White House and reported on two assassination attempts on President Gerald Ford that I always thought were entirely inexplicable. I mean, who attacks a man who so closely resembled a golden retriever? Then I was sent to San Francisco to run the *Sun*'s bureau and was responsible for covering the twelve states from Colorado to western Canada. It was great fun, partly because the *Sun* had a sink or swim approach to farflung correspondents and it let me come up with my own ideas.

I was on the West Coast for about eight years, at the end of which I had left the *Sun*, by then about to be purchased by the *Los Angeles Times*. I joined the Washington bureau of McClatchy Newspapers, which was then expanding its national coverage and wanted White House experience. I found the world of the White House press had changed. What I remembered as about a half-dozen women had expanded to about one-third of the entire group, and what pleased me most was that they were not there because they were women; they were there because they were good.

It was the beginning of the end of discrimination against women in what was considered a plum assignment in journalism. They led the way to equality by hard work and also by not pretending they were men. They were often better than the men they competed with, and the change was most marked in television, a brutally tough business where women like Martha Raddatz, Christiane Amanpour, Andrea Mitchell, and Judy Woodruff established themselves as standout journalists.

At the *Sun*, too, times had changed dramatically. Women were covering every beat, locally, nationally, and overseas. The paper that had hesitated so long in sending me to Washington was now readily appointing women as correspondents in Moscow, Johannesburg, Paris, and Jerusalem. Most of them excelled.

Alas, Mr. Dorsey is gone. But he left me a little legacy—one of the greatest compliments I ever received. Three weeks before he died, he sent me a brief note in the kind of spidery handwriting you rarely see any more, legible and graceful. He wrote briefly, "I should have written this a long time ago, but I wanted you to know I was proud of you. You made a lot of people look foolish."

He probably relished the thought that he'd been right about me and others had been wrong. I sent him an immediate reply telling him how much his letter meant to me and shed a tear before I put it away. If he had been well enough, I would have offered to go to Baltimore and buy him a Beefeater martini.

Time Travel

Arnold R. Isaacs

The generators that provided electric power in the Brazilian town of Porto Velho shut down at eleven o'clock every night, so at two-thirty in the morning, when I left the ramshackle little hotel where I'd been sleeping, the streets were completely black. I don't know why I didn't have a flashlight with me; power outages were a regular occurrence everywhere in Brazil in the 1960s, not just in the far reaches of the Amazon region. But I didn't have one, so I took a candle from a drawer in my hotel room and, holding it out in front of me, used its flickering light to pick my way along the eight-block walk to the railroad station.

The afternoon before, I'd asked a guard outside the station when the train was scheduled to leave. "Four am," the guard answered. I was lucky, he added; the train was the express. I asked when it would arrive in Guajara-Mirim, 230 miles away at the other end of the Madeira-Mamore Railroad. "Around ten o'clock," the guard said. My heart sank. Half the trip would be over before daylight? It turned out the guard didn't mean ten in the morning, though, but ten at night.

Eighteen hours to travel 230 miles. That was the express? I wondered how long the local train took. "Oh, two or three days," the guard shrugged. "*Se Deus quiser*"—if God wills.

When I got there to catch the train, the ancient woodburning locomotive was on a siding outside its wooden shed, firing up its boilers for the trip and sending plumes of glowing orange sparks into the warm, moist darkness. On the platform, crowds of passengers waited with their sacks and suitcases piled next to them, eating fresh-baked bread and drinking coffee bought from a row of vendors at little stands lit by candles or kerosene lanterns. The coffee was Brazil's universal *cafezinho*, little demitasse cups filled with a syrupy mix of sugar and rich, black coffee.

Standing on the platform, drinking my *cafezinho* in the flickering light from kerosene lamps and the sparks shooting up from the locomotive, I had a sudden sense of traveling back in time. The scene was exactly what I would have seen eighty or ninety years before somewhere on the Nebraska prairies, perhaps, in the Iron Horse era of American railroading. When the old wood-burner with its cylindrical boiler lurched from the siding onto the track right on schedule at four o'clock, with its string of wooden coaches rattling behind, it also looked as if it were arriving from the previous century. Passengers crowded into the cars and settled themselves and their bundles on the hard benches, and then, with a blast of the whistle that was strangely deadened in the damp night, we started our journey, trailing a shower of sparks behind us as the iron wheels screeched dementedly on the rails.

On a map of South America, the Madeira-Mamore Railroad appeared as a tiny vertical stripe seemingly from nowhere to nowhere, a slightly elongated speck in the middle of the great empty green heart of the continent. After fifty-seven years of operation, the railroad's days were already numbered when I rode it in early 1969. The motor road that would replace it was under construction, part of a major road-building program in Brazil's Amazon region. That green smear on the map was still almost roadless during my tour in the *Sun's* Rio de Janeiro bureau from 1966 to 1969; of the major projects planned, the only one yet completed (though not yet paved) was the 1,300-mile-long highway from Brazil's new capital, Brasilia, to Belem, near the mouth of the Amazon. But opening up the interior was a much discussed subject among Brazilians during my years in Rio, and the main focus of my reporting on this trip—my last before leaving South America for my next assignment.

The train story was about the region's past, not the future. But it was too colorful not to write. The railroad was a relic of the brief but heady Amazon rubber boom in the late nineteenth century and the first years of the twentieth, when the beginning of the automobile age created a soaring demand for rubber, then chiefly produced from wild trees in the South American jungles. The boom was at its height when construction began on the Madeira-Mamore. Built by Brazil to compensate for annexing a stretch of Bolivian territory farther to the west, the railroad was meant to give Bolivian rubber and other products access to the Amazon and eventually the Atlantic. But before the first train made the run in 1912, planters in Malaya and elsewhere in Southeast Asia had learned to grow rubber trees in plantations, producing rubber much more efficiently and much closer to ocean shipping routes. The Amazon bubble burst, and with it the main reason for the railroad. Its last stretch, a bridge crossing the Mamore River into Bolivia, was never built. So, at the end of my trip nearly six decades later, I was still in Brazil, looking across at Bolivia on the opposite bank.

Before leaving Rio, I would have sent a telegram to Baltimore saying that I would be out of touch in the Brazilian interior for a couple of weeks. (That meant *really* out of touch, in a way that's hard to imagine in the wired world we live in now.) I would not have mentioned the Madeira-Mamore railroad or any other possible stories. This, too, may be hard to imagine today, but it wouldn't have entered my mind to consult with the editors about such things, and it would not have occurred to them to think about what I was going to write—or what country I was in, for that matter—until my story began clattering out from one of the telex printers in the wire room.

The state of communications back then didn't allow any news organization to pester its reporters as they are regularly pestered now, but even then, the *Sun* was unusual in its hands-off style. When a major news event was happening, the *Sun's* editors trusted their correspondents to cover it as their experience and news judgment guided them. When there was no hard news, they relied on us to find interesting or enlightening subjects to write about. On rare occasions I would have welcomed suggestions or a bit more direction from the newsroom, but mostly the extraordinary freedom to choose where to go and what to write was a joy.

When I was assigned to Asia a few years later, I still didn't bother busy editors about what stories to write, and they still didn't bother me. By then the paper had its first full-time foreign editor, but the culture of noninterference hadn't changed. So, as one of many examples, when the Pakistani government lifted a decades-long policy banning foreigners from the remote region of Hunza, I am pretty sure I didn't ask for advance approval to go there on my next trip to South Asia from my base in Hong Kong. I just went.

Deep in the Karakoram mountains on Pakistan's side of the Kashmir ceasefire line, Hunza was (though not for much longer) the last of the quasi-independent princely states governed by local rulers in India and Pakistan under treaties dating back to the era of British rule. It lay on the route of the "friendship highway" linking Pakistan to China via the fifteen-thousand-foot-high Khunjerab Pass. At the time of my trip in the late spring of 1974, Chinese labor brigades sent by Mao Zedong's government were still working on the last couple of hundred miles of road on the Pakistani side of the pass. I hoped to go all the way to the border, or as close as I could get to a still secretive and isolated China. But I got only as far as Karimabad, the residence of the ruling Mir, a hundred or so miles short of the pass. There I was told that the road just ahead was closed by a landslide—a common occurrence, though I wondered if this one was a real landslide or a diplomatic invention to shield the Chinese laborers from prying foreign eyes.

Even if I didn't get as far as I hoped, Hunza was the kind of place I am drawn to: far from the world I know, taking me into an utterly different place and time. Karimabad, also called Baltit, certainly fit that description. Clinging to the walls of a deep valley, it looked out at steep terraced slopes where stone retaining walls enclosed slender strips of ground planted in mountain wheat or fruit trees. Far beyond rose the high mountain peaks, luminous with snow. "Spear-like poplars march in irregular ranks up the hillsides," I wrote in my story, "and jagged folds mark the courses of streams plunging toward the Hunza River, whose waters are clay-colored from the glacial silt carried in the current. On separate eminences rising over the river are an ancient fortress, now crumbling and unused, and the weathered-wood old palace, looking like a wildly misplaced Victorian mansion and hung inside with fading photographs of past Mirs and their families and British royalty of two or three generations ago."

After returning in a hired jeep to the mountain gateway town of Gilgit, I paid a lorry driver forty Pakistani rupees—about four dollars—to ride in the cab of his truck back to Rawalpindi. For the first two-thirds of the three-hundred-mile journey, we drove alongside the Indus River through a succession of jagged gorges carved out by the river on its way through the mountains down to Pakistan's northern plain. Hacked out of the steep rock walls rising from the river's banks, the unpaved roadway climbed and fell and climbed again, at times only one hundred feet or so above the narrow valley floor, and at other times closer to one thousand feet up. For most of its length, the road was only wide enough for a single vehicle. Bypasses were cut into the rock every few miles so trucks coming from opposite directions could pass each other, but often only after fifteen minutes or more of careful backing and filling with one vehicle brushing the wall on one side and the other with its wheels just inches away from the near-vertical cliff falling toward the riverbed far below.

After the first day's driving, still high up in the mountains, we slept at a rough camp where for one rupee—a dime—travelers could rent a string cot, called a *charpoy*, and a heavy quilt to keep out the cold thin air. After handing out the quilts, the camp attendants would catch some of the squawking chickens running around the grounds, wring their necks, and plop them into clay or iron pots to simmer in spicy curry sauce for an hour or so over hot coals. Guests dozed on their cots until the chickens were ready to be served, along with hot sweet tea and fresh warm flatbreads baked on the walls of the fire pits. After the meal you could pull your charpoy under the roof of a large lean-to if you wanted shelter, but May is bone-dry in Pakistan and with no risk of rain, so I dragged mine outside instead and slept under a sky full of astonishingly bright stars. It took two more long days to reach Rawalpindi— three days altogether. (Now, according to the guidebooks, it's an eight- or nine-hour drive.)

Besides that drive from Gilgit, I rode goods trucks or local buses in many other places, including a trip over the Khyber Pass from Peshawar to Kabul. Remembering those trips also brings back a sense of traveling through time, into a world that seems much farther in the past than a mere four decades ago. One reason those particular journeys seem so remote is that the places I went were still at peace, though not for much longer. The leftist coup and the subsequent Soviet invasion that plunged Afghanistan into decades of violence still lay in the future. So did the rising tide of religious intolerance, extremist terror, and officially sanctioned persecution of minority religious communities in Pakistan.

The road from Gilgit and others I rode on went through regions where nearly every male over fourteen had a rifle slung on his back, and the code they lived by was often a violent one. But the violence was local and private, not large-scale armed conflict or religious war. I traveled those roads with no sense of danger. Nobody was mad at me or the unimaginably distant place I came from. Unless I did something dumb like try to talk to a woman (hard to do anyway because they were almost entirely out of sight), no one had any reason to bother me.

When a truck or bus pulled off the road and the driver and everyone else got off for one of the daily prayers, I didn't pretend to join or do the bows and prostrations. I knelt or stood with head bowed, trying to appear respectful. It was obvious that I was not a Muslim, but I never saw any sign that anyone took any notice of that. I wasn't nervous about being identified as an infidel. It didn't cross my mind that there was anything to be nervous about. Today, friends who have lived and worked in the region assure me that most ordinary Pakistanis and Afghans still have no hostility to a non-Muslim foreigner, and in many areas—though not all—traveling is probably no less safe than it was a generation ago. Yet, in a time of widespread terror attacks and in a religious climate that is drastically more oppressive than in the 1970s, it is hard to imagine wandering now as I did then without any thought of conflict or possible danger. Forty years ago, I had no reason to think that any of those Pashtun men with their rifles riding in the back of the truck from Gilgit or along the road to Kabul would have looked at me and seen an enemy of their beliefs and their way of life. Today, looking at their sons and grandsons, I would not be as sure of that.

There's another reason, I believe, that remembering those journeys is like remembering another life in a remote past. Those were the last years before culture became truly global. When I left a major city and went someplace like rural Pakistan or the Brazilian Amazon, I left my world behind and entered a wholly different one, in a way that is much less possible in the present era. I didn't know that then, of course. But I recognize now that freedom from meddling editors in Baltimore was not the only thing that let me experience the world as freely as I was able to. The world itself was in many ways freer for the curious traveler than it is today, or so it seems to me, and I remain grateful that I saw as much of it when I did.

It would be nice if exotic adventures were the only things to remember from that part of my life. But there are other memories to reflect on, too. Among them are moments that taught me something about the nature of extreme poverty and the desperation and terrible demoralization that it creates.

One of those moments came in Haiti, then still under the ruinous rule of François Duvalier, the notorious "Papa Doc." I was riding through Port-au-Prince one night with a man I'll call Bob, who ran the Haiti office of a major international relief agency. In the center of the city—as I recall, within sight of Papa Doc's palace—Bob's car blew a tire. A moment before, the street had looked completely empty and still. But before we rolled to a stop, dozens of men were surging toward us out of the blackness, hoping to earn a few cents for changing the tire. By the time we got out of the car it was surrounded, the men jostling and shoving to get as close as they could. I was afraid we would be caught in a riot, but Bob, an old Haiti hand, knew what to do. After pushing his way around to the back of the car he opened the trunk, and arbitrarily pointing to one of the men, took out the jack and handed it to him. Most of the others dejectedly turned away, but one bigger and stronger-looking guy roughly grabbed the jack from the fellow Bob had selected, shoved him aside and set to work, while the first man stood by with pleading eyes.

When the new tire was on, Bob handed a couple of coins to the first man, nothing to the one who had changed the tire. Those were the rules of the street, apparently. The first fellow turned and walked away with his tip, maybe ten or twenty cents. The second stared at Bob, but not with any anger that I could detect. He just looked beaten and hopeless. After a moment he walked away, too.

Another lesson about poverty came six or seven years later on the other side of the world, in an abandoned factory shed in a place called Mirpur a few miles outside Dhaka (then usually spelled Dacca), the capital of Bangladesh. The factory was temporarily serving as a shelter for refugees from the countryside, fleeing a famine that ravaged Bangladesh and large areas of India that year. About three thousand people were crowded in the crumbling factory buildings and flimsy shelters on the muddy grounds. One of them was a man named Jaynal Abedin. When I met him, he was sitting stone still on the dirt floor. At his feet, wrapped in rags, lay the body of his youngest daughter. Father and child looked like a sculptor's image of despair.

Abedin's story was the same as everyone else's: no work in his village, no money to buy food. So he came to the city with his family to beg, then ended up in the Mirpur factory. They had been there about a month when his little girl died. He told this tonelessly, without any flicker of grief in his face or voice. Kneeling beside him, scribbling in my notebook as a camp official translated his words, I was a bit disconcerted at his lack of emotion, but before standing up to move on, I hesitantly offered a few words of condolence. In a startling transformation, Abedin suddenly began crying, in hoarse convulsive sobs that shook his whole gaunt body.

"They do not expect sympathy from anyone," the camp official said to me, noticing my surprised expression. Waving toward the other families huddled around us in the cavernlike gloom, he added, "Everyone here suffers so much." In that moment, I understood in a new way that poverty impoverishes the human heart, not just the body. Poverty did not just take Jaynal Abedin's child from him, but also the comfort he might have gotten from the sorrow of others.

Today, according to the statisticians, about a billion people around the world live in extreme poverty. That's a lower number than it was a few decades ago, chiefly because of improved living standards in China and India. I suppose we can tell ourselves that we've made progress. But a billion times the desperation of those men appearing out of the night on that Port-au-Prince street, or a billion times the misery I saw in Jaynal Abedin's face when he finally let it show, is still an awful lot of misery and desperation.

And then there was the war; wars, actually. Few others remember this, or ever knew it to begin with, but those who were there know that the wars in Vietnam and Cambodia were very different in circumstance and character. (The third Indochina war, in Laos, was different, too. But that war was run largely by the CIA in areas journalists could not get to, and with most details kept secret. We wrote what we could find out, but hardly ever—never, in my case—from the kind of firsthand reporting that was possible in the other two theaters.)

Vietnam's war was tragic, but Cambodia's was worse. One of many sorrowful memories is a scene on a wooden bridge near a place called Prek Ho, ten miles or so south of Phnom Penh. At the bridge, a group of soldiers' wives were standing in front of a roadblock, listening to the sounds of rifle and machine-gun fire from a few hundred yards away on the far side of the stream. The women had come with parcels of food for their husbands, who had been fighting for two days with nothing to eat—a common occurrence in that war. They knew their husbands had no food because the truck with their rations was still back at the unit headquarters. But the guard on the bridge would not let them through.

They had been waiting for several hours when I got there, hoping the firing would subside. But now they advanced toward the guard again, sobbing and wailing. For a tense moment it looked as though they were going to keep walking and dare him to shoot at them. Just then another soldier rode up on a motorbike. He was in the same unit as the women's husbands, and after a short conversation, they reluctantly handed him their parcels. They watched as he drove across the bridge toward the firing, then turned and started trudging back to their base.

I thought it was a good story when I wrote it for the *Sun* and later in my book *Without Honor*. I still think it was a good piece of writing, if I say so myself—vivid, moving, and showing something about the particular agony of that war. It wasn't until years later that I thought about the fact that none of those women were named in either the original story or the book. Probably I never asked their names. It's likely that many or even all of those women and their husbands had died by the time I wrote the book, either in the awful last years of the war or during the Khmer Rouge terror that followed. It is possible that no one was left alive who even remembered them. I still believe it was a good story, but I wish I had not left those women nameless. If I could go back in time and see that bridge again, I would ask their names and write them down.

In Cambodia, it was obvious for a long time that sooner or later the war would be lost. In Vietnam, by contrast, until the very last weeks it was hard to visualize the war ending at all, certainly not in any clear-cut, definitive way. From all the evidence, neither side was strong enough to win or weak enough to lose, and neither showed any sign of giving up, so it seemed the war would just go on forever. Battles didn't bring one side or the other any closer to winning or losing. They were like grenades thrown in a stream—after the ripples subsided and the dead fish floated downstream, the stream looked exactly as it did before. So in March and April 1975, when South Vietnam's army suddenly unraveled in a series of panicky retreats and the advancing North Vietnamese occupied entire provinces in a few days, it was hard to believe any of it was really happening. Remembering those last weeks is like remembering a dream, not something that actually took place.

There are moments that come back with brilliant clarity, like the strangled voice of the angry, humiliated sergeant in Tuy Hoa who had gotten separated from his wife and two of his children in the disastrous retreat out of the highlands, and his friend who I thought was going to throw a grenade at me. Or the swarm of refugees racing behind a water truck on the sandy beach of Phu Quoc Island, clutching empty tin cans or plastic buckets as they ran, determined to be first in line when the truck stopped. But as vivid as they are, those moments don't connect into any coherent narrative. They jumble and jostle in my memory, like lingering scenes from a dream after you wake up. It felt that way then, too.

The other odd thing about remembering those weeks is a strong feeling that I went through them alone and in silence, not speaking to anyone. It's not true, of course. I know exactly who was with me that day in Tuy Hoa, though we were separated when I ran into the guy with the grenade, and I know I was with a group of other reporters on that strange trip to Phu Quoc. Obviously we talked, but I have no memory of it, or of any other conversations I must have had with colleagues during those final days.

The story I remember most clearly from that time is one I didn't write, and that as far as I know no one else wrote either. The whole tale is too long and weird to tell here in detail, but the background is that a few weeks before the war ended, Graham Martin, the US ambassador, approved a clandestine evacuation for Vietnamese working for news organizations—this at the same time he was adamantly refusing to authorize evacuation of thousands of Vietnamese working for the embassy or other US government agencies. It's unprovable but not unlikely that by making an exception for media personnel, Martin was hoping to avoid any coverage of his efforts to keep the US mission's Vietnamese from leaving. I know of no explicit bargain, but for obvious reasons, the embassy's cooperation on our Vietnamese was a strong deterrent to any reporting on Martin's obstructive policy and the growing tension it was creating inside the mission.

Brian Ellis, the CBS bureau chief, coordinated the secret evacuation, which eventually involved about six hundred media employees and family members. I put four names on Brian's list. None of them actually worked for me. One was a woman who had put her half-American son on an earlier evacuation flight, terrified that the communists would kill all Amerasian children, and was desperate to get to the United States and retrieve him before he was given to an American family. One was the mother of my former interpreter, who was already in the States. The other two were a woman who had cooked for one of my predecessors and her daughter. They were trying to rejoin the woman's husband, who had deserted from the South Vietnamese army and was now in Hong Kong.

After giving Brian their names, I told them to check with me every few hours (no easy task in those pre-cell phone days; in my group, three of the four had no phone at all). This went on for several tense days until Brian sent word for me to gather them in my room and wait for the message to leave. When it came, they were told to walk separately to the square in front of the Saigon cathedral, a few blocks from the hotel, and wait there to be picked up and smuggled onto the airfield. I gave them as many dollars as I thought I could spare, walked down to the lobby and said goodbye, and watched them head up Tu Do Street toward the cathedral to begin their journey to a new unknown life.

The ethics of this affair were questionable, to say the least. The rules say that reporters shouldn't trade silence for special treatment, explicitly or implicitly, and it was clearly unethical to pass my four evacuees off as media employees when they weren't. But in the same circumstances today, I would do just what I did then. Sometimes the ethical decision and the right decision are not the same. I have no regrets about my choice, and even if I did, I would much prefer to remember unethically helping a few people rather than having to remember *not* helping people I could have helped, for no better reason than to sanctimoniously tell myself I was ethically pure.

Nine days after my evacuees left, on the morning of April 29, 1975, I woke up to the sound of communist artillery shells falling on Saigon's Tansonnhut Airport. A few hours later, I walked out of my hotel into the blazing midday heat, carrying a typewriter and a small suitcase. Everything else I left in my room, including the helmet and flak jacket I had bought on the black market years earlier. Then came a long wait on a downtown sidewalk, followed by a sweltering and inexplicably circuitous bus ride to the air base, and another long wait in the compound that was once the US military headquarters in Vietnam. At each of those stages, I was with people I knew. But again, I have no memory of exchanging words with anyone. At 3:36 pm I ran to a helicopter, scrambled on, flew up into a humid haze that turned the sky the color of platinum, and forty minutes later landed on the *USS Mobile* a few miles off the Vietnamese coast.

Many years later, I wrote a poem about that day. It mentioned the platinum sky and the helmet and flak jacket I'd left in the hotel. The last lines said:

> *I didn't leave the anger and sorrow.*
> *Those I took with me, and still have.*
> *Sometimes I wonder, if I could have left them behind,*
> *Would I? Half a lifetime later*
> *I still don't know.*

Long after the war, in 2000 or 2001, I had a conversation with a former high-ranking presidential aide who was certain he had seen live newscasts of the Saigon evacuation on television screens in the White House situation room. He looked incredulous when I pointed out that there was no live TV from Vietnam. In fact, I was a little surprised myself to realize how much the world of news had changed, and how quickly it had become unimaginable that scenes from such a critical event *wouldn't* be seen as they were happening.

Besides live TV from places like Vietnam, a lot of other things didn't exist when I was a foreign correspondent. There was no twenty-four-hour cable TV news, no Internet, no e-mail, no Twitter, and no YouTube. There were no cell phones, dumb or smart, or cell phone videos. Without all those things, there was nothing like the blizzard of fact-free or reduced-fact babble that now surrounds any major news event. It's also hard to remember now, but news in that world was not yet global. We didn't know everything that everyone else had reported, certainly not to the degree that journalists (and their editors) know today. Of course, reporters on a big story usually had a general idea what others were reporting and shared a collective sense of what the story was. But it was not as powerful and did not create a single, frequently oversimplified narrative of the event as quickly as often happens now.

Another difference is that many newspapers like the *Sun,* that once took international coverage as a serious obligation, no longer have foreign correspondents. For the *Sun's* owners, maintaining bureaus overseas was no doubt in part a status symbol. But their commitment to have the paper's own eyes on the world and to deliver knowledge and understanding to its readers through its own reporting also reflected an honorable sense of public responsibility—a recognition that journalism was not just a business but an essential institution for a democratic society.

That was a given for journalists in my generation. It is not as easy to see where that responsibility lies in the present era. The new-media gurus are right when they point out that today, sitting at our computers at home (something else nobody had forty years ago!), we have access to vastly more information from around the world than we did then. It is also clearly true that today's media give a voice to many more people, and transmit a much wider range of experiences, perspectives, and feelings than traditional journalism was able to provide. It is less clear how many readers take the trouble to find all that information or read it critically enough to sift valid knowledge from shrill argument or empty noise.

Overall, in a rapidly changing landscape, it's hard to tell where the road we are on is heading—to more knowledge and better public understanding of world events, or to greater confusion and faulty perception. In my mind, that is still a wide-open question. So is the meaning of the memories I've reflected on in this chapter. Were my years as a foreign correspondent part of a continuing narrative about reporting the world? Or are they like that ancient woodburning locomotive in the Brazilian jungle, a relic from a vanished past? That is an open question, too.

· 5 ·

More Fun than Getting Rich

Ernest B. Furgurson

The *Sun's* Washington coverage began in 1837 with letters from a single moonlighting postal clerk. When I joined the bureau in 1960, it had eleven full-time reporters. When I ended a dozen years as bureau chief in 1987, we had grown to fifteen.

Why?

Why did a Baltimore newspaper with the third-biggest circulation in a three-newspaper town make the effort and spend the money to be a more prominent Washington presence than other papers many times its size?

Over thirty-six years, I became well acquainted with the owners, publishers, and editors who decided what our paper would be, but none ever said to me "this is why we do this." At the working level, we talked every day about *how* to do it.

But the best explanation of *why* that I know of is rooted in the 1920 White Paper co-drafted by H. L. Mencken and Harry C. Black, who would become chairman of the A. S. Abell Company. Intended as a program for the "future course" of the *Sun*, the White Paper recommended a stronger push into Washington to increase the national stature of the newspaper. As noted in the 1937 centenary history, the "expansion" of the *Sun's* "circulation and prestige" in Washington "required, of course, a development of the Washington staff."

Whether that expansion was successful as a business proposition is unknown to me. I doubt it. But for many decades, when the *Post, Evening Star, Times, Herald, Daily News,* and other Washington papers were sleepy, sensational, or both, the *Sun's* authoritative coverage was thoroughly appreciated on Capitol Hill, at the White House, in the federal bureaucracy, and the capital press.

Starting in the 1960s, some of those somnolent bigger papers started waking up, in Washington and elsewhere. There were great upheavals at the *Washington Post* and the *Los Angeles Times,* for example—new editors, new publishers, and much bigger staffs. When I arrived in Washington, the *Sun* bureau was about the size of the *Chicago Tribune's* and the *New York Herald Tribune's*. The *Los Angeles Times,* just down the hall on the twelfth floor of the National Press Building, had two reporters and a secretary. By 1975, it had nineteen staffers, and in 1987 it had thirty, growing toward a peak of forty-two. The *New York Times*, which had twenty-two in 1960, nearly doubled to forty by 1987.

With such numbers, those papers could cover major breaking news and still commit to enterprise projects that demanded manpower without the certainty of success. At the same time, papers like the *Philadelphia Bulletin*, *Chicago Daily News*, *Chicago Sun-Times*, *Detroit News*, and *Boston Globe* made do with Washington staffs of half a dozen or fewer. They could cover the president, Congress, and their state delegations without feeling guilty if they missed something breaking elsewhere.

The *Sun* bureau seemed in the middle—not big enough to staff every major beat plus gambling on special projects that might or might not pay off, and not small enough to shrug at the chance of missing something that would lead the paper. (Our managing editor when I began, the fabled Buck Dorsey, said more than once that our job was "not to make the news, but to report it.") The bureau's unstated but understood daily effort was to see that the *Sun's* label was on every major story from Washington. In the capital and wherever the news led, we regularly covered the president, Congress, State Department, Pentagon, Supreme Court, economics, and politics, and as needs shifted, we often had two watching the White House, two or more on the Hill and on politics, and others following issues of the moment, such as education, the environment, and consumer economics. But we meant to offer readers more than our label, to do more than just being there. We wanted our correspondents to be or become authorities in their fields, to write with more depth and individuality than the press agencies that competed for space on page 1. Most days I think we succeeded.

Perhaps I was more sensitive than most about keeping the agencies off the front page. The only "rocket" I ever got from the home office while working overseas came after Nikita S. Khrushchev announced some Kremlin shift that was clearly old news. After being urged early in my Moscow tour not to send more than two pieces a day unless something startling happened, and having already filed twice, I passed up that routine story. Naturally, the weekend desk ran the AP's version out front, as prominently as if Lenin had risen from his tomb. When I got that highly unusual cable from Dorsey asking how this had happened, I reacted strongly. Still, down inside, I didn't forget.

Figure 5.1.   The Cuban Missile Crisis, October 1962.

Speaking of cables: in Moscow in the early 1960s, most other correspondents were filing by phone or telex, but in three years there, I never once spoke to Baltimore by that nineteenth-century device known as the telephone. I, and *Sun* reporters for years after me, had to file via the government telegraph office, which was downtown near Red Square. Before and sometimes after I got my Soviet driving license, that could mean slogging 1.3

miles and back through the cold dark streets at 3 am. Then, during the first part of my time in Saigon, I usually filed by tipping a Caravelle Hotel porter to hand-deliver my copy to the official Postal, Telegraph and Telephone office. Neither the central telegraph nor the PTT was speedy, and occasionally copy from Saigon never made it to Baltimore. But this reliance on primitive signals wasn't just a peculiarity of *Sun* duty in faraway places. Past the 1970s, in the heart of Washington, our bureau was still filing by telex, punched by a skilled operator whom we also took along to national conventions. Before catching up with the fading century, we went through a series of frustrating communications experiments that helped hurry our conscientious desk man Paul Ward, the Pulitzer-winning former diplomatic correspondent, to his death. For a long time, the *Sun* was not simply parsimonious about such matters; it was determinedly untrendy, shy of anything that might turn out to be a passing gimmick. Although the founder, Arunah S. Abell, had been full of bold ideas for getting and processing the news, in the 1880s his successors let years go by before daring to install the revolutionary Linotype machine, invented under their noses by the Baltimorean Ottmar Mergenthaler. In the 1970s, however, the *Sun* was among the first to invest in computers, adopting the Harris system to replace the venerable typewriter.

Parsimony: for decades, if not generations, the *Sun* was renowned in the business for the way it turned out a quality product while paying such scrimpy salaries. Many talented journalists came to the paper despite this because it offered a chance to work on a fine paper, perhaps to cover world affairs as a correspondent overseas or in Washington, which was more fun than getting rich. It's not at all surprising that one of the *Sun's* most illustrious foreign correspondents, Patrick Skene Catling, wrote a book about his adventures and called it *Better Than Working*.

In the early 1960s, the bureau was made up entirely of men (and one woman, Muriel Dobbin) who had worked with the paper in Baltimore. The only person hired from the outside in that decade was Charles Corddry, the veteran United Press International Pentagon reporter who joined us to replace Mark Watson, the Pulitzer-winning dean of military correspondents. When I became bureau chief in 1975, half the staff was older, half younger than I was at forty-six. One of the things agreed upon was that we would recruit talent both in and outside the paper, which meant we would have to compete with what others were paying in Washington. I'm happy to say that in the next decade, salaries went up steadily, and we hired more than a dozen experienced hands from Baltimore, the agencies, and bigger papers. At one period, during a hiring freeze, I interviewed dozens of applicants before the freeze broke and I could bring only one of them aboard. Lots of quality journalists wanted to work for the *Sun*.

Since we tried to staff the most important stories breaking in the capital, there was no great tension in daily relations with Baltimore, and seldom disagreement over what was coming from the bureau. We routinely sent them a schedule of what to expect, and they routinely asked to be sure that we were watching this event or that. There was occasional friction over the role of the lone correspondent assigned to the state congressional delegation and Maryland affairs. Organizationally, that reporter belonged not to the bureau but to the metro desk. On rare days when national news was heavy and state news was slow, we might borrow him to help us manage the load, and this did not always sit well with the metro editor back home. Some Baltimore staffers may disagree when I say that compared with the vast power struggles we heard about between the *Times* bureau and New York, and within some of the news magazines, peace and quiet was the norm between our bureau and the home office.

Ours was then a loosely edited paper, and we liked it that way. Ever since the days when newspapers were personal sheets published by the proverbial tramp printer with a shirttail full of type, there has been a built-in strain between the editorial and commercial sides of the business, the familiar church/state divide. Less obvious, but familiar within the trade, is the natural strain between editors in home offices and correspondents in the field, whether that field is as close as Washington or as remote as Dushanbe. In desert foxholes and at press bars in every newsy capital, there are doughty veterans complaining about those dolts back home who have no idea what it's like out here in the world, and of course there are veterans at desks back home congratulating themselves for saving those high-living prima donnas in the field from misspelling things like Ouagadougou. Dorsey was a lifelong deskman, an editor who had "never been outdoors," as we who had been sometimes put it. But he had our respect, and I think the reason why is that in his gruff way, he deeply respected even the youngest of us, and felt a fatherly affection for colleagues heading off into unknown situations. It became his habit to invite each newly designated foreign correspondent to a sendoff lunch at the Maryland Club in Baltimore. The eager reporter was certain to ask the venerable managing editor's advice about how to do the job at his new post, and Dorsey was certain to say, "That's up to you, we wouldn't be sending you if we didn't think you could handle the job." And that, I think, is also a vastly oversimplified description of relations between Baltimore and the Washington bureau well beyond Dorsey's retirement in 1966, when he was replaced by Paul Banker.

As bureau chief, I did little to change that pattern. Like my predecessors, I split my time between reporting and managing. I tried hard not to "bigfoot" our correspondents, a sin of which some other bureau chiefs were guilty when they stepped in to take away the biggest breaking stories from reporters who covered their beats day to day. For nearly seven years before I became chief, I had been writing three national affairs columns a week for the editorial page, and on changing hats I cut the column to one a week. Per tradition, I did set pieces like presidential conventions, debates, inaugurations, and occasional foreign trips, and often wrote analyses or color pieces alongside our correspondents' major stories. When things suddenly flew loose, I handled roundups and sometimes fed others my own reporting to back up their work. In emergencies, individual beats were forgotten while we scattered to cover the crisis.

There was the day Ronald Reagan and three others were shot as they left the Washington Hilton Hotel in 1981. Gilbert Lewthwaite, then our White House man, was a few feet away, and did an eloquent eyewitness account of that "frozen moment of sharp sound, soft smoke and sudden chaos . . . a sidewalk dripping a friend's blood and possibly life into a rusty grating." Fred Barnes, then our political writer, interviewed Secret Service agents and did a piece on special presidential security situations, and I wrote the lead, bringing in details from all directions, including our staffers at the hospital. The following winter, when an Air Florida jet crashed into the Potomac after taking off from National Airport in a rush-hour snowstorm, we scattered to hospitals and nerve centers on both sides of the river. Curt Matthews, our legal affairs reporter, and Bob Timberg, then a congressional correspondent, had to mush miles on foot past traffic jammed solid on the 14th Street Bridge to reach airline officials at a Crystal City motel. The ever-ready Lewthwaite did a deadline analysis of safety concerns at National Airport. They all fed me to wrap things up, and together we filed a complete package for the bulldog (mail and street sales) edition, which in those days was 6:30 pm. Of course, such all-out efforts are mounted in every city room when such emergencies break. But for me, it was always inspiring to witness the performance of old hands when adrenaline surged, to be reminded that however lofty their daily assignments, every one of them had started as a street reporter and still knew how.

I've been asked what our bureau budget was, to operate as busily as we did. I never knew, and never asked. The managing editor had his budget, and we got a noticeable slice of it. In the early 1980s, I estimated that we spent a million dollars a year. It was much more in political seasons, when we followed every major candidate and had one or two reporters constantly on the road doing state-by-state assessments. The airlines then typically charged one and a half times first class fare on political charters, which included bloody Marys, martinis, and cold towels day and night. Well past the 1960s, we still filed domestic copy by Western Union, which sent its own puncher with all such trips. Addressing each page of copy "baltsun npr collect," we ripped it out of our Olivetti and shouted "Western!" and the traveling puncher grabbed it out of our hand to rush it off. Traveling solo, at home or abroad, the first thing we typically did on arriving in any town, often before we started reporting, was to find the local Western Union or cable office; we were nervous until we did. Finally, at first on the road and then within the bureau, we started using primitive computers in the mid-1970s.

Early in the 1980s, our new publisher, John R. (Reg) Murphy, loosened the budget to authorize a deputy bureau chief who handled much of the daily routine. That gave me more freedom for reporting and getting out of town for my "USA" columns, and that fresh air inspired me to return to full-time writing. Thus, I was happy to rejoin the editorial pages in 1987.

Not all the bureau chief's duties were reporting or managing; I was also expected to represent the paper in press organizations and other doings that were not strictly journalistic. Some were fun, some less so.

Our top editors, publishers, and directors were proud of our presence in the capital, and looked forward to meeting presidents and senators at the black-tie White House Correspondents and white-tie Gridiron Club dinners. Dating way back, our correspondents have taken conspicuous roles in those groups—our Bill Knighton presided at the White House group's dinner the first time John F. Kennedy attended as president. Karen Hosler did so for George H. W. Bush. Fifteen *Sun* staffers have been members and three have been presidents of the much smaller Gridiron. In that club's 150-year history, every president of the United States except Grover Cleveland has attended its dinner and laughed, or pretended to laugh, at its satirical skits and songs. But it's hard to believe that any politician or club member enjoyed those annual hijinks more than did Gary Black, Harry Black's nephew and the company's longtime chairman. He was a principal reason why the *Sun's* flag flew so high for so long in Washington.

Gary Black not only enjoyed the Gridiron ritual—he entertained the whole mob in Baltimore beforehand. It was a longstanding tradition that the Gridiron members who performed the annual skit came to Baltimore to get their costumes and perform a dress rehearsal at the Maryland Club during a lunch hosted by the *Sun* with a menu that invariably included terrapin stew. The practice was broken under Murphy in reaction to complaints about the Maryland Club's exclusion of women. In any event, Murphy commented, "Nobody cares about turtle soup."

I must say that the greatest pleasure of heading the bureau, and of my other twenty-four years as reporter and columnist at the *Sun*, was to work with so many superb, dedicated, mostly unrecognized colleagues in Baltimore, Washington, and overseas. For most of that time, ours was still the third-biggest paper in a three-paper town—when the Pulitzer-winning foreign correspondent Price Day was editor-in-chief, he accurately described it as "the best unread paper in the country." In a way, being part of the *Sun* suddenly reminds me of my hitch in the Marine Corps many years ago: the Marines always have less manpower and materiel than the Army, so they aren't equipped to do everything, but what they do, they do with vigor. Some of the *Sun* people who made that true for us were colorful characters, like the hard-charging bureau chief and old Asia hand Phil Potter, and others just did their fine work quietly, like Al Sehlstedt, who covered the space age before and after the moon landing, and . . . There were so many—I can't list them all, but beyond those mentioned above, I must remember Hank Trewhitt, our peerless diplomatic correspondent, who was my closest friend on the paper, and Joe Sterne, who covered the world and then Washington with modest confidence before taking over the editorial page, and . . . There are so many, and I owe them so much.

· 6 ·

Learning from the Best

Tony Barbieri

Long before I knew how to write a lede, work a story, develop a beat, or cultivate a source, I learned how to be a newspaperman by watching some of the most distinguished journalists in the country.

In 1968, I was a student at George Washington University in Washington, DC, and by chance I fell into a job as what was then known as a copy boy at the Washington bureau of the *Baltimore Sun*. This job was the lowest rung it was then possible to occupy at the newspaper that would be my one and only home in a thirty-six-year journalism career that I ended as managing editor.

Even fifty years ago, such a story—copy boy to managing editor—would have been regarded as farfetched, but that's the kind of place the *Sun* was, and delightfully remained, well into the new century.

The *Sun's* Washington bureau was quite an operation back then—an L-shaped series of dusty two-person cubicles on the twelfth floor of the National Press Building. In addition to a dozen or so correspondents, there was a bureau manager, receptionist/bookkeeper, two part-time key punch operators, and several part-time copy boys, all under the direction of the chief of the Washington bureau, the legendary Philip Potter.

Tall, rail-thin, white haired, and abundantly profane, Potter could make a casual "good morning" sound like a challenge to an argument. He had made a name in Washington, and nationally, for being one of the few Washington journalists to take on Senator Joseph McCarthy when the Wisconsin demagogue was at his most dangerous. He was also known to be close to Lyndon B. Johnson (figure 6.1). Those two facts alone made Potter one of the highest profile journalists in Washington and a regular panelist on Sunday morning news shows. On one of my very first evenings on the job, I was sitting at the receptionist's desk when I heard Potter calling loudly and impatiently for someone named Dennis.

I failed to answer, not being named Dennis, until the bureau manager tapped me on the shoulder and explained gently, "He's talking to you." It seems that one of the copy boys two or three years earlier had been named Dennis, and Potter had never bothered to update his mental contact list. So for the next year or so, I answered to Dennis.

When I finally hustled into his office, he barely looked up from his typewriter and said, "Get over to the White House and wait for a copy of the advance text" of a speech the president would be giving in a few hours.

Get over to the White House? I can do that?

Yes, indeed I could do that, and lots of other things as well. My new status as even the lowliest employee of a newspaper bestowed on me the right to go places other people couldn't go, to find out things before other people knew them, and to look at the powerful and exalted people who made the news through a different lens. Now I could stand outside and look in, mostly with disapproval, at the way the world worked. Now I could be in the company of smart, witty, and colorful people who smoked, drank a lot, and told wonderful stories. It was for many of these mostly bad reasons that I suddenly decided I knew what I wanted to do with my life.

It was in these early days at the *Sun* that I first encountered a twenty-seven-year-old John Carroll, newly returned from a stint in Vietnam as a war correspondent, where he had made a name for himself covering the siege of Khe Sanh. Cool, laconic, and possessed of a dry, self-effacing wit, Carroll was the exact opposite of the volcanic Potter. He would soon leave the paper and then two decades later return to the *Sun* to make his mark as editor.

It was from watching journalists like Potter, Carroll, and others in the bureau who were kind enough to tolerate my questions that I learned how newspapermen ought to behave.

On the one hand, there was the breezy insouciance and brash irreverence with which they regarded the pompous and vainglorious politicians they covered. It was not exactly Mencken's "the only way to look at a politician is down," but neither was it with any hint of the awe that a then-twenty-year-old George Washington undergraduate considered the idea of senators, cabinet members, and Supreme Court justices. Let a president dare to give a major domestic policy address, and a correspondent would wander by cynically inquiring, "Did he point with pride, or view with alarm?"

But I also saw the other side of journalism at the *Sun*—the competitiveness, the fanatical devotion to accuracy, fairness, and balance, the craftsmanship and skill it took to spin a lovely soft lede on deadline. These were the important things, the things not laughed off with the latest political speech. I saw this every day when, as the bureau's gofer and sometime researcher, I was sent digging through files to check someone's middle initial, or confirm it was a senator's third term.

Decades later, Carroll captured this dichotomy beautifully in a lecture on journalism ethics at the University of Oregon, a lecture I have assigned to every journalism ethics class I've ever taught. In it, Carroll talks of the fun, cynical humor, and lassitude of the newsroom as some of journalism's ostensible appeals. But he says the "looseness of the journalistic life, the seeming laxity of the newsroom, is an illusion. Yes, there is informality and humor, but beneath the surface lies something deadly serious."

I learned from Carroll about this seriousness when he returned to the *Sun* to become editor in 1991, and I was lucky enough to be given a job that brought me into close contact with him nearly every day. It was from Carroll that I learned that the art of putting out a quality daily newspaper involved far more than strong reporting, great writing, and smart editing.

It meant good, sharp, strong headlines, photography that went with stories, and captions that added value to the picture. It meant hitting deadlines so that on the nights when we needed to be late the composing room would trust us. It meant flawless production—no typos, no dropped lines, no incorrect jump pages, not even a pica too much white space between the last obit and the first death notice on page B12.

Beyond insisting that all this be perfect, Carroll wasn't particularly engaged in any of it. When I became assistant managing editor for news—a job that basically dealt with the nuts and bolts of putting out the paper, from selecting the front page stories to space allotments to machines that would break in the night—Carroll and his managing editor, William K. Marimow, made it clear they preferred to focus on other things.

Thus, I was deputized to be the newsroom's representative on a standing committee that was otherwise comprised of vice presidents from the business and production sides—circulation, printing, advertising, marketing, and so forth—all people a couple levels above me in the paper's hierarchy.

"Just make sure you don't let them do anything that hurts the paper," were Carroll's instructions. I had a quick flashback to my first day as a copy boy in Washington and Potter ordering me to "get over to the White House." I can do that?

Yes, I could, and it wasn't so tough. Despite skepticism from my newsroom colleagues, I found people on the business side to be quite conscious of the *Sun's* reputation for quality and who were determined to avoid conflicts with the newsroom.

This was an attitude that came from the top, from publishers like William F. Schmick Jr., when the paper was family owned, or Michael E. Waller after it had been acquired by Times Mirror.

Not long after I became managing editor, I got a phone call from a car dealer who was furious about the paper's coverage of an issue involving him.

Because the man's dealership was a major advertiser, I thought it prudent to give Waller a heads-up on the complaint.

"Whenever something like that happens," Waller instructed me, "tell them that when they buy an ad in the *Baltimore Sun*, they are buying the best and most effective advertising in the Baltimore region. But that's ALL they're buying."

Some of the most important things I learned, and now teach, about the role of a news organization in its community I learned from hearing the similar experiences of others at the *Sun*—"Here's what Old Man Schmick did when someone tried to threaten him. . ."—or from my own later experiences with Waller. Keep politicians, businesses, and even the most nobly-intended civic groups at arm's length. The appearance of a conflict of interest is just as bad as a real conflict.

My first contact with a managing editor was when I was still a copy boy in Washington and had only the dimmest notion of what one did. My education began when Potter ordered me to "call Banker and tell him I'll have a six-hundred-word analysis" that hadn't been scheduled. Paul Banker was the managing editor, at the time the highest ranking news executive at the paper. As a part-time copy boy in the Washington bureau, I was the lowest. I had never met Banker and he of course had no idea who I was, but I'd overheard enough to know that he was a remote and intimidating presence.

Now I had to call the fearsome Banker, introduce myself, and tell him he had to tear up his front page to accommodate a late story from Washington.

Through encounters like this, I began to get a better understanding of Baltimore: not only the newsroom operation itself, but also the strangely exotic city in which it was located, a mere thirty-eight miles away. The idea began to grow that some day I might be able to get a job there.

For many reporters at the *Sun*, service in Baltimore on the local staff was a necessary stepping-stone to the prestigious jobs as national or foreign correspondents for a nationally influential newspaper.

The Washington bureau and the Baltimore newsroom frequently seemed to be at war. Bureau correspondents rarely mentioned anyone in Baltimore except to complain about them. "Goddamn copy desk changed my lede without asking me." Baltimore, I discovered later, returned the affection.

Still, these feelings were not unanimous at either end of the parkway. Reporters on the local staff shamelessly clamored when a bureau posting came up. And bureau correspondents, especially younger ones with more recent service on the local staff, made no pretense about whose coverage was central to the paper's mission.

As my graduation from George Washington University approached, I told several correspondents in the bureau that I had abandoned the idea of going to law school and wanted to become a reporter. Some advised that the best path for me was to get a job at a small paper and learn every aspect of the craft. Others felt a wire service job was the best place, where I would learn how to get it first, get it fast, and get it right. The only unanimity among my advisors was that an inexperienced person like me had zero chance of getting

Figure 6.1.   President Lyndon Johnson and *Baltimore Sun* Washington bureau chief Philip Potter confer at the White House, 1968.
Courtesy of the White House (Jack Kightlinger), 1968.

hired at the *Baltimore Sun*. Besides, they said, "Banker has a rule" against hiring copy boys as reporters.

The issue of my future course was settled quickly when Potter overheard one of these conversations. "Why the hell do you want to start at a weekly in some godforsaken place in West Virginia," he asked. "Why don't you start at the *Sun*?"

Well, we all explained, not only did I not have any experience, I had not worked at either my college or high school newspaper and had, actually, never written a single word for publication. Potter didn't care.

"I'll call Banker," he said, and disappeared into his office.

It was thus that I found myself a few days later aboard a Trailways bus bound for Baltimore, wearing my only suit, bearing a pathetically thin resume, and consoling myself that at least I'd get to see what a real newsroom looked like.

I remember nothing of my interview with Banker. Possibly, I was too terrified. Or, perhaps I never even had an interview with Banker. All I know is that a few days later, I received a phone call from Banker's secretary telling me to report to work on such and such a date and that my salary would be $127 a week.

Going from the Washington bureau to the newsroom in Baltimore was no mere trip up the Baltimore–Washington Parkway. In a very real sense, I was leaving one newspaper and joining another. Leaving the *Baltimore Sun*, the distinguished newspaper read by the high and mighty with broad and deep national and foreign coverage, and joining something called the Sunpapers.

No one in Baltimore called it the *Baltimore Sun*. Officially, the journalism organization at 501 North Calvert Street was the Sunpapers. That's what it said on the front of the building. That's what was written on the side of the delivery trucks. That was the phone book entry. The journalists in the building took great care to distinguish between the *Sun*, the *Evening Sun*, or the *Sunday Sun*; virtually no one else in Baltimore cared.

Confirmation of this came when anyone called the paper's switchboard—Lexington 9-7744—and was greeted with "Good afternoon, Sunpaper." The chief operator was a woman named Miss Thornburgh whose nasal voice and unique enunciation of the word "Sunpaper" was ceaselessly imitated in the newsroom. There were no doubt several Miss Thornburghs, for they sounded alike to me and she could not have worked round the clock. There was no sir, ma'am, or miss to anyone calling the Sunpaper—everyone was Hon. "This is the pope calling from Rome, I'd like to speak with Mr. Banker." "Just a second, Hon."

In the first days of 1980, I was sent from Moscow to Kabul to cover the Soviet invasion of Afghanistan. The Russians had for some reason allowed foreign correspondents to enter the country, but had cut off all communication with the outside world—no telephone, no telex, no wires, and no cables. Then, suddenly, the blackout ended, and the heretofore useless phone in my hotel room rang in the middle of the night.

"Hello, Bal-berry? Sunpaper calling, Hon. O'Mara (the foreign editor) wants to talk to you." Miss Thornburgh had gotten through to Kabul.

Going to work every day didn't really become fun until I was assigned to cover the frantic ninety-day sessions of the Maryland General Assembly in Annapolis and there encountered the Baltimore pols who still held formidable power in the state.

These were people with nicknames like Soft Shoes and Bip; a state senator whose legal name was American Joe (he renamed himself after a family tavern in East Baltimore); a city delegation which included two brothers, of whom it was said, one can read, the other can write; a delegate who conceded to being under pressure to win reelection because he'd already traded next year's votes; and a senator who objected to being accused of conflict of interest because the bill he introduced "doesn't conflict with my interest."

Running it all with an iron grip was Marvin Mandel, the brilliantly manipulative governor. Annapolis reporters not only had to cover what Mandel said and did, but also had to spend at least an equal amount of time trying to figure out what he *really* was doing and then—days, weeks, or sometimes months later—digging out what he *really, really* had done. And even then know that we probably missed something.

What multiplied the fun of Annapolis was the chance to work with Richard Ben Cramer, a journalism prodigy just out of Johns Hopkins. Cramer went on to win a Pulitzer Prize at the *Philadelphia Inquirer*, and then left daily newspapers to become a successful freelance writer and author. His book on the 1988 presidential campaign, *What It Takes*, influenced a generation of American political writers.

Even today, much later and a few years after Richard's death from cancer, my mental picture is of Richard pounding away at a typewriter in the overcrowded press room in the basement of the State House, a huge grin on his face, a cup of black coffee steaming to one side of his desk, and an unfiltered Camel smoldering on the other, unable to stop laughing to himself at the story he was spinning for the next day's readers.

My second job interview with Banker occurred when I applied for an opening as Moscow correspondent, and unlike my first eight years earlier, I remember every word of this one.

Banker's first questions were about why I wanted to go to Moscow. There then followed one of the endless silences with which Banker modulated his conversations. He must have smoked half a Marlboro while looking out his window, but I was determined not to crack and start blurting out inanities.

Finally, he broke the silence. "Can you cook?" he asked, apparently concerned that as an unmarried man I would be at risk of starvation without a wife to prepare meals for me. Well, sure, a few things, I replied uncertainly. And that was that. Interview over.

My last conversation with Banker occurred a few days before I left for Moscow in March 1979. The phone rang in the kitchen of my house in Annapolis. Banker wanted to know why I had included a stove in the shipment of my household goods to Moscow when we had just sent a new stove to the paper's apartment.

After hemming and hawing, I finally confessed that the stove really wasn't for the apartment, it was for the *Sun's* Russian driver in Moscow, Leonid, who had just renovated his apartment and wanted an American-made stove.

"It's for Leonid? Well, why the hell didn't you say so?" Banker shot back, and abruptly hung up.

Leonid Lovtsov was more than just a driver—the guy who drove the big black office Ford and stood in line for tickets—he was the Soviet version of an alchemist. Leonid could turn bottles of French brandy and cartons of American cigarettes into prime seats for the Bolshoi Ballet, expedited treatment from the bureaucracy, or one kilo tins of Beluga caviar. Leonid made long lines disappear and miracles happen.

Some of Leonid's miracles had involved people at the highest level of the *Baltimore Sun* who had encountered Leonid on their tours of *Sun* bureaus. Gary Black, chairman of the board of the A. S. Abell Company, was a particular Leonid fan. The two got on famously—the millionaire aristocrat from the Greenspring Valley and the four-hundred-ruble-a-month Soviet driver who somehow managed to procure Black's preferred room on the second floor of the historic Hotel National on Red Square.

Of all the stories that illustrate the overused but utterly true assertion that the old *Sun* had been like a family, the stove for Leonid story is my favorite. Not only did the out-going and in-coming Moscow correspondents conspire to get Leonid his stove, and not only was the managing editor okay with buying Leonid a stove and paying to ship it halfway around the world, but the managing editor clearly thought I was a moron for thinking there might be something to be hidden about the whole scheme.

This atmosphere extended not only to the highest ranks of the newsroom, but to the highest ranks of the company itself. Every foreign correspondent lived in trepidation of the day when he or she would be on the receiving end of an official visit from Gary Black, and every correspondent came away from those visits having gotten to know a warm and generous man—but one who inhabited a different world from the rest of us.

Up until the mid-1970s, *Sun* foreign correspondents themselves traveled first class. This practice led to one of the more celebrated stories in *Sun* lore. In the late 1960s, William F. Schmick Jr., the *Sun's* publisher, was touring Asia with his wife. In Hong Kong, they joined the *Sun's* veteran bureau chief, Peter Kumpa, and John Carroll, who was then based in Saigon. Kumpa and Carroll were then to accompany the Schmicks to their next stop, Bangkok, aboard the same flight.

Carroll liked to recall how he experienced something between embarrassment and terror when he and Kumpa rose at the boarding call for first class passengers and he realized the Schmicks were flying coach. Kumpa was unfazed, calling out to the paper's top executive, "See you in Bangkok," as he and Carroll got on the plane. Kumpa later brought glasses of champagne from the first class cabin back to the Schmicks in coach.

To a large extent, the degree to which foreign correspondents leave a mark during their tenure depends on what is, or is not, happening on their patch during their time. In this I was enormously lucky.

I was privileged to cover what I argue was the beginning of the end of the Soviet Union and its empire—the visit of Pope John Paul II to his native Poland in June 1979.

The Pope drew millions to his outdoor masses and homilies during an exhausting nine-day visit in an early summer heat wave. His appearance touched off a revival of Polish nationalism that, a year later, would explode to the surface when a little known electrician with a walrus mustache named Lech Walesa slipped into the giant Lenin Shipyard in Gdansk to lead a strike against Poland's hated communist regime.

Stories like this were inspiring to me. On the steaming streets of Manila a few years later, I saw a crowd of nuns and schoolteachers, dentists, and accountants kneel in front of the tanks Ferdinand Marcos had dispatched to quell "people power" protests against his regime. The tanks, driven by Marcos's elite Philippine Marines, stopped dead in their tracks. A few days later, Marcos was out as president.

The next year it was another Asian capital, Seoul, but the same theme: the middle class, students, businessmen, professionals, braving clouds of tear gas and ranks of riot police to demand free elections and an end to the sham democracy the South Korean generals had been selling. The generals caved and within a few years, Kim Dae Jung, the country's leading dissident, was elected president.

Reporters, particularly foreign correspondents, try to affect an attitude of jaded cynicism and detachment. I could never quite manage this, not when covering good versus evil struggles such as those in Moscow, Poland, the Philippines, and South Korea. I was constantly amazed—and angered—when I was in the Soviet Union to read the patronizing ridicule that faculty room leftists in the United States and West European intellectuals would heap on Ronald Reagan when he called the Soviet Union an "evil empire" or predicted that Marxism was headed for the "ash heap of history."

I was no Reaganite (though I did possess a VHS of one of the Gipper's films, *Bedtime for Bonzo*, which gave me my fifteen minutes of fame in the Moscow ex-pat community), but of course the Soviet Union was evil. I never met any foreign correspondent who doubted this after even a few months of covering the struggle of dissidents for greater human rights, or of Jews for the right to emigrate, or of ordinary Russians to find meat and vegetables.

I remember once walking in a narrow alley around midnight to meet a dissident source. As we rounded a corner he was simply snatched off the street by a carload of KGB thugs who appeared out of nowhere. I know they were KGB because I asked one of them for his identification, which he cheerfully produced. When I demanded to know why the person was being arrested, he laughed and told me to call KGB headquarters in the morning. What was a joke to him was part of the job for me, pointless as the exercise was.

One of the more egregious methods the Soviets used to persecute dissidents was confinement to a mental hospital for "treatment" under the theory that only a lunatic would think there was something that needed improvement in the Soviet Union. A brave and incorruptible Soviet psychiatrist objected to this abuse and spent months gathering information about it, which he made available to Western correspondents, including me.

Predictably, as soon as our stories appeared, he was pulled off a train, arrested, and sentenced to a term in a labor camp.

One Sunday a year later, I got a call from the jailed dissident's wife. She was calling from a pay phone outside our apartment building. I rushed down into the minus-twenty-five-degree weather to find not only the dissident's wife, but three or four plainclothes cops.

She said her husband had given her a statement and told her to ask me to get it out of the country for him. To do so would violate standard ethical strictures against participating in stories we cover, not to mention the explicit orders of my editors in Baltimore—"whatever you do, don't get involved with dissident politics." But not to do so would have meant dismissing a request from the wife of someone who had been sent to a labor camp partly because of a story I'd written.

Out of sight of the KGB men for a moment, she ripped out the lining of her coat and handed me her husband's statement, which I tucked into my mitten. Later that week I slipped the statement into the outgoing mail of the US Embassy's diplomatic pouch—another violation of the rules—and have not regretted it for a moment, then or now.

When people learn that I spent my entire journalism career at one newspaper, the assumption is that I am either extremely loyal or simply inert. In fact, neither is true. I'm merely selfish. Just about every time I wanted to do something new, try a new challenge, do something different, take my career in a different direction, I got that opportunity at the *Sun* without having to move on to another newspaper.

The biggest of these changes came after nearly ten years as a foreign correspondent, when I decided to give up reporting to become an editor.

The newsroom to which I returned to be city editor in 1988 was vastly different from the one I had left. The journalists the *Sun* had begun to hire set a level of experience and competence on the local staff that perhaps would have ruled out hiring me and others like me back in 1970. The paper was much more editor-driven that it had been before—a major upgrade to replace the cranky day city editor who began each morning cleaning his desk with a feather duster.

Though I had spent nearly five years covering the Soviet empire and five more in East Asia, I barely watched the bank of TV sets in the city room in Baltimore when the Berlin wall came down and when the Tiananmen Square demonstration was crushed in Beijing. I was too busy learning to be an editor, from the small things like rewriting police briefs to the big things such as grasping the idea that an editor's most important contribution often comes before a single word has been written.

After three or four years of this, I thought I knew a lot about the newspaper business, an erroneous impression that disappeared the day I was handed over to John O'Donnell to be trained as night editor. O'Donnell may not have been the most famous journalist ever to work at the *Sun*, but he was one of the most versatile, and certainly the most underpaid when one considers what it took to replace him.

O. D., as he was called, was the night editor—the person who was in charge of the newspaper after most editors went home. He would come in shortly before four, in time to chair the page 1 news meeting. At this point he would choose the stories for the front page. He would then deal with the space and deadline requirements of the various sections. He would then take a ruler and pencil and design the front page on a grid. He would then choose and size the photographs for the front page. He would give a serious read to all the major stories in the paper to make sure they were journalistically sound. He would go to the composing room to close the first edition.

Within two years of O'Donnell leaving that job, no fewer than four people were doing what he had done alone: a day news editor, a night news editor, a page designer, and a photo editor. (O'Donnell himself returned to reporting, and in 2003 was a finalist for a Pulitzer Prize in explanatory journalism.)

When I became managing editor in 2000, I was, at last, prepared. There were no angst-ridden weeks or months while I tried to cope with the bewildering challenges of a new job—getting into the White House, finding Pigtown or Parkville, learning Russian verbs of motion. I was one of a handful of people still at the *Sun* who could put out the paper by myself—write and edit a story, design a page, size a photo, close in the composing room, tell an advertiser to get lost, and placate a reader over a mistake in an obit. I knew and had worked with most of the people in our newsroom and knew how the rest of the company worked. Just as important, I had a strong relationship with the editor who had appointed me, Bill Marimow.

For the first time in my career, the paper's boss was not a remote and intimidating presence like Paul Banker or someone who had known me since I was a copy boy, but a contemporary and a colleague. Marimow had won two Pulitzers for investigative reporting at the *Philadelphia Inquirer* and, as an editor in Baltimore, wielded a relentless intelligence that missed nothing and found its way to the core of even the most complicated stories.

For Marimow, a good day as editor-in-chief of the paper was getting through the meetings, bureaucracies, and paperwork with enough time left over to work on a story with a young reporter in one of the suburban bureaus. He regarded the hiring and nurturing of young journalists as the most important thing an editor could do. We had plenty of talent to work with, too. The *Sun* had always attracted an unusual number of ambitious journalists who could write their own ticket at any newspaper in the country. But then at some point in the dozen or so years Carroll and Marimow ran the newsroom, the *Sun* had its moment as the country's "hot" paper. We suddenly seemed to have our pick of the best young reporters, photographers, and graphics artists in the country.

The day in January 2004 when Marimow was fired by a publisher who assumed, correctly, that he, Marimow, would never be willing to oversee the curtailment of the *Sun*, was the day that I realized I would have to leave the newspaper where I had been working for more than three decades. That night, I went to Marimow's house in Poplar Hill, a shaker of martinis in hand. Sometime during that boozy evening, I also sought the advice of John Carroll, who told me he felt there was no reason to hope the *Sun* would remain the kind of paper we had both admired. But he advised me to stay for a few more months and do my best to help the bright young people we'd hired. I followed his advice and stayed on until August.

It would be difficult to argue today that had the *Sun* had different, smarter, or more nimble owners and managers, it would have been immune from the powerful forces that, in a stunningly short time, destroyed the financial model that had supported quality journalism in the United States. But because the *Sun* had for so long been a paper that punched above its weight—a paper that had ambitions and reach far beyond its size, and had the talent and resources to achieve those ambitions—the fall, when it came, was harder and the bitterness more personal.

When I left the paper on August 30, 2004, the *Sun* employed about four hundred journalists. It still had five foreign bureaus and a twelve-person Washington bureau. In the previous year, we had won a Pulitzer Prize for beat reporting and had been finalists in two other categories. When the invasion of Iraq began, we sent eight reporters and photographers to the war zone. For a series on the abuse of student visas, we sent a reporter to Micronesia; for a piece on a Johns Hopkins public health project on vitamin D, we sent a reporter to Nepal.

Performance like this for a regional paper was rare in American journalism and a source of enormous pride for generations of *Sun* people. When the paper was acquired by Times Mirror in 1986, executives in Los Angeles went out of their way to say how gratifying it was for them to acquire a paper with this proud history. So it was with a sense of disappointment and anger that we gradually came to realize that our new owners in the Chicago's Tribune tower did not share this view at all, and seemed to look at us with contempt for harboring ambitions beyond those of Tribune papers in Ft. Lauderdale or Orlando.

Within a few years after Tribune bought Times Mirror and us in 2000, the *Sun's* foreign bureaus and the large Washington bureau were gone—understandably, considering the financial condition of the company and the industry. Less understandably, the *Baltimore Sun* was to change to a paper oriented toward local news—though its muscular metro staff was to be cut drastically. Inexplicably, the two most "local" sections in the paper—metro and features—were eliminated. Editors in Baltimore would soon have to justify it to Tribune executives when world or national stories were run on the front page.

By 2008, the company was in the control of Sam Zell, a Chicago real estate mogul who declared that Tribune's distinguished lineup of newspapers suffered from "journalistic arrogance." He put the day-to-day running of the company in the hands of a former DJ and Top 40 radio executive who had to be booted from his job after the *New York Times* disclosed that he had engendered an atmosphere in Tribune headquarters of crude sexual innuendo and smutty frat boy humor. Zell's tenure ended in the largest bankruptcy in the history of the American media industry.

None of this had yet happened when I left the paper, but clearly hard times were not far away. Shortly after Marimow's firing, the exodus began, as one smart young reporter after another left. For me, the saddest day came during my last weeks as managing editor, when I had to preside over the farewell cake at the city desk for the paper's best reporter, Scott Shane. Bearded, soft-spoken, and scholarly, Shane looked more like a post-doctoral student in an applied physics lab than an accomplished journalist. His twenty-year career at the *Sun* had included local coverage, the Moscow Bureau, and many of the paper's most important projects. He had been courted off and on for years by the nation's leading papers. When Shane finally decided to take an offer from the *New York Times*, it felt to me like a door was closing on a fine experience that had slipped by all too quickly.

Foreign Assignment

Black Baltimore

Antero Pietila

I always wanted to be a foreign correspondent. In 1969, I got my chance: the *Sun* hired me to cover cops in Baltimore. There I was, a bashful twenty-four-year-old journalist from Finland, working in an alien language in a strange country. With a reporter's notebook in my back pocket, a dog-eared street guide in my hand, and my front pockets loaded with nickels (for pay phones), I rummaged through neighborhoods in a company car equipped with a two-way radio. Police districts, fire stations, and funeral homes served as my lodestars. As a rule, regardless of previous experience, one's career at the *Sun* in those days kicked off with covering cops. New hires who did well moved on to write obituaries, then to general assignment or to cover beats. This was the way one learned the city and how to ask the right questions. Such as, after an apparent suicide jump: Was the window open or closed? If you got a byline during your probationary period, you were doing real well.

I had first become acquainted with the *Sun* five years earlier. I was in college in Finland in 1964, when I saw *Time* magazine's ranking of top US dailies. The *Sun* was among them. This is what Henry Luce's news magazine said about Charles H. (Buck) Dorsey Jr., managing editor at the time: "His style is the style of Arunah Shepherdson Abell, the vagabond printer who started the *Sun* in 1837. . . . The paper remains aloof, aristocratic, old-fashioned, proud, and something of a snob—just the way Baltimoreans like it." Curious, I contacted the *Sun's* business office, which airmailed a front section to me in Finland. The paper looked archaic; its typography was even grayer than the *New York Times*. Peculiarities of the *Sun*—there were many. There was not a single local story on the front page. Instead, the broadsheet opened with dispatches from its bureau in Washington and from staff correspondents in London, Moscow, Bonn, Rome, New Delhi, Rio de Janeiro, Hong Kong, and Saigon, and, if it could not be avoided, wire service stories. The most prominent local stories began on the *back* page of the second section, jumping inside. So well-read was this "local front page" that the bottom half was sold at premium rates to advertisers, whose copy was limited to one column width. Ad headlines were set in hollowed out type, so as not to distract from news stories. The ads were all type; no pictures were allowed. As a service to readers, a hangover cure recipe ran on the front page every New Year's Day. Later that day the paper was confronted with an annual dilemma: selecting the first baby born in the new year. Babies were only considered mentionable if born to a married, white mother. Sooner or later, a qualifying baby was found. This practice lasted until the early 1970s. Editorially, the paper was rather conservative. Decades before, it had voiced white supremacist opinions, but then slowly but steadily changed its position on civil rights. In 1947, the paper received the local Sidney Hollander Foundation's annual award for promoting equal rights because of its "removal of racial designations from news headlines, and for the support of justice for Negroes." If the award was a carrot, there was no stick: racial designations in crime stories continued until June 1961.

Scott Sullivan hired me. He was city editor, a 1954 Gilman School graduate, a magna cum laude Yalie with a Phi Beta Kappa key and chain. He had a second bachelor's degree as well as a master's degree in modern European history from Cambridge. He had also studied at the Sorbonne. Sullivan didn't exactly urge me to join the paper. "Let me say at the outset," he wrote, "that I have serious doubts about whether your English has reached a point where you could comfortably handle the kind of work that would come your way here. Nevertheless, your background in and obvious knowledge of foreign affairs are of interest to the *Sun*, and your assiduity in seeking a job here has been impressive. I would be glad to talk with you about the possibilities any time that you can manage to come to Baltimore, always bearing in mind that your lack of familiarity with the language could count heavily against you." I took the Greyhound bus from Washington where I'd had an interview with the *Post*, and overnighted at the YMCA. The *Sun* interview consisted of a comprehensive general knowledge test and a story that needed to be rewritten. Being unaware of the *Sun*'s rules of style, I wrote my story in a breezy tabloid fashion.

An undergraduate degree was a minimum requirement for getting a reporting job at the *Sun*. My distinction was that I came from Finland and was reputed to be the only reporter in the morning newsroom who had not gone to a private college; my master's degree was from Southern Illinois University, Carbondale. In other ways as well, the *Sun* was a discriminating paper. The company hired very few Jewish journalists until the 1950s, after Philip B.

Perlman quit in 1917 for a law career that led him to be Harry S Truman's solicitor general. When I arrived the year after the 1968 race riots, the morning paper had no black reporters, and only a handful of women.

The *Sun* was a time capsule. A huge mural in the lobby confronted visitors. It depicted the city in 1837, when the paper was born. The city was spread as a panorama in the distance while in the foreground, on what appeared to be farmland, an elderly bareheaded black man, clutching his hat to his body, stood respectfully before a lordly white couple and their daughter. (In the 1980s, after complaints of racial condescension, the work was hidden behind a false wall.) The longtime lobby attendant was a diminutive African American, Bernard E. Barney, who always wore a dark suit and tie. He began operating the front elevators in 1925 when the paper's offices were downtown. In the new Calvert Street building the elevators were automated, but years later when I reported to work, Barney remained an institutional mascot of sorts, standing in front of the twin lifts, greeting visitors. The family of the *Sun's* board chairman made bets on his behalf at racetracks and casinos over the years and gave him the winnings. Another African American constant was a janitor named Johnson—that's what the name tag on his overalls said—who came by the newsroom every afternoon, asking gentleman reporters whether they wanted a shoeshine.

The lobby mural accurately depicted the past of Maryland, a slave state which reluctantly stayed in the Union. Within a month after the outbreak of the Civil War, Union troops occupied Baltimore, an important port city and the hub of the only railroad line from the North into Washington, DC. Under military rule, pro-Confederate newspapers were closed. A number of journalists were thrown into the dungeons of Fort McHenry along with other assorted suspected rebel sympathizers. The *Sun* escaped unscathed. Although dramatic events unfolded in Baltimore and fighting raged in western Maryland, the paper produced hardly any notable reporting; its heart was not in it.

After the war, the paper reflected the sentiments of a city which viewed itself as the largest industrial and commercial center of the upper South. "The white race is the dominant and superior race, and it will, of course, maintain its supremacy," an editorial assured in 1913. "The attitude of the Southern man and the attitude of an average Baltimorean toward colored people is one of helpfulness. He sees in them not simply wards of the nation but descendants of those whom he and his ancestors trusted and respected for their loyalty and affection."

When Maryland's Democratic Party tried three times, between 1905 and 1911, to deprive blacks of voting rights, the *Sun* supported the effort. "The amendment is aimed to rid the electorate of Maryland of the illiterate and shiftless negro," one editorial explained. "It is the amendment's aim to place the electorate upon a higher plane, to make this State a white man's State, and not let thousands of votes of thoughtful white men be killed by the ballots of ignorant negroes."

The paper campaigned for racial separation. When blacks began penetrating white west side city neighborhoods off Pennsylvania and Druid Hill Avenues, the *Sun*, through provocative stories, letters, and racially motivated advertisements, created the specter of a "negro invasion," the only newspaper in town to so agitate. The city council sprang into action, making Baltimore in 1910 a national leader in residential segregation. Richmond, Norfolk, Birmingham, Atlanta, Louisville, St. Louis, New Orleans, and Dallas were among cities copying Baltimore in mandating residential segregation by local laws. One letter of inquiry came all the way from the Philippines, where the US occupation authorities wanted to know how Baltimore had done it. The *Sun* also advocated legally binding restrictive covenants that allowed neighborhoods to exclude blacks and Jews. Even after the Supreme Court in 1948 made such covenants legally unenforceable, the *Sun*'s real estate ads for more than a decade included "White" and "Colored" classifications. "Restricted" meant that the premises—whether for rent or sale—were not available for blacks or Jews.

The year before I joined the *Sun*, Martin Luther King Jr. was assassinated in Memphis, and, like many other cities, Baltimore paid. The Palm Sunday weekend mayhem left six persons dead and seven hundred injured. More than a thousand businesses were ransacked and destroyed, commercial strips were wiped out in nine neighborhoods, a large number of homes were set afire, and more than five thousand people were arrested. The National Guard and regular Army patrolled downtown. A year later, physical wounds were still raw; psychological scars unmistakable. By custom, everyday life remained rather segregated. So demoralized was the city and so dispirited its residents that image makers came up with a hokey nickname, "Charm City," to describe the gritty industrial town. After years of white flight, black strivers also started running. During my first three summers, the city was on edge. I remember getting this advice: if you are filing in a tense situation, don't close the door of the phone booth because doing so turns on the light and pinpoints you as a target for a gunman.

When I grew up in Finland, that country was so homogenous that eye and hair colors marked the biggest differences among a population of fewer than five million people. Only about 1,500 Jews lived in the land of a thousand lakes and the midnight sun. There were no blacks. I found Baltimore's diversity exhilarating. These were the days of ethnic festivals, an antidote against all the gloom that followed the riots. I learned about East Baltimore's white ethnic groups who were melting into the mainstream and losing their immigrant traditions. I met African American middle-class women and men who, after moving to Forest Park, Windsor Hills, and Ashburton, created a garden club as one of their first acts (the For-Win-Ash Garden Club still existed in 2016).

In other neighborhoods, I saw evidence of creeping slumification and the emergence of a permanent underclass. The city was in the midst of a demographic upheaval. During World War II, so many workers had flooded the factories and shipyards that the estimated 1942 population reached 1.2 million, about double of what it would be in 2015. The biggest group of new-comers consisted of some 250,000 men, women, and children who poured in from the Appalachian hills and hollows. Most returned home after the war—to dismal-sounding hamlets like Bald Knob and Granny Dismal. By contrast, black war workers and their families—primarily from the Virginias and Carolinas—came to stay. The migration of blacks continued into the 1980s, statistically masking the fact that, except for incoming blacks, the city was losing population (and its political clout) to the burgeoning suburban counties. As whites deserted city neighborhoods, blacks from the influx moved in, facilitated by real estate speculators who made a killing by fanning racial fears.

The borders of "Baltimore's Negro Archipelago" of a dozen island-like neighborhoods were quite inflexible. The main concentration of blacks was historically on the west side, where all classes shared the same streets during segregation. All black institutions, too, were on the west side, except for Morgan College. The black concentration on the east side was smaller, clustered in parts of Fells Point and Oldtown. East side residents were reputed to be "country," recent arrivals from the south.

All that changed during Christmas holidays in 1944, when the first blacks crossed West Baltimore's customary demarcation line, Fulton Avenue. A landscaped median strip ran in the middle of the thoroughfare. Rowhouses on one side of the street were all occupied by blacks, the other side by whites. The breach caused panic and the emergence of "blockbusters," real estate speculators who hovered over white neighborhoods looking for distress auctions and other scared sellers whose rowhouses could be acquired cheaply and then flipped to a black at outlandish profits. The more blacks who were planted into a neighborhood, the cheaper houses became for speculators to acquire from frantic whites. Blockbusting spread rapidly after Baltimore desegregated public schools in the fall of 1954, the only big city to implement the Supreme Court ruling system-wide without delay. In a typical case, a speculator acquired a rowhouse from a white for $7,500—less than the appraised value—and then sold it for double the price to a black. Blockbusters knocked on doors and leafletted by day. At night, they made telephone calls, spreading rumors about crime, and exhorting a homeowner to sell because prices would never be this good.

As a result of the federal government's redlining of Baltimore and 238 other cities in the 1930s, banks and other financial institutions generally did not lend to blacks, and charged exorbitant rates for whites living in the inner city and other changing areas. Redlining grew out of a New Deal attempt to stabilize a Depression-era housing market, mapping neighborhoods by credit risk that federal officials calculated on the basis of race, religion, ethnic group, and class. Maps were color-coded from lowest to highest risk: green, blue, yellow, and red. Red was hazardous. If you were black, it was likely you lived in a neighborhood colored red—red-lined—and chances were you couldn't get a conventional mortgage loan.

In this atmosphere, blockbusters thrived. They got their financing from syndicates of investors, usually headed by lawyers, who saw racial change and wholesale flipping as manna from heaven. In neighborhoods where banks didn't lend, the blockbusters offered mortgages with high interest rates and used dubious rent-to-buy arrangements with payments due weekly. In 1954, a *Sun* reporter, Odell M. Smith, wrote about the practice. Titled "Housing Racket," his investigative effort was unusual because it was long and ran as a series, starting on the back page, of course. Smith extensively reported on deceptive practices, naming complainants but not identifying the real estate operators by name. Fifteen years later, Douglas Connah Jr., a copy editor, encountered similar reticence. In 1969, the *Sun* devoted much of one Sunday's Perspective section to his law school paper on blockbusting, but editors removed the names of all speculators from the story. That soon changed, and the paper distinguished itself. In the 1970s and 1980s, housing reporting by James D. Dilts and Mark Reutter was detailed, insightful, and gutsy, with names and all. (Reutter's own childhood neighborhood, Edmondson Village, had transitioned from almost all-white to nearly all-black in two decades: from 16,343 whites and 45 blacks in 1950, to 18,650 blacks and 679 whites in 1970.)

In 1978, at Reutter's invitation, I became part of a team effort. The "Corridor in Transition" series we wrote focused on Liberty Road, a one-time turnpike cutting through Baltimore County all the way to Pennsylvania. Beginning as Liberty Heights Avenue in the city, it was an extension of Druid Hill and Pennsylvania Avenues, where neighborhoods from the 1910s onward had transitioned from Christian white to Jewish white to African American. By the time the 1968 riots came, Reservoir Hill, Auchentoroly Terrace, Mondawmin, Ashburton, and Howard Park had gone through that rotation pattern. After the riots, blacks, too, joined the flight. Homeowners fled Park Circle and Pimlico, where a lower socioeconomic element of blacks replaced working- and middle-class blacks (and whites), thanks to more generous and inclusive mortgage programs by the federal government. Blacks headed for Lochearn, the first neighborhood beyond the city line in the Liberty Road corridor. Colonials and ranches lined leafy streets scattered with Protestant churches. Until 1951, Lochearn banned Jews from residency, and when they came, Christians began to flee. Now Lochearn was going through another stage in the ethnic rotation cycle.

Reutter and I saw the telltale signs of racial panic everywhere along Liberty Road: forests of "For Sale" signs on streets still inhabited by whites. Our series characterized the black migration as "a milestone in recent Baltimore history." That it was; blacks were now moving to the 95 percent white county, which almost surrounded the city. Baltimore County Executive Dale Anderson tried to stem the influx. He ordered real estate agents to report to the police any sales or rentals they made to blacks. The real estate industry now designated Liberty Road as an expansion area for blacks, who were effectively barred from the rest of the county by minimum-lot restrictions and high prices. "Steering" was the new strategy. Available houses were no longer shown to whites; instead, blacks were channeled in. During the turnover, tensions were palpable, but white friendliness was not unknown. "They were friendly up to the day they moved out," I quoted one black suburban pioneer as saying. In other words, integration along Liberty Road was a brief phase between desegregation and predictable resegregation.

In Baltimore City, the demographic changes were especially stark. The 1950 census counted 949,708 Baltimoreans, a little less than one-quarter of whom were African American. A decade later the black population accounted for one-third of the city's 939,024 residents. In 1970, after a net exodus of some 150,000 whites, blacks formed nearly one-half of Baltimore's 905,759 population. By 2014, the city had shrunk to 620,961 people, 63 percent of whom were African American.

Similar changes rapidly led many other cities to elect black mayors. Yet in Baltimore, just three years after the riots, voters chose as their mayor the white city council president, William Donald Schaefer, who served four terms before his election as governor and then state comptroller. As mayor, even after the racial transition, Schaefer continued to live with his mother, Tulula, in an Edmondson Village rowhouse among a handful of white holdouts. He was an honest man, an eccentric bachelor. His political godfather was Irvin Kovens, who ran a phenomenal fundraising and patronage machine from a dusty installment sales furniture store on West Baltimore Street. He also sponsored two future governors, Marvin Mandel, a Democrat, and Spiro T. Agnew, a Republican (both of whom were later disgraced in scandals, as was Kovens himself). The cigar-puffing Kovens called Schaefer "Shaky," a friendly reference to the

candidate's nervousness in early campaigns. Kovens was well connected. Together with Jimmy Hoffa's Teamsters, he owned racetracks and part of the
Caesar's Palace gambling casino in Las Vegas. Thanks to Kovens, Baltimoreans
were well represented among the casino's roster of investors.

Among Kovens's friends was William L. Adams, an African American
transplant from North Carolina. As teenagers, the two ran the streets of East
Baltimore, where the Kovens family operated a grocery store. By the age of
sixteen, "Little Willie" was a numbers boss, an operator of illegal lotteries. In
the boom years of the 1950s, when Pennsylvania Avenue's nightlife rivaled
Harlem's 125th Street, he owned many clubs there and promoted the bright-
est jazz stars from Count Basie to Billie Holiday. He also controlled another
important stop on the so-called Chitlin' Circuit: Carr's Beach in Annapolis,
a segregation-era amusement park which drew thousands of revelers each
weekend from Washington and Baltimore. Thousands more listened to live
broadcasts on black radio. Adams became the first truly important African
American business figure in Baltimore. Kovens even offered a piece of the
Caesar's Palace action to him. Adams declined, and later regretted this
missed investment opportunity. Never mind, there was plenty of money to
be made elsewhere.

Most black-owned taverns bought liquor from Adams's wholesaler or
accommodated his vending machines. As a silent partner, he bankrolled funeral homes and beauty parlors, a supermarket chain, and the Parks Sausage
Company. He also branched out into construction and real estate development. His patronage powers were considerable, mostly in the Fourth District,
a formerly Jewish area that transitioned into black. He had his representatives on the liquor and zoning boards and on the planning commission.
Increasing Adams's influence was his wife, Victorine, a soft-spoken former
school teacher. After marrying Little Willie (his nickname a salute to the
title character in the gangster movie *Little Caesar*), she opened a pioneering
fashion shop, Charm Center, on Pennsylvania Avenue. Instead of having to
go to Philadelphia or New York (because blacks could not try on clothing in
Baltimore stores), black lawyers, doctors, and ministers now could buy the
latest fashions for the women in their lives right in Baltimore. Her Charm
Center taught social graces to adults and children alike. Her work made her
popular, creating a base of support that vaulted her first to the Maryland
legislature and then, in 1967, to the City Council as its first elected woman
member of any race. At a time when the racial balance of power was about
to shift, her organization, Woman Power, Inc., trained candidates for elected
and appointed offices.

Beyond this outline, little was known about the history or activities of
Willie Adams. He seldom deviated from the protective behavior he adopted

during his numbers days. He left as few fingerprints as practicable. He kept a low profile and gave no interviews. He drove cars that were respectable but not fancy. He dressed modestly. His big home near Lake Ashburton blended into the surroundings. In other words, he was a man who did not want to call attention to himself. As a result, no one had published a solid profile of Baltimore's premier black powerbroker (or extensively profiled current and future leaders).

I set out to change that. I wrote a four-part series in 1979 on the black power structure. Its title: The Afro-Baltimoreans. Willie Adams was a central figure because he was connected to most everything. Before the government's Small Business Administration existed, he filled that function with his silent partnerships. He was connected to the Masons and even to the *Afro-American* newspaper. During civil rights arrests, he quietly provided bail money and financed lawsuits that opened municipal golf courses to blacks.

I had been introduced to Adams at political meetings, but he had not made himself available for an interview. When I approached him to talk about my project, he declined. Circumventing him, I began interviewing business associates and combing through yellowed newspapers in the *Sun* morgue, compiling lists of his operatives who had been arrested in numbers raids (Adams himself never spent a day in jail). I then followed their career paths and found them, or their relatives, often still fronting as licensees of his taverns, night clubs, and other businesses. Adams took no chances: he always asked his front men and women to sign an undated liquor license transfer application just in case. Luckily, I had documentation, including pictures, of many of Adams's associates, because the Sphinx Club (pronounced Spinks), a selective membership club on Pennsylvania Avenue, published anniversary books. That was Willie's club.

As I snooped around, I was sure that curiosity about what I was doing would draw him out. I knew I'd got to him when Henry G. Parks, his partner in the meatpacking business, said, "I don't know why Willie wants me to talk to you because nothing good will come of this." After a career as a city councilman, Parks had concluded that it was a mistake for any black to seek publicity, particularly a businessman. Nevertheless, he talked, as eventually also did Adams, inviting me into his home. But Parks was right. Soon after my series appeared, Adams was charged with numbers violations. The supposed wiretap evidence was laughable and the case went nowhere.

Only later, while researching my 2010 book, *Not in My Neighborhood*, did I realize that Adams had secretive friends in high places far beyond Kovens's orbit. In 1938, while doing banking on North Avenue, he ran into the new Equitable Trust branch manager, John Luetkemeyer. Adams was quite a celebrity in those days; Philadelphia mobsters had recently firebombed

Little Willie's Bar, his numbers headquarters on Druid Hill Avenue. So when he and Luetkemeyer saw one another, they had something to talk about. They began conversing regularly. One day Luetkemeyer was promoting a pet idea of his, consumer credit. Adams listened, then said, "You know, Equitable and others don't lend to us." He offered a solution. He handed $40,000 in cash to Luetkemeyer, and instructed the banker to put the money into a safe deposit box and keep the key. This is the way Adams became the first black to have a line of credit at a Baltimore bank. After the war, Luetkemeyer, a battle-hardened Marine wounded in the Philippines guerrilla operations, rose to head Equitable, the city's second largest bank. He was also elected the state treasurer three times. Thus, he was one of the three votes on the Board of Public Works, which vetted and voted on every major state contract. His friendship with Adams continued under the radar. He served as a board member of Parks Sausage when the firm was private. When Luetkemeyer died, mourners were astonished to see Willie Adams as a pall bearer.

Hustling and politics had always mixed. As early as 1893, the *Baltimore News* documented the Democratic Party's illegal lottery racket that employed two thousand runners, netted millions, and left a staggering 65 percent as profit for the backers whom police protected, thanks to generous bribes. Much of the numbers activity was white. Adams's rapid rise was due to a vacuum left by the death of Thomas R. Smith, a Democratic boss who had the main franchise in black areas. Smith could hardly read or write, but he was a big man. The *New York Times* said he was Baltimore's "Black King." On election days, he distributed cash freely to keep black Republicans—the majority of black voters in an overwhelmingly Democratic city—from going to vote. He also knew how to stuff ballot boxes after the polls were closed. He operated out of his twenty-six-room hotel on Eutaw Street, where a shrine greeted visitors. It consisted of a life-size photo of Joe Gans, the great lightweight boxer from Baltimore, surrounded by pictures of Smith's patrons—the white Democratic bosses John J. (Sonny) Mahon, Senator Millard E. Tydings, and John S. (Frank) Kelly, nicknamed "Slot Machine" and "King of the Underworld," whose bust was there for all to see. In 1938, Smith died of natural causes. His brother took over the numbers operation but was gunned down while counting profits at a Druid Hill Avenue Democratic club. Other gangland slayings followed. Adams survived this war, emerging as the main numbers figure in black Baltimore.

Much of this story was startlingly new to readers of the *Sun*. My 1979 series identified a dozen black powerbrokers. Aside from Adams and Parks, they included Allen Quille, a cousin of Victorine Adams and the second-largest parking lot operator in the city and a prominent fund-raiser for Israel; US District Judge Joseph C. Howard; Charles T. Burns, principal owner of the Super Pride supermarkets (and a cousin of Thurgood Marshall); state Senator Verda F. Welcome, a one-time Adams ally who turned against him; and Samuel T. Daniels, grandmaster of the Prince Hall Masons. Also on the list were the owners of the *Afro-American*, the Baltimore-based newspaper that included local and national editions and editions for Washington, Newark, and Richmond.

The Mitchell family dynasty was on the list, of course. The matriarch was Lillie M. Jackson, whose daughter, the attorney Juanita Jackson Mitchell, married Clarence M. Mitchell Jr., a one-time *Afro* reporter who rose to become a legendary NAACP lobbyist in Washington. One of their sons was state senator Clarence M. Mitchell III; another, Councilman Michael B. Mitchell. Yet another relative, Parren J. Mitchell, was Maryland's first African American congressman. They all were west siders. Representing the east side on the list were City Councilman Clarence H. (Du) Burns (who would be appointed Baltimore's first black mayor after Schaefer won the governorship), and state senator Robert L. Douglass, chairman of the Black Caucus in Annapolis.

The series also described emerging leaders. They included first-term state delegates Howard P. Rawlings and Larry Young, and two activist pastors, John R. Bryant and Wendell H. Phillips. Less known were the lawyer Larry S. Gibson, a school board member who became a law professor and behind-the-scenes political mastermind, and Catherine Pugh, who would serve on the city council and in the Maryland Senate. Then there were businessmen, including Theo Rodgers, a Harvard Business School graduate who worked for General Motors and a data processing company before Adams hired him as the corporate secretary of Parks Sausage. Adams had a daughter; in Rodgers, he found a son. The two operated the A & R Development Company—as in Adams and Rodgers. Adams, in many eyes, was tainted by his past, but Rodgers was another matter. Over the following decades, he served on the National Advisory Council at Federal National Mortgage Association (Fannie Mae), as trustee at Johns Hopkins Medicine, Johns Hopkins Health System, University of Maryland Foundation, McDonogh School, Baltimore Community Foundation, and the Baltimore Symphony Orchestra. He stayed out of politics—and media scrutiny. "I don't talk to the press," he often repeated. Due to his noncooperation, thirty-five years after the *Sun* published my 1979 series on Baltimore's black powerbrokers, a comprehensive subsequent profile of Rodgers had yet to appear. My series was the talk of the town—foreign correspondence on a local topic. I was going places; the *Sun* sent me overseas to catch another dream.

Nearly three years later, I returned from South Africa, and was studying Russian to go to Moscow. One 1983 spring morning at about six o'clock,

I was walking my future wife's black poodle around the Lake Ashburton water reservoir when I spotted Adams in front of me, deep in his thoughts. My footsteps awakened him. Startled, he turned around. He did not recognize me. His bluish-gray eyes were filled with apprehension seeing a white stranger in his neighborhood, clearly thinking no good can come of this. I said good morning and introduced myself. He was in no mood to talk and neither was I, realizing that I had invaded his private space. Seventeen years later, I bumped into him at an event involving a parade of antique Cadillacs on Pennsylvania Avenue. Adams was an organizer. He lived in a luxurious warehouse for rich old people; friends said his memory was fading. I introduced myself. There was no glimmer of recognition, so we talked about Cadillacs. Then he stopped in mid-sentence, his eyes on mine.

"So you are the fellow who likes to walk around the reservoir," he said.

• 8 •

Cradle of Corruption

Frederic B. Hill

Maybe I was preparing questions for the governor. Perhaps I was reporting on driving regulations. I can't be sure. What I do remember for certain was the telephone call.

On a mid-January day in 1971, I was pleased to be sitting in the press room in the basement of the state capitol in Annapolis. After five years covering the Baltimore police districts and several suburban counties, I thought I had finally made it, now one of three reporters assigned to cover the Maryland General Assembly for the *Sun*.

The telephone call was from my city editor, William F. Schmick III. Schmick said he wanted me to go back to Baltimore County. The "Desk," that all-knowing authority reporters did not dare to question, had received tips about possible corruption in an unfolding rezoning process.

I had just spent two years covering Baltimore County, the sprawling suburban jurisdiction that surrounds the city of Baltimore. I had covered its dominant Democratic political machine: its school board, its liquor board, its planning and zoning board, and many issues in between.

The last thing I wanted was to return to Towson, the county seat. What had I done to deserve this demotion? Schmick assured me that it was not a setback, that I would return to the State House after "looking into" these reports for a few weeks.

By early 1971, Baltimore County was engaged in its very first county-wide effort to rationalize future land use by adopting a comprehensive set of new zoning maps. The county was the site of explosive population and building growth in the 1950s and 1960s stemming from highway construction, including a new beltway, and predominantly white flight from the city's troubles and rising taxes. The county's population had more than doubled to 621,000 in less than two decades.

Every single piece of land in the county was subject to rezoning, and due to rapid growth and the expectation of more, much of it was owned by speculators, from Baltimore to Bermuda. Any change in the zoning law from an agricultural designation, say, to housing development or to high-density, commercial or industrial use could be a windfall for the developers or those to whom they might sell the rezoned land.

After more than two months of research into county land records and interviews with dozens of officials, lawyers, professional planners, civic leaders, and others, I wrote a week-long series of articles on the zoning process. My research revealed a blatant pattern of favoritism and tradeoffs between wealthy real estate developers and the Democratic machine led by the county executive, Dale Anderson. Rejecting two-thirds of the major recommendations of professional planners for balanced, economically feasible growth, the machine's representatives on the county council had backed a rezoning plan that would yield millions of dollars in higher land values for the most generous contributors to their election campaigns and possibly lead to helter-skelter development.

The articles electrified a placid county populace. Numerous neighborhoods, whose schools and roads were already crowded and in disrepair, revolted against such extensive rezoning and new housing developments. A countywide hearing shortly after the series ran in mid-March 1971 led to an outpouring of public anger. "I haven't seen this many people at a county hearing since the last public hanging," quipped one Towson lawyer.

The *Sun's* series and the resulting public outcry forced the reversal of many of the council's politically motivated zoning changes and led to major reforms in the county government. A November 1972 referendum broke the Democratic organization's stranglehold on the council election process—which was rigged to favor the Democratic machine that had dominated county politics for decades. No longer could council members win elections based on a countywide vote, a system that diluted the strength of Republican concentrations in parts of the county. Election outcomes now would be determined district-by-district, allowing Republicans a fairer chance to win.

The series, which was nominated for a Pulitzer Prize, stimulated popular engagement in county government to unusual levels. By exposing the cozy relationship between county politicians and dozens of developers, engineers, and architects, it was a prelude for a series of investigations of corruption by federal authorities which reached the highest level of the American government.

George Beall, the (Republican) US attorney at the time, attributed an initial inquiry into corruption in Baltimore County to "anonymous telephone complaints" to his office and to the Internal Revenue Service in the year after the *Sun's* zoning articles were published. The first federal investigation, beginning in January 1973, led to Anderson's downfall. A second probe that grew out of the Anderson case would force the resignation of Spiro T. Agnew as vice president of the United States. Agnew had been Anderson's predecessor as Baltimore County executive.

Having once condemned his accusers as "damn liars," Agnew agreed on October 10, 1973, to leave office and plead "no contest" to a single tax evasion charge—an arrangement that allowed the government to disclose his acceptance of "substantial cash payments" (hundreds of thousands of dollars) from engineers and architects while he was Baltimore County executive, governor of Maryland, and vice president (figure 8.1).

Five months later, lashing out at "a God-damned bunch of pinkos," Anderson was convicted on similar kickback charges involving many of the same people as in the Agnew case. Anderson was found guilty on thirty-two counts of conspiracy, extortion, and income tax evasion on March 20, 1974, after a trial in which his own administrative officer testified that the two men had squeezed engineers and architects for payoffs and kickbacks in return for favorable decisions on contracts. Nearly $40,000 in cash had been given to Anderson in white envelopes.

The testimony of the administrative officer, William E. Fornoff, who pleaded guilty to a tax charge in return for no jail time, was backed up by several engineers and architects—at least four of whom had provided evidence against Agnew the summer before Anderson's trial. The county payoff scheme was so extensive that Anderson and Fornoff sometimes lost track of who had paid whom. Ordered once to give a non-bid job to a particular engineer, Fornoff testified that he told Anderson that was impossible: "I reminded him I'd already given it to someone who's paying us."

Anderson was eventually sentenced to five years in prison; he served a year and six weeks.

At first focused mainly on Anderson, the federal investigation broadened to encompass corruption in the county government. The feds issued subpoenas to dozens of engineers and architects on two successive Monday mornings in January 1973; they also subpoenaed what turned out to be truckloads of county records. Russell T. Baker Jr., an assistant US attorney at the time, recalled, "It had never been done before, at least in Maryland; but we gave the tree a huge shake. And it worked." Engineers and architects had been making payoffs from 1 to 5 percent of non-bid contracts to high county officials for years.

Under threat of prosecution, Fornoff and two engineers, Jerome B. Wolff and Lester Matz, described the awarding of county contracts and the

The Weather
Variable cloudiness today, fair tonight. High, 78; low, 58. Yesterday's High, 76; low, 52.
[Details and Map, Page C14]
Vol. 273—No. 127—F

THE SUN
FINAL

BALTIMORE, THURSDAY, OCTOBER 11, 1973

66 Pages   10 Cents

AGNEW RESIGNS

Russia resupplies Arabs; U.S. aids Israel

Tel Aviv claims recapture of Golan Heights

Airlift | Mideast

By JAMES A. KEAT
Washington Bureau of The Sun

From Wire Services

Tax evasion draws fine, probation

By BENTLEY ORSICK and THEODORE W. HENDRICKS

Spiro T. Agnew leaves Baltimore's old Post Office Building after announcing his resignation.

The case against Spiro Agnew

SUMMARY

INTRODUCTION

Major news elsewhere

Orioles stay alive

Reaction:

Nixon talks of successor	Capitol Hill is subdued	State Leaders sympathetic
By ADAM CLYMER	By ALBERT SEHLSTEDT, JR.	By FRED BARBASH

Other Agnew news

Index

payment of kickbacks. Overwhelming evidence of systematic corruption during the Anderson and Agnew administrations was emerging.

The lead prosecutor in both cases, Assistant US Attorney Barnet D. Skolnik, told me the zoning series spotlighted corrupt practices in Baltimore County and "triggered some of the tips" that came in during 1972. Agnew's downfall, Skolnik said, was "a direct result" of the investigation into Anderson.

Agnew was not the focus of the initial investigation. But not long after the investigation began into the Anderson regime, Wolff and Matz revealed there was a more significant potential target than Anderson: the vice president of the United States. They were prepared to give evidence against Agnew—in return for immunity. Beall, Skolnik, and the Baltimore prosecutors set aside the Anderson probe for a time and concentrated on the Agnew allegations. Soon they had sufficient evidence to inform Elliot Richardson, the US attorney general, of the new turn of events and the much higher stakes.

Once convinced of the evidence against Agnew, Richardson and his staff pushed for immediate action. With the growing Watergate scandal threatening the presidency of Richard Nixon, they were concerned about having a suspected felon (Agnew) next in line to succeed an embattled president.

Over the next three months the Justice Department engaged in protracted negotiations with Agnew's lawyers, who threatened to explore an unpredictable impeachment process. Finally, Agnew, the tough-talking advocate of law and order, agreed to resign and admit to tax dodging. Skolnik later said, "We were very fortunate" that all this took place when "the very principled" Richardson was attorney general. Ten days after Agnew's resignation, Richardson himself resigned rather than fire special Watergate prosecutor Archibald Cox as ordered by Nixon in the dramatic "Saturday Night Massacre."

The system of payoffs under Agnew was described in detail in sworn affidavits outlined in the 1973 federal summary of facts that was part of the vice president's resignation package. More came to light in a 1981–1982 civil case brought by three taxpayers and the state of Maryland to force Agnew to pay back his ill-gained funds.

Wolff, the engineer who was state roads commissioner when Agnew was governor, and I. H. (Bud) Hammerman, a wealthy developer and close friend of Agnew's, outlined the kickback system. Wolff told prosecutors that Hammerman kept 25 percent of a bribe for himself, gave 25 percent to Wolff, and 50 percent to Agnew.

Just before Agnew's resignation, Hammerman said in a sworn statement, "The engineers knew what was expected of them. We spoke only of 'political contributions,' but the engineers knew better than I how the system worked, that is, cash payments, through me . . . were necessary for them to receive substantial state contracts. The contributions were always in cash." (In occasional calls, Agnew, or "Spiggy" as the Baltimore prosecutors referred to him privately, would ask his friend Bud how many "papers" had been collected. One "paper" meant $1,000.)

Matz testified that he once delivered an envelope with $10,000 in cash to Agnew in the vice president's White House office—continuing a long-running scheme that went back to Maryland contracts.

As a result of the civil suit, a lower court ruled that Agnew, who had paid only $13,551 for unreported taxes when he resigned, owed $248,735 to the state of Maryland ($147,500 in bribes; $101,235 in interest). The decision was upheld by the Maryland Court of Special Appeals.

Wolff and Matz were granted immunity in return for their cooperation, and were not prosecuted, although charges were brought against both Hammerman and Allen Green, another contractor who admitted paying $50,000 directly to Agnew. Both men were convicted of tax evasion and drew sentences of eighteen months and one year in prison, respectively, though Hammerman's sentence was later vacated. A higher court determined that Hammerman, who had admitted to being Agnew's "bagman," should not be treated more harshly than Agnew himself, and that his critical evidence had helped clinch the vice president's resignation.

The convictions of Agnew and Anderson came as no surprise to longtime observers of Maryland politics. Six of the most prominent politicians from Baltimore County who won or ran for high office in the year 1962—from county executive (Agnew) to US Senate to clerk of the county court—were convicted of criminal offenses within the next decade.

One of the most consequential was A. Gordon Boone, powerful speaker of the Maryland House of Delegates who was convicted of mail fraud in 1964. (In Maryland's special genealogy of corruption, Boone was succeeded as speaker by a popular Baltimore City delegate Marvin Mandel. Mandel, as speaker, would become governor when Agnew left the office to become Nixon's vice president. Mandel would then be convicted on mail fraud and racketeering charges. Agnew, as we have seen, resigned the vice presidency under threat of federal indictment.)

In 1972, Senator Daniel B. Brewster, a county resident, became only the second US senator in sixty years to be convicted while in office. He was found guilty of accepting $14,000 in "illegal gratuities" from mail order interests but later pleaded "no contest" to a misdemeanor charge and was fined $10,000.

Nor was corruption limited to the county. The 1977 federal conviction of Governor Mandel in a secret scheme to bolster the value of a rundown racetrack hardened Maryland's image as one of the most corrupt states in the country. A national humor magazine suggested putting "cradle of corruption" on the state's license plates. At Maryland–Virginia football games in the late

1970s, the University of Virginia student band would announce "a special guest" at halftime, "the governor of Maryland," and a student would run out on the field dressed in a convict's black-and-white striped suit.

For nearly ten weeks in 1971, I did not contribute a single article to the paper as I conducted my research and wrote my stories. A *Sun* rewrite man, Louis Peddicord, helped polish the seven-part series, and Schmick spent much time and effort in editing it and laying it out on the front page (where local articles seldom appeared in those days).

The stakes were high—orderly growth, a need to tie demands for new roads, sewers, and schools to the county's resources, and millions of dollars in land values.

Slowly, in my research, I began to find a direct correlation between political contributions and zoning decisions. My work was aided by the fact that Baltimore County had just held an election in November 1970, with hundreds of thousands of dollars in campaign contributions going to the Anderson machine—all of them a matter of public record. The names of the donors and the amounts they contributed were invaluable. (The county executive and all his Democratic council candidates had been easily elected.)

In many cases, the county's professional planners had rejected requests for major rezoning by wealthy developers, but the planners' decisions were overturned by the machine's councilmen, all beneficiaries of the developers' election-campaign largess.

Other instances of favoritism showed up. A small number of politically connected lawyers represented the largest developers—signaling that they were the "go-to" lawyers for a favorable outcome. Planning officials, angered by the intense political pressure, became helpful sources. The articles demonstrated the extent to which the public interest in professional planning and the welfare of county residents were, in effect, being sold to the highest bidders.

Most of the payoff testimony against Anderson in his 1974 trial came from engineers and architects, not the landowners or developers. But all of them stood to benefit directly from the warped rezoning process—landowners and developers from the increased land values, and contractors, engineers, and architects from all the work to be assigned by developers and the county for roads, sewers, and so forth.

The stakes in the rezoning process and the overlap between the Anderson and Agnew scandals are illustrated by the involvement of the same high-rollers in political contributions and bribes to the two men.

One major donor to the Anderson organization in the 1970 election was Bud Hammerman, the developer who was to be a key witness against Agnew. He was seeking a favorable zoning ruling on large tracts of land he had an interest in.

Two rezoning cases serve as examples of how the political pressures worked in the redrawing of the county maps. Two developers, Jacob Friedman and Leon Crane of Miami Beach, had donated generously to the Anderson campaign. A year later, they sought eight zoning changes involving 190 acres of land. County planners rejected seven of them. The machine's obedient councilmen overrode six of the seven decisions.

In another contentious case, the owner of a 612-acre parcel at the intersection of the Baltimore Beltway and I-70, Ragan Doub, wanted rezoning of the whole parcel to manufacturing/light industrial. Anderson, who seldom took public positions on such matters, backed Doub's request. In response to a question about it at a press conference, Anderson snapped, "We don't sell favors around here."

In the ensuing comprehensive process, county planners opposed the use sought by Doub and prospective developers, basing their decision on both land use guidelines and an earlier Court of Appeals decision. To no one's surprise, the county council gave the developers the blank check they sought.

Prospective developers of that tract included Harry W. Rodgers III. Rodgers, who held a lucrative lease on the sprawling Social Security complex on land once owned by Doub, had been a notable contributor to the Anderson campaign in 1970. Rodgers was tried and convicted a few years later in the racetrack bribery scheme, along with Governor Mandel.

My editor made good on his promise to send me back to the General Assembly in 1972, and I'm glad he did. With barely a week left in the legislative session, I uncovered evidence that Governor Mandel's closest political associates might be the hidden owners of a small racetrack that the governor was pressing the legislature to award additional racing days worth millions.

My April 3, 1972, article revealed that Irving (Tubby) Schwartz, a right-hand man of Irvin Kovens, Mandel's chief fund-raiser and close friend, owned a small share of Marlboro, a half-mile racetrack in Prince George's County. At the time, Schwartz admitted to ownership of an 8.5 percent stake; years later, after the indictment of Mandel and his confederates, it proved to be thousands of shares. He also held shares for Kovens and the governor's other closest pals, including W. Dale Hess, a real estate speculator and key figure in Tidewater Insurance, a company that profited immensely from state bond contracts. Another owner of Tidewater, also indicted, was Harry W. Rodgers III.

The initial Schwartz disclosure prompted an uproar in the General Assembly that final week. Democrats and Republicans, led by two state senators, Julian L. Lapides (D) and Jervis S. Finney (R), demanded hearings. They blocked much of the governor's legislative package until they could obtain more information on the true ownership of the track.

Mandel allies in the General Assembly ignored the mandated 12 am closing time on the final night of the session, April 11, in a last-ditch effort to force approval of the racetrack "consolidation" bill. But Lapides and Finney continued a bipartisan filibuster, and the Senate president, William S. James finally declared adjournment—well past midnight.

I moved to the Washington bureau later that year and covered the trial of Senator Brewster, another step in the federal investigation of corruption in Maryland. Other reporters for the *Sun*, the *Evening Sun*, and the *Washington Post* continued to investigate the racetrack ownership and the efforts to swing lucrative racing days to Marlboro and its owners. In the end, the same federal prosecutors who nailed Agnew and Anderson gained grand jury indictments of Mandel, Kovens, Hess, Rodgers, and two others on mail fraud and racketeering on November 24, 1975 (figure 8.2).

The governor's lawyers maintained that his friends never told him they had acquired ownership of the racetrack, and that they were merely rewarding Mandel with "gifts" to compensate for his low salary—not paying him off for his efforts to benefit them. The federal attorneys, led by Skolnik, did not see it that way. They argued that Mandel's secret share in a lucrative lease held by Hess and Rodgers on the sprawling Social Security complex in suburban Baltimore county, part ownership of two hundred acres of Eastern Shore

Figure 8.2.   Federal investigators set their sights on Governor Marvin Mandel and his cronies in 1975, the year of release of the film *Jaws*.

waterfront for which Mandel paid $150, and substantial financial help with a costly divorce were direct bribes for throwing the weight of the governor's office behind the racetrack scheme and doubling its value to more than $4 million.

"None of the increase," the *Evening Sun* editor Brad Jacobs later observed, "would be creditable to business acumen, all of it rested on legislative manipulation. Because the Governor held a legislative majority in his palm, he was the pivotal point."

The governor, Kovens, Hess, and Rodgers were found guilty on August 23, 1977—after a second trial. (The first was declared a mistrial after attempts to bribe jurors.) The governor and the other three were each sentenced to four years in jail. In April 1980, the Supreme Court refused to hear their appeal. The original trial judge reduced Mandel's sentence to three years, and the governor went to prison on May 19, 1980. Mandel served a little more than eighteen months before President Ronald Reagan commuted his sentence in December 1981.

In 1987, Mandel's conviction, and those of the other defendants, was overturned by a US District Court judge in a ruling, based on a similar Kentucky case, that whatever the governor's actions, they had not led to tangible economic loss to the state of Maryland. The judge, Frederic N. Smalkin, did not contest the evidence of bribery, but he ruled that federal prosecutors had stretched mail fraud and racketeering laws too far.

"The evidence of concealment of ownership of Marlboro shares and Mandel's secret financial arrangements certainly showed that something fishy was going on, perhaps even dishonest," Judge Smalkin declared. "Mandel might well have been bribed. His co-defendants might well have bribed him. But, however strong the evidence of dishonesty or bribery, the jury was told it could convict for something that did not amount to a federal crime." Congress moved swiftly months later to close the loophole in the federal mail fraud statute, passing legislation which made clear that the law was meant to cover "an intangible right to honest" government.

The corruption uncovered in the Mandel case was examined in Brad Jacobs's book, *Thimbleriggers: The Law v. Governor Marvin Mandel.* (A thimblerigger is an operator of a shell game designed to deceive and cheat.) Jacobs places the racetrack conspiracy in historical context, in line with century-old political machinations and turnabouts which put Mandel in the governor's mansion and led to his trial in the stricter, post-Watergate environment. It also provides marvelous details of the tragi-comedy that led an ambitious and often effective politician to "fade into history as Maryland's first governor to busy himself, in his post-Annapolis years, stacking other convicts' clean underwear."

The Sun's reporting on Anderson, Agnew, Mandel, and their cronies by many reporters in the 1970s was part of a long tradition of taking on political corruption and malfeasance dating back to the late nineteenth century.

This tradition was alive and well when I joined the paper in 1965. The *Sun* had just published a sweeping series on wrongdoing in the Baltimore City Police Department. The series, by Richard Levine, led to a housecleaning of the department—and, incidentally, made it more difficult for young reporters to deal with the police for many years.

Later investigations included outstanding articles in 1976 by Steven M. Luxenberg and Mark Reutter on the charity scams of the Pallottine Fathers and a 1985 series on mismanagement and fraud in Maryland's savings and loan industry by Brian Sullam and Ellen Uzelac. The first resulted in the criminal conviction of the Pallottine's chief priest and was a finalist for a Pulitzer Prize; the latter prompted prosecution of several bankers. Convicted of embezzlement, Jeffrey Levitt, president of Old Court Savings and Loan Association, went to prison for six years; Jerome S. Cardin, a wealthy developer and backer of Dale Anderson, was sentenced to fifteen years in jail and given a substantial fine for stealing $365,000 from the thrift. Cardin was paroled after one year due to ill health.

Among other noteworthy projects was a series by John O'Donnell in 1999 on the invidious real estate practice of flipping, the systematic buying and quick-selling of bottom-line properties mostly to low-income people. O'Donnell and two colleagues were recognized as Pulitzer finalists in 2003 for articles on Baltimore's low rate of convictions in homicide cases.

The scale of corruption in Maryland, which Jacobs termed "cash register politics," appears to have lessened in recent decades, though some observers say it has just taken new and more subtle forms.

A number of recent studies surveyed good government practices and risk of corruption in all fifty states. Maryland came out with mixed results. One of the most comprehensive, published in July 2015 by the Edmond J. Safra Center for Ethics at Harvard University, focused on illegal corruption and what it called "legal corruption." Maryland received a high grade in outright illegal corruption (bribe-taking, etc.), but ranked among the worst states in legal corruption—such as the awarding of favors by public officials in return for substantial campaign contributions.

In July 2015, the *Washington Post* reported that former governor Martin O'Malley, then a candidate for the Democratic nomination for president, had accepted $148,000 in speaking fees from a California company that had received a $3 million non-bid contract from Maryland's three-member Board of Public Works—of which O'Malley was the most influential decision-maker. There is no proof of a quid pro quo, but the perception of a tradeoff, as the *Post* editorialized, is very "concerning." Noting that the arrangement for the speaking fees came shortly after O'Malley left office, the paper concluded: "Notwithstanding the governor's sincere interest in the subject matter (interactive mapping software), there's the appearance of a payback."

The Ivory Tower

Barry Rascovar

When four Democrats began their run for governor in 1978, three were given a chance. They were well-known and had strong constituencies in Maryland's largest jurisdictions: the city of Baltimore, populous Baltimore county, and fast-growing Montgomery County in the Washington suburbs.

The fourth was Harry R. Hughes, a former state senator from the rural Eastern Shore who had a handful of volunteers as campaign staff, no backing from any politician of influence, and a poll number that barely showed a pulse. So dim were his prospects that Harry McGuirk, a wily state senator from Baltimore known as "Soft Shoes," got a lot of knowing laughs when he called the Hughes campaign "a lost ball in high grass."

And so it seemed until the editorial pages of the *Baltimore Sun* and its sister paper, the *Evening Sun*, rescued the Hughes campaign from the tall fescue. The two papers combined in an unusual series of editorials to promote Hughes as an antidote to the corruption tainting Maryland politics. Hughes won the primary, the general election, and served two effective, basically scandal-free terms in the State House—an editorial writer's dream.

All this, plus the overhanging history of the *Baltimore Sun's* venerable editorial page—reverberations from H. L. Mencken, Frank R. Kent, Gerald W. Johnson, and Price Day—was on my mind a year later as I drove to Baltimore for a meeting with the editorial page editor, Joseph R. L. Sterne.

For eight years, I had covered local, state, and national politics in Baltimore and Washington. Now, Sterne, a respected reporter who would run the editorial page longer than any other editor, wanted to interview me for a job as his deputy.

Whether it was the police beat, working on the *Sun's* city desk, or covering the State House, I loved the world of news reporting, where facts speak

93

for themselves. Opinion writing? Not in my career plans. I was clueless about the inner workings of this curious department, which some reporters sarcastically called the "Ivory Tower."

To say the least, I was a little bit intimidated by the department's history, its national influence, and storied former inhabitants.

The editorial page was a leading factor in the *Sun's* rise to prominence in the early decades of the twentieth century. The Baltimore papers (both the *Sun* and the *Evening Sun*) got a huge boost thanks to Mencken, America's most influential man of letters in the 1920s and 1930s.

As editor of the *Evening Sun* editorial page, the sage of Baltimore enjoyed infuriating priggish segments of the middle and upper classes with his biting ridicule. From there, and as editor of the national magazines *American Mercury* and the *Smart Set*, Mencken blasted away at hypocrisy and hooliganism, moneyed folks and the uncultured, the "booboisie," all political pretensions, and the mountebanks who ran for public office.

Mencken resigned from the editorial page just before America's entry into World War II due to his pro-German sympathies. But there were several other stars in the *Sun's* editorial firmament. Among them were Kent, who, after a path-breaking series on the Versailles peace talks at the end of the First World War, launched the nation's first syndicated political column, the "Great Game of Politics"; Gerald W. Johnson, an erudite Southerner; and John W. Owens, winner of the 1937 Pulitzer Prize for editorial writing.

In those days, the *Sun* leaned Democratic, sometimes with a Southern twist. It backed Franklin D. Roosevelt in 1932, but soon fell out with him over the New Deal. The paper did not endorse him again, and it became more sympathetic to the Republicans. That changed when the more liberal Price Day took over as editor-in-chief of both papers in 1960.

Day, a former war correspondent who won the Pulitzer Prize in 1949 for reporting from India, nudged the *Sun* closer to a liberal outlook on most issues, though he often had (for that epoch) conservative positions on the economy and national security.

Price Day focused his editorial page on the nation and the world, and was not much interested in local problems. "I'm not the editor of potholes," he once told Sterne, his deputy. No wonder the *Sun* failed to take the lead on many Baltimore questions.

* * *

I had joined the *Sun* as a reporter in 1969 when Day still ran the editorial page. Now, ten years later, I became the deputy editorial page editor.

I soon absorbed the lesson that under Sterne's leadership, which would last twenty-five years, the editorial department operated as an enlightened despotism. On major issues, he set policy, and for good reason. The *Sun's* publisher—unlike the situation at most newspapers—bestowed on the editorial page editor near-total authority and responsibility to speak for the institution.

Indeed, Sterne says he never once received an order from the publisher to slant an editorial a certain way, and, with the exception of presidential endorsements, that he never consulted with the publisher before declaiming on matters affecting big advertisers, the paper's own finances, or burning social issues. Such journalistic independence was rare in America, and still is.

Sterne recalls one collision with the paper's overseers. He was asked to accompany the publisher William F. Schmick Jr. to the downtown office of William E. McGuirk Jr., the influential boss of Mercantile Bankshares Corp., which held in trust much of the A. S. Abell Company's stock. The A. S. Abell Company owned the Sunpapers. McGuirk, who sat on the newspaper's board (and would become its last chairman) minced few words. "I think your editorials are a load of shit," the banker said to Sterne. A sharp, half-hour exchange followed about economic policy as McGuirk tried, and failed, to bully Sterne. Afterward, Schmick quietly told his editor, "Well, he certainly didn't intimidate you."

Similarly blunt economic discussions between McGuirk's successor at Mercantile, H. Furlong Baldwin, and the *Sun's* editorial writers flared occasionally over legislative efforts in Annapolis to cap bank interest rates and open Maryland to big, out-of-state financial institutions. Baldwin's passionate arguments received polite consideration, but nothing more.

As editor, Sterne used his experience in Washington and overseas to keep a firm hand on essays dealing with foreign policy, national security, economics, and the presidency. He believed in extensive research and reporting, writing most of these editorials himself, sometimes more than one a day.

Sterne gave his six-person staff freedom to shape the newspaper's voice on other issues—mainly local editorials, but also scientific advances, the arts, medicine, popular culture, education, national politics, and legal affairs.

All this got thrashed out at 10 am meetings that could last from twenty minutes to an hour or more. Each writer suggested a topic and how to approach it. Next came a barrage of pointed questions. In this Socratic dialogue, Sterne made sure proposed editorials held up under intellectual scrutiny. He also wanted the writer to know where the editor stood. That was key because Sterne believed in rigorous editing. He, with my assistance, wanted to make sure every piece was consistent with past *Sun* positions and could be defended when upset readers—elected officials, CEOs, or lobbyists—came knocking, sometimes quite literally.

The quick-tempered governor William Donald Schaefer once got so enraged at a critical editorial that he showed up in the *Sun*'s lobby at the crack of dawn, demanding to see Sterne. When the guard on duty said the editor wouldn't arrive for several hours, an exasperated Schaefer stormed out of the lobby muttering to himself. Actually, the two really liked one another. Schaefer would accuse Sterne of trying to "destroy" him. Sterne would reply that most politicians would kill for the kind of press Schaefer got in the *Sun*.

Putting together a short or long editorial can take even an experienced writer much of the day. Most of that time is consumed by researching and interviewing experts, advocates, opponents, and newsmakers. The hoped-for result is an engaging essay covering all relevant elements, analyzing matters concisely and persuasively.

It's no easy task. Many experienced *Sun* reporters found themselves uncomfortable writing editorials. They liked reporting just the facts rather than producing a think-piece that took a strong stand on issues.

Those who gravitate to editorial writing prefer topical essays that size up events. The staff I joined included Edgar L. Jones, whose writing focused on individuals who made Baltimore's infrastructure and school system work; Daniel Berger, a former London correspondent who followed foreign affairs; Theo Lippman Jr., a wry Georgian who wrote about national politics and civil rights, and produced a droll, award-winning column; Jerome Kelly, a veteran local political reporter and Neiman Fellow responsible for suburban issues; and Richard Gilluly, who covered science and health issues. A veteran Associated Press foreign correspondent, Stephens Broening, ran a lively, high-toned Op-Ed page. And Tom Flannery, flanked by Mike Lane on the *Evening Sun*, provided marvelous cartoons in the tradition of Edmund Duffy, winner of three Pulitzer Prizes, and the idiosyncratic Richard "Moco" Yardley. Kevin Kallaugher (KAL) would join the staff when Flannery retired.

Three to four editorials appeared every day, seven days a week. Writers also handled proofreading and makeup duties, as well as editing letters selected for publication. The work was always interesting but intense. Sterne boasted that his writers had such skills they could "cover the universe."

* * *

As editor, Sterne had few ideological guideposts, preferring a pragmatic approach. The *Sun*, while endorsing Richard Nixon three times for president, nevertheless excoriated his efforts to cover-up the Watergate scandal. After Nixon resigned and received a pardon from Gerald R. Ford, the paper supported Ford's action, arguing that the nation needed to return to normalcy. This stood in sharp contrast to the *Evening Sun*'s editorial declaring, in effect, that the Nixon pardon was sinful.

After Ronald Reagan's election in 1980, the *Sun* derided his economic and domestic policies as well as his bellicosity toward Soviet Russia. The newspaper strongly supported Reagan's accord with the Soviet leader Mikhail S. Gorbachev limiting nuclear weapons.

On civil rights, Sterne's predecessor, Price Day, had abandoned the foot-dragging, "all deliberate speed" approach toward school integration advocated by earlier editors. Further back, the *Sun* had endorsed blatantly racial policies and backed residential segregation well into the 1950s. Slowly but surely, Day moved the newspaper firmly behind the 1964 Civil Rights Act and a ringing endorsement of Lyndon B. Johnson—the first time in eight elections the *Sun* had supported a Democrat for president.

Early on, Day also questioned the wisdom of US involvement in Vietnam. His skepticism about the war intensified as casualties and setbacks mounted. But Sterne and his deputy at the time, John E. Woodruff, a Vietnam correspondent and expert on Asia, held out hope for a turnaround of American fortunes—to no avail.

"It's inevitable," Sterne says, "that you're going to be wrong on some editorials."

Under Sterne, the editorial page took on more of a Baltimore flavor. The *Sun* editorialized daily on controversies at City Hall and the State House. There was staff resistance when Sterne enthusiastically supported then-Mayor Schaefer's efforts in the 1970s to transform Baltimore's rat-infested wharves into a gleaming waterfront mall—the Rouse Company's Harborplace. As usual, the editor got his way.

Nationwide acclaim greeted the opening of the Inner Harbor pavilions in 1980, spurring a remarkable Baltimore renaissance. It marked a turning point for the *Sun*, too, which rapidly assumed a prominent role in shaping public opinion on state and local issues—much as it had done when battling Baltimore's political "rings" in the late nineteenth century.

This renewed editorial focus on local developments culminated in the historic endorsement of Harry Hughes in 1978—at the end of a decade marred by a series of scandals that led to the downfall of Vice President Spiro T. Agnew, the former governor of Maryland, and the conviction of his successor in the State House, Marvin Mandel.

The *Sun's* unusually strong editorial advocacy that year persuaded voters to shatter Maryland's dominant, and often corrupt, Democratic machine that had controlled the state pretty much since Civil War days. It showed what can happen when a newspaper is willing to risk its reputation for the common good.

* * *

Election endorsements offer newspapers unusual opportunities to influence the course of political events. Not many voters pay careful attention to what hundreds of candidates are saying as Election Day approaches. They look for guidance from respected sources, such as established daily newspapers.

In this arena, the *Sun* offered informed advice, frequently supporting experienced reformers. Just before political Judgment Day, the newspaper traditionally prints on the editorial page a list of its choices—candidates, bond issues, charter amendments—suggesting readers take this list with them when they vote.

For decades, the *Sun* inveighed against the city's bosses and their political puppets. To a surprising degree, voters heeded the newspaper's direction.

The power to endorse in local contests rested mainly with the editorial writers. Staffers spent the pre-election summer interviewing dozens of aspirants, parsing candidate questionnaires, and preparing for a Grand Inquest—a marathon meeting of the editorial boards of both the *Sun* and the *Evening Sun*.

It was the only time they met jointly, to agree on a single slate of candidates so as to appear coherent. For the rest of the year, morning and evening staffs went their separate ways—the *Sun* taking a more studied and cautious path, the *Evening Sun* a colorful, free-wheeling approach.

Advice from the writers who had researched each race normally prevailed, but not without heated arguments. On most elections—mayor, governor, congressman, or senator—the editorial page editors took the lead. Presidential endorsements were another matter. The publisher reigned supreme, almost routinely supporting the Republican nominee. Price Day, who had created a liberal editorial voice for the newspaper, met repeated opposition to Democratic candidates, dutifully making the trek every four years to the publisher's suite where he was instructed to support a Republican for president.

This became especially difficult for Day in 1960, when the publisher informed the editor that the *Sun* would be endorsing Nixon over Day's choice, the Democrat John F. Kennedy.

Day accepted this as part of the system, but ran into a particularly strong headwind from his staff that year. No one was willing to write the endorsement editorial. Philip Wagner, the most conservative writer on the staff, finally agreed—and even he had trouble generating much enthusiasm for Nixon. Wagner concluded his endorsement by writing that the newspaper's concerns over Kennedy's domestic policies "outweigh the doubts about Mr. Nixon"; faint praise, indeed.

That brings us to the 1978 statewide elections. Sterne ruled the *Sun's* editorial page; Bradford Jacobs, the blue-blood descendant of a Civil War governor, ran the *Evening Sun*'s. The campaign took place in the shadow of multiple corruption scandals. Successive governors had been disgraced—Agnew and Mandel. Reform was in the wind, the gubernatorial candidates failed to impress.

Jacobs, who later wrote an elliptically styled book detailing Mandel's illegalities in the context of Maryland's shady political history, was a longtime chronicler of the state's nefarious "b'hoys." He was horrified at the prospect of endorsing the heir to the formidable Mandel machine—the patrician, well-meaning but hapless acting governor, Blair Lee III.

Lee, who had refused to sever his ties to Mandel's entourage, was the heavy favorite. As endorsement time neared, Jacobs approached Sterne with a bold suggestion. He wanted the newspapers to back a candidate then dead-last in the polls, Harry Hughes.

Without question, Hughes was the best of the bunch: a former Senate majority leader and budget chairman, co-author of a pioneering tax-reform law, and a highly regarded transportation secretary who had resigned from the Mandel administration over political efforts to manipulate a $24 million subway contract.

Yet Hughes's rag-tag campaign barely registered with voters. His support stood at 4 percent in all surveys.

Jacobs argued this was the time for the newspaper to put its credibility on the line and endorse Hughes—even if it meant backing a loser. What if the A. S. Abell publications endorsed the best candidate in the race and did

Figure 9.1. Harry Hughes scores a hole-in-one off the head of Senator Harry McGuirk.
Mike Lane, courtesy of Baltimore Sun Media Group, all rights reserved.

so early and often? What if the two newspapers ran Hughes endorsements on their *front pages*?

It was a cheeky proposal, typical of Jacobs. His outrage and desire to make the Sunpapers the loudest booster of Hughes's anticorruption, "good government" crusade struck home with Sterne.

"Brad said we should endorse Hughes, that it was the right thing to do even if he didn't win," Sterne recalls. "I told Brad I would support him to the hilt. When we were on the verge of a decision we asked [Publisher Donald] Patterson if we could visit him that evening at his home near Annapolis. We told him the most honorable candidate was Hughes. Patterson said 'fine' and gave his approval."

This decision was fraught with peril. It went against the political common wisdom and the business community's strong support for a known quantity, Blair Lee. The newspaper could turn into a laughingstock.

Sterne's deputy, John B. O'Donnell, wrote a lengthy Hughes endorsement, which his boss worked over for two days until both men were satisfied. The editorial ran August 20, a Sunday, the biggest circulation day. It appeared two weeks early—but not on the front page as Jacobs had urged. What did appear on page 1, though, generated almost as much buzz: a top-of-the-page box headlined, "Sun Endorsements for Governor":

> In the Democratic primary the paper endorses Harry R. Hughes in the belief that he is the one candidate with both the experience to govern Maryland and the capacity to rid state government of a political system that in the last decade has helped give it a reputation for corruption.

The editorial, along with that startling front-page announcement, created a political tsunami.

Hughes's backing nearly tripled by the time pollsters contacted voters the next day. The "lost ball" had been found (figure 9.1). Thanks to a solid performance in televised debates, where Hughes talked policy while others bickered, the *Sun*'s choice kept gaining ground. Enough new money flowed into his campaign to reprint two hundred thousand copies of the Sunday endorsement. The two-column, 1,600-word editorial ran the entire length of the page and began this way:

> The 1978 gubernatorial elections offer Marylanders a needed opportunity to break cleanly with the politics of the past. For too long this state has been plagued by a system that has fostered corruption, petty and monstrous. It is a system that has ended in the criminal conviction of Maryland's last two elected governors. It is a system oiled by private profits gleaned from the manipulation of political power. It is a system that has demeaned this state in the eyes of the nation, and it must be broken.

All four Democratic candidates portray themselves as men unsullied by the system. But only one—Harry R. Hughes—seems to have the experience and capacity both to overcome the system and to govern. Although his campaign to date has lagged behind his major competitors, many citizens regard him as the best in the field—if only he could win. The *Sun* considers him the best of the Democratic candidates. To help him win, this newspaper offers its early and enthusiastic endorsement.

A day later, Brad Jacobs got his wish, a front-page *Evening Sun* editorial heaping more praise on Hughes and castigating the powers that had corrupted government in Annapolis. Entitled "A Case for Hughes," Jacobs's endorsement noted, "The candidate armed with the sturdiest promise for running Maryland's government honestly and well, Harry Hughes, apparently is being overlooked by party voters." It described him as "no whirlwind campaigner, no backroom money-raiser, no spinner of utopian dreams [but rather] a proven leader on both the two broad avenues a governor must travel, legislative and executive."

The clincher came at the end:

A vote for the right man is never wrong.

Hughes, in his autobiography, admitted that by mid-August what his struggling campaign "needed the most was a miracle"—and it arrived with the glowing editorial endorsements. It went "beyond my wildest expectations. . . . Here was the most influential newspaper in the state swinging its power through an unprecedented front-page endorsement to a candidate who has never risen higher than about eight percent in any of the pre-primary polls. It was a stunning rejection of Lee, the front-runner. . . . Suddenly I was seen as a viable candidate. . . . The editorial got people to thinking for the first time that, 'Maybe he can win.'"

One week before the September 13 Democratic primary, a *Sun*-commissioned poll showed Hughes in third place, still fourteen percentage points behind Lee, but with 22 percent of voters undecided. Undeterred, the *Sun* editorialized again on the Monday before Election Day:

Harry Hughes can win. He will win if the tens of thousands of Marylanders who normally stay home from the polls come out tomorrow and vote.

Come out they did. Hughes, with 37 percent, upended Lee by three percentage points. His margin of victory was twenty thousand votes. Hughes breezed to election in November and served two terms as a progressive, principled governor.

The final tally in the primary was Hughes 213,457 (37.2 percent); Lee, the Montgomery County patrician, 194,236 (33.8 percent); Ted Venetoulis, Baltimore County executive, 140,486 (24.5 percent); and Walter Orlinsky, president of the Baltimore City Council, 25,200 (4.4 percent).

The newspaper's strong and early support made the difference. Sidney Hollander Jr., a veteran Baltimore pollster writing in *Public Opinion Quarterly*, analyzed the impact of the *Baltimore Sun's* support for Hughes. His conclusion: the editorials indeed had swayed Maryland's large group of undecided citizens "who hesitated to vote their convictions because they were afraid of 'throwing away' their votes. The newspaper endorsement made Hughes a plausible candidate and the voters did the rest."

Debate has persisted ever since about the *Sun's* editorial power to influence elections. For years, Hughes chafed when asked about it, especially after cynics referred to him as "Son of *Sun*." Was he lifted from political obscurity by the power of the pen?

Gene Oishi, Governor Hughes's first press secretary and an alumnus of the *Sun's* reporting staff, gets the last word: "Nobody," he said in the early days of the Hughes administration, "likes to think he was elected by a newspaper."

· *10* ·

The Bay

Tom Horton

Mother Nature is a capricious goddess. Before I had worked at the *Sun* enough months to get my name on stories, two years before I became its first full-time environmental reporter, thirty-four years before I'd file the last of thousands of pieces for the paper on Chesapeake Bay, came the biggest environmental story I'd ever cover.

The first warning came from the Associated Press the morning of June 20, 1972. A modest hurricane had lost strength after striking the Florida panhandle. Downgraded to a tropical storm, it might make for a soggy day or two as it moved through the mid-Atlantic. Readers of the *Sun* were probably more intrigued by the burglary that week of the Democratic National Committee headquarters at the Watergate office complex in Washington.

But Tropical Storm Agnes would dominate the news pages as it swelled to a rain event such as the Bay might experience, on average, a few times every thousand years.

Beginning the afternoon of Wednesday, June 21, Agnes would soak Maryland and Virginia, where water tables were already saturated and reservoirs brimming from a very wet winter and spring. Then, moving north through Pennsylvania, the storm unexpectedly hooked back south and stalled. It dropped unimagined rainfall across much of the Chesapeake's 64,000-square-mile watershed, which drains lands extending north to Cooperstown, New York, across one-third of Pennsylvania and into West Virginia. Had the 2,500-square-mile Chesapeake been an enclosed reservoir, Agnes would have raised the water level in it two feet. "The most massive flooding in the history of the eastern United States," said the Federal Office of Emergency Preparedness.

One hundred and twenty-two people died in Agnes's path, including the three young children of Carlotta Shelton of Ruxton, a Baltimore suburb. She was swept away (and survived) as she struggled to extricate them from her car, surrounded by floodwaters engorging the Jones Falls. The Patapsco River ran twelve feet deep down Ellicott City's main street. Near Port Deposit, where the Susquehanna River delivers nearly half the Bay's freshwater, explosives were placed to blow a section of the mighty, 116-foot-high Conowingo hydroelectric dam if its stability could no longer be controlled. "Like projectile vomiting . . ." says my notes from that day, as I watched the deep brown, sediment-laden Susquehanna belching from all fifty-three of Conowingo's floodgates. The river's force moved the near mile-long dam a quarter inch on one side, closing US Route 1, which crosses it, for months of repairs.

Agnes struck the Chesapeake a massive blow. The Bay has surprisingly little water in it to absorb pollution washing from a watershed covering one-sixth of the Atlantic Seaboard. From Tidewater Virginia at its mouth to Havre de Grace near its head, the Bay is about a million feet long and up to one hundred thousand feet wide—but only twenty-one feet deep on average. In 1972, few thought of the Bay's vulnerability to farflung activities across the landscape; but Agnes foreshadowed the need to understand and manage the whole ecosystem.

The storm hit unusually early in hurricane season, when the Bay's fish, crabs, oysters, and seagrass meadows were all spawning and flowering and at their most vulnerable. Polluting, smothering sediment washed into the Susquehanna, Potomac, James, and dozens of lesser tributaries and blasted them with as much dirt in a few days as the Bay normally receives in a few decades.

And more than dirt: the watershed had been under increasing assault for years, from suburban development and intensifying chemical agriculture, to deforestation, wetlands destruction, and concentrations of manure from industrial strength dairy and poultry operations. Agnes pulled the trigger on this, coming after a decade of drought, with scant pollution runoff from the land. To this day we struggle to reverse many of the declines ushered in by that mammoth deluge. It gave me an appreciation for the limits of science. You might have measured sediment inputs to the Chesapeake for centuries, and thought you understood how it worked, then overnight, BAM!

Hired just out of the Army in April 1972 with virtually no journalism or writing experience, I was thrown into the all-hands-on-deck coverage of Agnes. I had a fair knowledge of my native Maryland's rural landscapes, but more important, my GMC pickup had sufficient road clearance to probe into remoter flooded areas.

Agnes was an indelible immersion in the power of nature. I crawled out over railroad trestles bridging the gap at Harpers Ferry, West Virginia, where the Shenandoah River normally slides peaceably, clear and shallow, into the main Potomac. A loaded coal train was parked there, apparently in the hope that it would anchor the bridge. The whole affair was vibrating hard enough that I stood up only very tentatively for a better view. The two rivers collided roaringly in sharp, standing waves several feet high, tossing sections of turkey houses like matchsticks; refrigerators, oil drums, massive uprooted trees, and boats ripped from their moorings.

Agnes was also a crash course in the power and camaraderie of a big and talented newsroom to come together in crisis; dozens of normally independent reporters working in concert under pressure to deliver the big story. I was hooked—still young and carefree enough to marvel someone would pay you to do this. I was also certain, as the floods subsided and I returned to the police beat and obituaries, that I preferred reporting from the outdoors, and loved the long leash the newspaper afforded reporters in the field to go wherever the story lay.

In 1974, I became the *Sun's* full-time environmental reporter, a news beat that scarcely existed four years before, employing then fewer than a

Figure 10.1. Tom Horton interviews a crewman of the oyster-bearing skipjack *Rebecca Ruark*, on the Choptank River in 2013.
Courtesy of David Harp, Chesapeake Photos.

dozen journalists around the country. It was a big, new commitment of time and news space. No limits were placed on coverage, which over time would take me from rainforests in Amazonia to drought-ravaged western Sudan, and rainbow reefs of corals in Australia. But the beat would focus on Chesapeake Bay. The Bay was in the *Sun's*, Baltimore's, and Maryland's DNA.

"Baltimore lay very near the immense protein factory of Chesapeake Bay, and out of the bay it ate divinely," H. L. Mencken wrote of his boyhood there in the 1880s, recalling "prime hard crabs . . . at least eight inches in length, with snow-white meat almost as firm as soap . . . any poor man could go down to the banks of the (Patapsco) . . . and come home in a couple of hours with enough crabs to feed his family for two days." (A century later, I would report several hundred urban crabbers were still at it, a few near the Hanover Street Bridge netting up to four bushels a day; but none near eight inches, and mounting concerns about how many it was safe to eat.)

Our state dog was the Chesapeake Bay retriever, the Chesapeake oyster skipjack the official state boat, and the bluecrab and rockfish were the state crustacean and state fish, respectively . . . even the state fossil came out of the Bay's cliffs in Calvert County; and "Go Terps"—what other state university would have the diamondback terrapin, cosmopolite of Chesapeake marshes, as mascot? My Eastern Shore boyhood, devoted to hunting and fishing and marsh mucking, to dipping spring-run herring in the creeks, and grabbing bullfrogs by hand from old gravelpits at night, complemented this. My mom, who worried about her teenager's inattention to formal schooling, observed, in her late eighties: "Well, you were training for the *Sun*; we just didn't know it."

Indeed, a fond memory is the day I emerged, wet and muddy, from "researching" a story on the April spawning migration of herring, home from the sea, mounting Rock Creek through the District of Columbia, halted only by a little dam behind the National Zoo. I clumped into the *Sun's* suit-and-tie Washington bureau in hip boots and sat down at a typewriter.

The Chesapeake's tidewater tentacles extended the life of the oceans and the rivers deep and broad into our landscape and history and culture—what the poet Alexander Pope termed "the genius of the place." And if there was any genius in the way we would cover environment at the *Sun* in the decades that followed, it was to recognize that the meat of the beat was often not about breaking news and filing daily.

That was a stretch for a traditional newspaper of four decades ago, but timing is all, and the times were changing. The first Earth Day in 1970 remains one of the biggest turnouts of citizens in support of any cause in our nation's history. That same year President Richard Nixon created the Environmental Protection Agency—EPA ("eppa," he called it)—to oversee strong new clean air and clean water laws passed by huge majorities of both the US House and Senate. William Warner in 1976 would win a Pulitzer for *Beautiful Swimmers*, about blue crabs and the Chesapeake, and James Michener followed with the best-selling *Chesapeake* in 1978.

The University of Maryland was hiring a new generation of bright young aquatic scientists, PhDs trained in systems analysis and new ecological approaches to comprehending dynamic and complex environments like the Chesapeake, where ocean water collided with the flows of forty-odd rivers, a classic mixing of salt and fresh that makes an estuary.

My career and theirs would overlap joyfully. My editors allowed me the downtime to spend many days afloat and afield with researchers, and in their laboratories and classrooms, learning as I'd seldom learned during an indifferent four years at Johns Hopkins. I learned also from remarkable women like Ajax Eastman, Beth Hartline, Fran Flanigan, and Judy Johnson of Baltimore. They and others were the full-time volunteers who carried the environmental movement before the rise of professional organizations. I was once informed that I was expensing more than anyone on the metro staff subscribing to magazines, newspapers, and science journals, from local to international. It was not a complaint.

Also changing was the bountiful Chesapeake I'd taken for granted most of my life—losing oxygen, losing vital seagrass, and wetland habitats, losing waterfowl and seafood. By the late 1970s, an unprecedented five-year research effort into the reasons and solutions was underway. In 1983, an historic summit meeting among EPA and the states of the vast Chesapeake watershed concluded that business as usual wasn't going to cut it; restoration of the Bay to something like I knew as a kid in the 1950s would become the driving force of environmental programs. The Bay beat was here to stay.

The environmental movement was a different animal than the ones newspapers were used to covering—radical at its core—about humans learning to coexist with the rest of nature, about the right of citizens to healthy air and fishable, swimmable waters (and denying any right of corporations to pollute). It was about what you did on YOUR private property being connected and obliged to OUR Bay; about limits to eternal growth of the human species and economy on a finite world.

It was easier to speak of such things when I began the environment beat than it is now. Environmental organizations shy from talk of limits. Easier now, perhaps, to get money and members with "growing greener," "growing smarter," and "sustainable growth" campaigns that imply we can have our cake and eat it, too. They are mostly good campaigns—just not enough to actually restore places like Chesapeake Bay.

The Chesapeake restoration seemed to me an exciting, world-class experiment. We had taken a place with a world-class environment, screwed it up big time, and were hell bent on pulling off a startling recovery, even as the region boomed with new growth. If the richest, most powerful nation in the history of the world couldn't manage this in a place that lay at the (Potomac River) doorstep of its capital, then where on earth could we expect to learn to live sustainably?

Around 1976, a story came along that exemplified and foreshadowed the greater Bay experiment. It involved a remarkable local political leader, Bernie Fowler, and a courageous Bay scientist, Donald Heinle. Both lived and worked near the mouth of a major Chesapeake tributary, the Patuxent River. Theirs was superficially a classic struggle between rural, seafood harvesting downstreamers, watching their way of life decline because of pollution from burgeoning development upstream across central Maryland. But the Patuxent's fate would be seminal to the future direction of the whole Chesapeake.

Maryland and the EPA had endorsed a plan to govern the river's water quality for the twenty years to come. It acknowledged that as much as 80 percent of the Patuxent's flow from upstream would be water issuing from rapidly expanding sewage treatment plants. But the river could still thrive with proposed, high-tech removal of phosphorus from the sewage. Phosphorus is a plant nutrient that was overfertilizing lakes and rivers nationwide, murking their waters with algae and depleting aquatic oxygen. The plan for the Patuxent was premised on science that was "about where Newtonian physics was before Newton," the state's own water quality consultant told me in an interview.

And it would likely finish off the lower Patuxent's marine life, according to cutting-edge research being conducted by Don Heinle and his colleagues at the University of Maryland's Chesapeake Biological Laboratory at Solomons. Heinle had said as much to the locals, led by Bernie Fowler, a Calvert County commissioner who had known the river intimately when it was healthier. Removing phosphorus worked in freshwater, where EPA back then had its expertise; but in estuaries the chemistry was different, a mix of saltwater and fresh; and sewage treatment plants would also need to remove nitrogen, the other major plant nutrient in human waste flows.

This was technologically tough and fearsomely expensive—and unproven in the eyes of Maryland and the EPA. But it had massive implications for the whole Chesapeake, and for that matter for hundreds of other increasingly polluted estuaries around the world.

Heinle, who worked for the state, was forbidden from talking to the press. He would have friends notify me to show up when he was giving a private briefing, or where he would be "asked" for his opinion on nitrogen at an unrelated meeting. Not since Rachel Carson and DDT in the early 1960s had a daily newspaper given such space to chemistry lessons. I was tipped that Heinle's boss, Peter Wagner, had gotten a call from a high state official at something like 3 am, demanding Heinle be fired. I called Wagner to confirm. A long pause, then: "I can't confirm that call because I get so many . . . they run together." Years later when he retired, Heinle gave his successor a wooden shield with my phone number across the front of it.

He and Fowler agreed it would be tragic if the state's major Bay laboratory let a river die on its threshold. Armed with an affidavit from Heinle and other scientists, the Southern Maryland counties sued in federal court to overturn the state-federal water quality plan. In 1979, a judge junked the plan. The state's top water quality official was stripped of much of his authority. A new agency was set up under a new governor, Harry Hughes, who pledged to do whatever the Patuxent needed. The goal was to return it to the clarity Bernie recalled as a young man in the 1940s, when he'd wade out shoulder deep after soft crabs and could still see his toes on the bottom.

I did not get onto that terrific Patuxent story through dogged enterprise. I read about it in the *Washington Post*. The *Post* always had the resources and the talent to bury me, but they never followed up on the story. Throughout my career, with a few notable exceptions, the estimable *Post* did not share the *Sun's* unflagging commitment to covering regional environment.

The Patuxent's story isn't over yet. Bernie Fowler, at ninety-one, was ready to lead yet another annual "wade in" the summer of 2015. It's a ritual he began after the lawsuit thirty-five years before, where supporters of the river hope to see their feet, shoulder deep, as he once did. Most years they are lucky to get to knee deep. The river keeps reducing pollution per capita, keeps adding people—"walking south on a northbound train," a singer friend on the Patuxent termed it.

And wonky as it sounds, the big issue there, nitrogen, turned out to be the "perfect" pollutant for an inquiring environmental reporter. Wherever humans have settled on a modern, intensive scale along coastlines, it has become the primary water pollutant—some 450 documented "deadzones," bays without adequate oxygen, worldwide now.

Nitrogen comes from most everything humans do: flushing, farming, driving, heating and cooling, and manufacturing. It is hard to control, dissolving in water, escaping underground to emerge, sometimes decades later, in rivers and bays. It is limitless—extracted from earth's atmosphere of which it is 78 percent; unleashed whenever we burn fossil fuels. Earth and its waters have become awash in nitrogen—one of the biggest human meddlings ever with the planetary environment.

To restore any balance will require reining in the full scope of human activities on the planet—a story with real legs. Indeed, in 2000, the *Sun* won a prestigious Overseas Press Club award—best international environmental reporting in any medium—for a globe-girdling series, "Nitrogen's Deadly Harvest" that I reported with Heather Dewar and Frank Langfitt.

The 1980s were the Reagan years, sobering after the enormously hopeful environmentalism of the 1970s. I got a foretaste when the *Sun* sent me to Wyoming in late 1980 to find out who James Gaius Watt was, Reagan's little-known nominee to head the Department of the Interior. Watt seemed opposed to virtually everything I'd assumed even a conservative environmental official would think important. God was obviously deeply important to him, but newspapers back then still assumed politicians kept their religion separate. I worried the story I filed might seem harsh before the guy even had a chance in office. In retrospect, it was too soft. Watt came on like a gleeful bulldozer. He would be gone in a few years, his major accomplishment perhaps the recruitment of legions of new members to environmental groups opposing him.

Watt aside, he and Reagan represented a lasting turning point. Republicans in my experience had been at least as instrumental as Democrats in fighting for the Chesapeake: Arthur Sherwood, who founded the Chesapeake Bay Foundation; Senator Charles McC. Mathias Jr., who spearheaded the Bay restoration effort; the Eastern Shore resident and Nixon EPA administrator Russell Train, who blocked oil refineries from Baltimore. Before Reagan I don't recall covering the environment as a partisan issue. Nowadays it is depressingly so. Republican party positions now often leave Democrats the only game in town, free to offer environmentalists half a loaf.

Wetlands were a special target of the Reagan administration, which saw protecting them as infringing on private property rights and an impediment to economic development. But wetlands are among the most ecologically valuable components of places like Chesapeake Bay, not only as a habitat that underpins hunting and fishing and seafood harvesting; but also in their ability to remove large quantities of nitrogen from the estuary. Wetlands for me were also personal. The place where I grew up encompasses some 40 percent of the entire Chesapeake's marshes. They are the landscape where, returning from the western shore, something inside whispers, "home."

In 1983, I broke a national story on the *Sun's* front page (April 10) documenting how the Reagan administration was systematically dismantling federal protection for millions of acres of the nation's wetlands. The piece, and a subsequent editorial by Theo Lippman, raised alarms across the country, ultimately helping blunt the assault. More than thirty years later, I was addressing one of the nation's largest environmental groups when an older official extended his hand: "The *Sun* nailed that Reagan wetland story."

The more immediate reaction in 1983 was less salutatory; a blustering phone call from Reagan's point man in the wetlands wars, Assistant Sec-

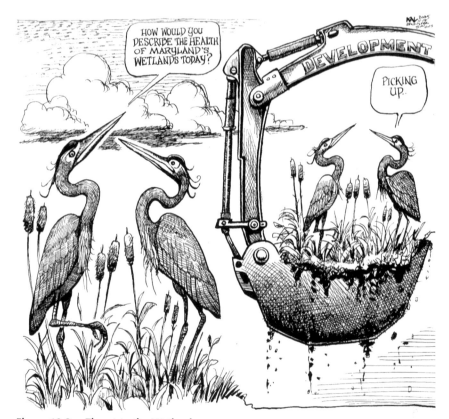

Figure 10.2.   Threat to the Wetlands.
Courtesy of KAL.

retary of the Army William R. Gianelli. He assured me he would take my transgressions up with the people who ran the *Sun*. He demanded a meeting at the Pentagon, where I spent a long morning alone at one end of a huge conference table, ringed at the other end with all manner of Reagan officials objecting to my reporting. The theme of the day seemed more intimidation than factual objection.

And frankly, I was a little shaken. Reporters have to develop thick skins, but by temperament, I was more nature writer than muckraker, more educator than investigator. But the *Sun* stood behind me, a quality I would appreciate several times. It is hard to overstate how important that is for doing a reporter's work.

Wetlands landed me on the firing line again several years later, with a wealthy land developer screaming he would "get me . . . if it took everything (he had)." He had at least a couple billion dollars. His name was Paul Tudor Jones, a Wall Street securities trader who, ironically, had done a lot more good than harm to nature, preserving land and donating heavily to environmental organizations. But in extensive efforts to "improve" his Dorchester County hunting property, Jones had been forced to pay what was then the largest fine in the history of wetlands enforcement.

The story wasn't even about Jones, and it wasn't even initially for the *Sun*. It was a freelance piece for *Audubon* magazine. And it focused on Bill Ellen, Jones's property manager, who inexplicably ignored warning after warning from federal regulators to stop dredging and filling wetlands. By the time I interviewed Ellen, he was in federal prison. If Jones had ordered him to push ahead and take the fall, Ellen never said.

The storyline was the anatomy of an "eco-martyr," the creation of which had become an effective tactic of the antiregulation, property rights crowd nationwide. They were having great success—*Wall Street Journal*, talk radio, American Farm Bureau publications—portraying people like Ellen as innocents crushed by brutish federal environmental regulators. I wanted to take a close look at the case, a look that ultimately showed Ellen was anything but naive or innocent; but that would also expose some flaws in regulatory enforcement. I had interviewed Jones at his Greenwich, Connecticut, mansion, a session I think both of us taped. I left thinking for all that it had gone amicably.

Then things got weird. For months I went back and forth with *Audubon* editors, who always seemed to come up with more changes, more questions, more rewrites . . . all normal to a point, but this? I called a friend, a former environmental journalist, who worked at *Audubon*, not on my story. "Have they paid you?" he asked. "Yes." "Then forget the story. It's not gonna run." I could never prove why. I knew Jones was close to *Audubon's* chairman, and that he contributed significantly to the organization. The magazine made no protest when I withdrew. I never asked to write for them again.

What occasioned Jones's screaming at me, several times over the phone, once on Christmas Eve when I finally had to hang up on him, was that the *Sun* ran the story in its entirety. This had not been our agreement, he charged, apparently believing the interview I had with him could lead only to an *Audubon* story whose content he could control. I think he was outraged because despite his billions, he had no way to influence the *Sun*.

Was the *Sun* that un-influenceable? People ask whether there were any sacred cows on my beat, subjects the paper wouldn't go after. The only one I experienced, I tell them, was other newspapers. I had three stories killed by the paper in some thirty-five years, and all involved competitors (like a column on how the *Washington Post* screwed up a story on the Nature Conservancy). Perhaps it really isn't smart to sling ink at folks who buy it by the traincar-load. Overall, when it counted, the *Sun* had your back.

What I wrote most about was neither wetlands nor nitrogen. Chesapeake Bay is, above all, a good eating part of the world—fat oysters, savory crabmeat, toothsome striped bass, and delicately flavored shad roe, just to highlight a few. Readers of the *Sun* expected a constant and reliable flow of news on how all of these iconic creatures were faring. And I was never just writing about fish. The people who caught them were unique—*watermen*, we called them, men (mostly) of whom I once wrote:

> [P]reying on oysters, crabs, rockfish, eels, clams, terrapins, even bloodworms . . . the Chesapeake waterman is a true top of the food chain predator, the closest thing to a great white shark this estuary supports, the nearest subculture in America to the hunter–gatherer society we left behind on land nine thousand years ago.

It was not just seafood we Marylanders wanted. We wanted oysters on the half shell caught by salty captains under full sail in century old wooden skipjacks; not just rockfish stuffed with crab meat, but rockfish and crab meat that come from little towns and islands where old English still tinges the speech, and the quaint harbors are the stuff of nostalgic photographs.

I grew up around watermen and respect them; but if they think you are coming between them and what they catch for a living, well. . . . I once was "invited" by a skiff full of burly shad netters to "put your f'in boat to the bank and we'll pound your ass." I politely declined, throwing my engine in reverse, hollering that it was the state proposing a moratorium on their livelihood. I was just writing about it. That failed to soothe them, and I fled upriver, my interview concluded—forever as it turned out —the moratorium took effect that month in 1978 and it remains in place. My kids, in their thirties, have never experienced catching shad, one of the great enthusiasms of my growing up.

A similar situation loomed years later with rockfish. A few netters agreed to talk after dark at the end of a long dock in the remote fishing town of Rock Hall. On the way over, I picked up the biggest, strongest friend I had to accompany me. The interview this time was polite, almost subdued. I think at least some of them realized the fish really were in trouble.

The rockfish moratorium that ensued was a bitter pill for watermen, but a valuable lesson for managing the Bay. Unlike the shad, government had funded the science and collected the data to draw the line and stop taking rockfish before it was too late. When the rock rebounded nicely a few years later, effective management plans with scientifically determined quotas and strict regulation were applied. None of this is popular, but where we do it, fish come back.

And where we don't . . . the Chesapeake's oysters are testament. While the last few years have seen an uptick in harvests, the shellfish remain at 1 percent or less of their historic abundance, and few think that current catches are sustainable. With the blue crab, the Chesapeake's last great fishery, I am quite hopeful we have gotten our act together in time. Excellent science has enabled setting responsible catch limits in both Maryland and Virginia. No moratorium appears on the horizon. Watermen will argue that if the rest of society would ever clean up Bay pollution, they could catch more seafood without "overfishing." I have a lot of sympathy for that argument. In the short term, it has been easier to reduce their catches than to restore the Bay's overall health.

My full-time reporting on the Chesapeake lasted until 1987 when I moved with my family to Smith Island, a watermen's community ten miles out in the Bay. I wanted to experience it while it lasted, before young people leaving and sea level rise erased the unique, centuries-old culture there. I would return to the *Sun*, hired by John Carroll, who told me, "This newspaper should own the Chesapeake Bay." I would write some 650 columns between 1993 and 2006. I ended my last one this way:

> If I have offended anyone during my years writing on the environment, I have mostly meant to. If I have made anyone think we should act as a part of nature rather than apart, good; good too, especially good, if I have made anyone feel a little less crazy and alone for suffering anguish at seeing open land skinned alive and shackled with asphalt and buildings.
>
> If I have made anyone lose hope in saving the Bay, for that I apologize. The great tension of my career was always between lamenting all we're losing, while celebrating all that's left and precious . . .
>
> Thanks . . . to this newspaper, which always gave me a long leash.

11

You Better Be Right

Steven M. Luxenberg

Paul Banker loomed over my desk. Looming over desks was not the managing editor's usual posture. He loomed over the newsroom, but he accomplished his looming from a distance, like an eagle surveying the forest from his treetop aerie. Every reporter knew he was there, in his corner office, probably smoking a cigarette, watching us and doing whatever the morning newspaper's top editor did to keep his operation running. I felt his presence, but as a twenty-three-year-old reporter with no seat at any table other than one in the *Sun* cafeteria, there weren't many reasons for the two of us to look each other in the eye, let alone have collegial chats.

Now, on a late December afternoon in 1975, the Presence stood calmly at my desk, clutching a rolled-up sheaf of paper. To say that Banker was terse was to understate the case. He was not a man of few words. He was a man of no words, at least in my (small p) presence. Reporters joked about his penchant for silence, how it would be a nightmare to find Banker waiting alone at the elevator for a ride from the fifth floor to the lobby. Would he say anything at all? Would you? Would you resort to the weather—"Nice day, Mr. Banker"—or just stare at the buttons, *4, 3, 2, Lobby*, cursing Otis for making an elevator that was as plodding as Pimlico race track after a spring downpour? Would you dare to mention, um, the *news*?

The Presence did not strike fear in our hearts, at least not in mine. He struck bewilderment. He was a riddle, wrapped in a mystery, inside an enigma, to borrow shamelessly from Winston Churchill's description of Russia at the dawn of World War II. Maybe Banker was less perplexing to his inner circle of editors. But from my lowly position, he was an enigma, buried in a paradox, dressed in a seersucker suit. He was there, but he wasn't *there*. We mostly glimpsed him, like astronomers tracking a distant star.

He had been a reporter—a good one, from what I later read. His dispatches from overseas showed a nose for news, an eye for detail, and an ear for how people talked. But he didn't spend time talking with his reporters. Perhaps he was a prisoner of his own chain of command. Occasionally, like Moses on the mountaintop, we received his words, relayed by disciples. "He wants . . ." or "He doesn't like . . ." or "He says to get rid of . . ." or, happy day, "He's taking it for the front page." No need to identify "He." I'm sure the editors sometimes said "Banker" or even "Paul." But nearly forty years later, "He" is what I remember.

He was not a father figure. Not that I didn't respect him. He wielded his authority with a stoic integrity, and while three decades of age and experience separated us, I endorsed his core beliefs, absorbed largely by osmosis: fairness first, accuracy always, specifics not speculation, facts not frills. (This chapter might never have made his paper.) As I watched, as my thinking evolved, we sometimes disagreed on how to apply his standards. He saw limits where I saw opportunity. Like most of us, he had his blind spots, which brought the two of us to loggerheads later on. Perhaps this was merely generational; I like to think not. Eventually, I came to believe that editors could be more than enigmas, that reporters thrive best in newsrooms bubbling in ideas and debate and frisson, that a difference of opinion is not an act of rebellion, and that leaders can be laconic, but only sometimes and not if it undermines the mission of creating great journalism. (Memo to any twenty-three-year-olds reading this: your turn.)

He was probably shy. Others later told me so, and I can see that now. At night, in winter, when he slipped on his beige raincoat and left his newsroom in the hands of others, he would stride toward the elevator, his chin slightly down, probably praying (I imagine now) that we wouldn't screw it up before morning. His route took him within close range of my desk. I watched him go, sometimes. He was tall and broad-shouldered, graying at the temples, a crew cut short enough to blend in at the Naval Academy, a glint in his eye, and the permanent hint of a smile, as if the world were amusing to him but it would be undignified to say so.

The Presence wasn't smiling now, as he loomed, although the glint was there. He tossed the sheaf of paper on my desk: it was the story that Mark Reutter and I had filed a few hours earlier, the latest in our run of investigative pieces about a Baltimore-based Catholic order called the Pallottine Fathers, their mammoth fund-raising operation that sent a pittance to the poor, and their questionable investments. After a month of work, several out-of-state trips to dig into land records, and a half-dozen front-page stories, this was the first time that Banker had approached one of us directly. For some reason, on this one, he didn't want to rely on others to convey his words.

I waited. He spoke.

"You better be right," he said.

We were not on a movie set. This is not my version of the screenplay, crafted for tension and drama. Banker did not have a flair for the dramatic, although I'm pretty sure I held my breath as I waited for him to say more. Most newspaper editors are not terse. Most do not talk in four-word sentences. But I kid you not. That is what he said. That is all he said.

You better be right.

* * *

I didn't belong in the *Sun* newsroom, not really—or perhaps more kindly, not yet. I arrived during an uncomfortably humid week in the summer of 1974, a month before the Watergate scandal toppled a president and made journalism seem especially alluring to my generation of job seekers. In those days, when the newspaper business was expanding rather than shrinking, newspapers of the *Sun's* caliber had no need to take a risk on an unknown applicant fresh from college. It could hire someone with five or more years of experience at a first-rate regional paper, people good enough to work anywhere, if only enough top-tier jobs had existed to accommodate them. The *Sun* could do better than a kid so wet behind the ears that he was in danger of drowning, as my *Sun* colleague Mike Bowler once quipped about himself.

Why was I there? Bill Schmick, that's why. As the city editor, he ran the *Sun's* local staff. He was thirty-three when he hired me, and his father was the publisher. Everyone in the newsroom called him Billy, a youthful nickname that fell away after he left the paper. I only mention the long-ago name now because during the too-short time I worked for him, that's how I knew him. He was Billy, just as the Presence was Mr. Banker.

Schmick had a different philosophy about hiring, or so he told me. He believed that newsrooms needed reporters of all ages, not just veterans, not just high-fliers who had been stars in Annapolis or Providence or Louisville, not just hotshots who viewed the local staff as a brief stop (they hoped) en route to a foreign bureau or Washington. The *Sun* newsroom was far too white and far too male, but that was beginning to change, slowly. As a white guy, I didn't add to the diversity in those ways, but my youth helped lower the average age.

Another plus, unmentioned but understood: youngsters would readily do some of the mundane tasks that help a newspaper come out every day, work that the grown-ups grumped about. Everything—police reporting, obits, weekend festivals that were fun but demanded a dollop of ingenuity to make into an interesting story—seemed fresh and daunting to me. Paul

Banker probably felt the same way when he started at the *Sun* as a college student, working summers before joining the Navy during World War II.

Banker's father had been a *Sun* editor until his death in a 1938 boating accident. Banker had lived in Baltimore since age six, and knew people in town. I had no such advantages (or disadvantages). Yet here I was. "They pay me to do this," I told my parents in Detroit. "I almost can't believe it." I think I heard my father, a furniture salesman working on commission, roll his eyes over the phone.

For my first year, I carried an index card, my story list at the ready. I was certain I would be fired if I couldn't recite my works-in-progress on demand. Reporters were paid to bring news to the newspaper, weren't they? If an editor made a surprise raid, demanding to know what I had coming, my list was my shield. Needless to say, mine were the only eyes that ever saw that card. But even after my probationary period passed and my fear of firing ebbed, I kept a list going, my security blanket and alarm clock.

Serendipity, that constant newsroom companion, tossed me into the Pallottine story. One morning in November 1975, Mark Reutter read a report in the *Washington Post* that sent him scurrying to his own files. A $54,000 Pallottine loan, funneled through intermediaries, had helped Maryland's governor, Marvin Mandel, with his divorce settlement. This was a head-snap of a story. A Catholic order indirectly financing a politician's divorce? What chain of events had brought these unlikely parties into the same room?

Mark, a twenty-five-year-old reporter on the *Sunday Sun* who specialized in investigations with a consumer bent, had written about the Pallottines a year earlier as a particularly secretive charity. The order was raising money for its foreign missions serving the poor, but its reports offered the barest of bones on its activities. The Pallottines had rebuffed Mark's questions, refusing to open the parish door to him on one visit, which merely piqued his interest. He now suggested a thorough look. I was recruited from the daily newsroom. We would report to Schmick.

Our first task: getting a handle on the size of the Pallottines's fundraising operation. We knew they were sending out a huge number of appeals from their unmarked warehouse in a Russell Street industrial park, just south of downtown. Based on Mark's experience, knocking on the door clearly wasn't going to work. We needed another entrance. We found it through the US Postal Service.

We learned that the Pallottines, as a nonprofit bulk mailer, were required to file daily logs of their output. Based on that public record, they would pay the correct postage at the discounted rate. A formal request to the Postal Service brought us, within a few days, photocopies of two years' worth of logs. Late into the night, we tabulated the results. Our creaky calculator could not display more than eight digits, so when the total topped one hundred million, we had to start again. Soon, citing industry experts, we had reported that the order's direct-mail operation was collecting between $8 million and $15 million annually. The experts based their estimates on the volume of mailings (106 million pieces in 1974, by our count) and the likely response rate. But only three cents of each dollar were reaching the Pallottine missions. The rest was being consumed by fund-raising costs and a plethora of investments we had unearthed, many in real estate, including motels and trailer parks in south Florida.

The Pallottines, as an independent order, answered to the Vatican. The Baltimore archdiocese, the oldest in the United States, had no control over the order or its fund-raising operations. This proved deeply embarrassing to the archbishop, who found himself confronted with disconcerting questions about what this Catholic order was doing on his patch. He called for an independent audit, with the Vatican's acquiescence, and promised to release the results.

The Pallottine fund-raising appeals, featuring desperate children, brought thousands of envelopes a week from around the country. Some donors sent just five dollars, writing apologetically that they couldn't afford more. Some scrawled notes, asking the priests to light a candle, or say a prayer. Employees said they were instructed to extract the money, no need to keep track of requests for candles or prayers. One mail sorter, a devout Catholic, could not bring herself to throw away all the letters. We published some she had saved.

That story resonated like none other, especially among Catholics. Real estate investments, as well as the Mandel loan, were about money and power. The letters gave the story humanity, as well as gravitas. Disregarding requests for prayers and candles did not sit well within the archdiocese.

About the same time, a document came my way that took us in a new direction. It revealed yet another hidden enterprise, but with a notable difference: the venture bore the names of four men with connections to the Mandel administration, and listed the priest in charge of the Pallottine fund-raising operation as holding a share of the business in his own name. This document offered the first hint of a personal stake for the head Pallottine priest, the Very Rev. Guido John Carcich. It was possible, of course, that the priest had invested his own money or intended to turn over any profit to the order. As usual, the Pallottines weren't commenting. We filed the story, prominently noting the caveats.

This was the story that brought the Presence to my desk on a late December afternoon in 1975. It ran the next day, at the top of the front page, under the headline, "Pallottine aide holds secret investment."

You better be right.

* * *

Journalists are fond of invoking lofty principles to explain what we do—the First Amendment, the right to know, holding institutions accountable. Yes, yes, and yes. But among ourselves, in the privacy of the newsroom, the best reporters also are aware that unflattering stories about important institutions can be nerve-wracking for people up the newspaper's hierarchy. Words to the unwise: don't hand anyone the ammunition to shoot you down.

Banker had a sense of the two reporters stirring up trouble with their Pallottine stories and whether we were up to the job. He hardly knew us, but he had observed us, and at a meeting with the archbishop had demonstrated his support for our reporting. But what about the publisher? The chairman of the board? The board of directors? They must have wondered, at least fleetingly, about these guys, both younger than twenty-six, and their Pallottine stories. Can we trust them? What if they make a mistake, a serious mistake, putting the paper and its reputation at risk?

You better be right.

Since our first Pallottine story I had been fretting about being right. Even at twenty-three, I understood that the stakes were high, that we were being watched carefully by the Catholic community, some of whom were out-

Figure 11.1.   Paul A. Banker, managing editor of the Sun (1966–1985).

raged by what we had reported, some of whom were doubtful. Fortunately, we were working so hard, pulling at the threads, that we didn't have a lot of time to worry about the pressure we might be under. Schmick let us know that if we produced solid stories, well-documented and fairly reported, he would have our backs.

Schmick had his own burden to carry. As the publisher's son, never a comfortable position, he was always subject to snickering about favoritism. He had worked as a reporter, both locally and overseas, before becoming city editor. But as long as Schmick's father was publisher, there was no escape from being William F. Schmick III, aka Billy.

I had no standard for comparison at the time, but I couldn't have asked for a better editor on that investigation. Schmick stood out in that newsroom, in that era. He was curious, attentive, and often ahead of us in seeing the bigger picture. Most mornings during those first few heady months, he would grab us as soon as he saw us. What's next? What do we know? What don't we know? What should we know?

He was our champion, but he wasn't a cheerleader. Only much later, after I had become an editor myself, did I understand and appreciate the difference. We needed a sounding board, a devil's advocate, a mentor, a skeptic. He played all those roles. He challenged us, pushed us, vexed us, and restrained us. Only after passing his tests could he act as an advocate, and our stories surely needed a confident advocate during the daily news meetings. I can't recall trying to hide anything from Schmick. I do remember thinking: How can he protect us if we don't protect him?

Schmick was far from perfect. As he will tell you himself—as any editor worth the title will tell you—he made some mistakes during his time as city editor, real lulus, including a few that make him scratch his head now and wonder, "What was I thinking?" I was on the receiving end of one such lapse; perhaps that was part of the bond between us. We were both young and inexperienced in our jobs, improvising as we went along.

Throughout that winter and spring, our Pallottine stories were a front-page staple. The *Sun's* foreign staff expanded our investigation, visiting the Pallottine missions in Tanzania, Japan, and India. They found "no organized social or charitable programs at the small, remote enclaves," the newspaper reported.

In June 1976, the Pallottine audit came out, and to our relief, our stories held up. The audit confirmed the investments we had found, and revealed more. The amount going overseas was the same as we had reported, 3 percent, and the fundraising experts we had consulted had been on the money: the Pallottines had raised $20.4 million in eighteen months, which worked out to about $13.6 million in a year, at the upper end of our $8 to $15 million estimate. We had been conservative in reporting such a large range. It had almost felt foolish at the time. Now it felt good. *Anything* in excess of $8 million would have felt good. Anything less would have made us wrong, even though we had called it an estimate.

You better be right.

The Pallottine story was far from over. A state prosecutor would open a criminal investigation, which eventually led to the chief priest's guilty plea for misappropriating $2.2 million in charitable funds. His eighteen months' probation included one year working as an aide in the Maryland Penitentiary hospital. Mark and I continued our digging, but without Schmick, who left the paper several months after the audit. We were on our own, more or less.

We kept asking ourselves: What do we know? What don't we know? What should we know?

The Presence mostly loomed elsewhere during the summer of 1976, but in the fall, I had a new assignment that would send him rocketing into my orbit. Mandel went on trial in federal court for alleged corruption, accompanied by five codefendants accused of benefiting from their friendship with the state's top politician. Coverage of the trial would dominate the front page for the duration, with oodles of inside space devoted to the many details. Competitors from the *Evening Sun*, the *News American*, the *Washington Post*, and the *Washington Star*, as well as TV and radio, would be there to chronicle each day's fireworks.

The *Sun's* lead reporter would be the tenaciously flinty Robert A. Erlandson. He was the obvious choice: he had competed hard against the other papers in covering the Mandel investigation, producing an assortment of scoops, and he knew the case better than anyone else at the paper. For reasons that mystified me, I was asked to serve as junior partner. I had helped investigate some aspects of the Mandel story before indictment, and I had a beginner's grasp of the legal issues. But I had never covered a major trial before. I was not the obvious choice.

I hoped, instead, to be an inspired choice. The trial offered a chance to deepen my deadline skills and stretch my writing abilities. I envisioned trying my hand at profiles or legal analysis. But no, that wasn't the idea. The editors, worried about handling the extra volume of copy that the trial would generate, wanted me to attend the morning session only. I would return to the newsroom, put together a summary, and have it ready for Bob. He would write the "top" of the story, even if the morning had produced the day's most important developments.

While the plan made sense, it wasn't smart. Missing the afternoon session meant I was always behind, like a student who attends half of each class and then has to borrow someone's notes. Or maybe the better metaphor is Alice, in Wonderland, having to run twice as fast just to keep up.

I kept pace by staying late, reading the voluminous trial transcripts. It wasn't the same as being there. I felt like a drop-in; the trial felt like a grind. Tired was not a fine way to start my morning. Determined to keep sharp and avoid stenography, I thought about how to improve my summary. What was I missing?

Corruption trials often involve complex and arcane details, hard to fathom in real time and hard to reduce to an easily digestible news account. The Mandel case swirled in complication, particularly on the prosecution side. (Pause for wondering readers: Mandel and the others were convicted after two trials. Their convictions were overturned on appeal. All very complicated, like nearly everything in that case, and not relevant here. Google awaits you.)

The prosecutors knew that confusing the jury was a danger, and they worked to present their evidence clearly. But they didn't pay much attention to the clock. They didn't think about "morning" or "afternoon." A witness might testify for an hour or a day, then the defense would have its shot. When the morning session ended, and I turned into a pumpkin, a witness might be in mid-testimony. I tried to keep two questions in mind as I wrote: What did the new testimony add to what we knew? How did it relate to the charges? Small picture, big picture.

As the case neared its end, I realized that the prosecution hadn't yet presented direct evidence on one count involving a codefendant. I noted that fact in my portion, unaware that it might summon the Presence.

Toward late afternoon, he loomed once again, printout in hand. His exact words haven't stuck with me, but I'm sure they totaled more than four. Essentially, he asked, "Why did I write that paragraph about what the prosecution hadn't done?"

It took several heartbeats to gather my thoughts. Flustered, I said something about how it was a fact, it wasn't speculation, that it helped readers to understand the progress of the case.

He absorbed that. He gathered *his* thoughts. Finally, he said something like, "We write what they do. We don't write what they don't do."

I protested. Maybe I didn't explain myself well. I tried to say that I was adding something of value, that there was no bias in saying it, that I wasn't implying the prosecution had fallen down on the job. It must be possible to fix the sentence, I said. Surely, sometimes, what doesn't happen is news, too.

Unconvinced, he shook his head. "Take it out."

It went out. I lost the battle, and the readers lost what I was trying to convey. But months later, I realized that I won something more valuable.

I had stood my ground. Banker had listened, taken me seriously, and debated my point—which helped me understand why I disagreed with him then, and why I disagree now. The earth had not crumbled.

He was no longer the Presence. He was the managing editor, and we had just engaged in a back-and-forth discussion—a genuine disagreement. I wanted more, and would succeed on rare occasions, but sparring was neither his forte nor his comfort zone. Still, I had glimpsed the kind of newsroom I longed to work in, and I was determined to help build it, whether it was here or somewhere else.

Happy day.

12

A Free Hand Abroad

Gilbert A. Lewthwaite

In 1971, I made an entirely unexpected career switch from the *Daily Mail*, London, to the *Baltimore Sun*, a transatlantic venture which, on reflection, strikes me as akin to swapping a Jaguar for a Jeep: the first sleek, impressive, powerful; the latter staid, prestigious, reliable.

I knew nothing of America or American newspapers, but I was soon to learn a lot about both. One thing became clear as soon as I walked through the doors of the *Sun's* office on North Calvert Street: as much as the *Daily Mail* appreciated style, the *Sun* demanded substance. It is perhaps not too simplistic to say that on one side of the Atlantic the media showed a surfeit of flair and a lack of application, while on the other just the opposite balance held sway.

The *Daily Mail* was a direct descendant of England's penny press, committed to intense, effective reporting, but also eager to print gossip, ever-ready to publicize celebrity, and so anxious to promulgate its conservative views that it made little or no distinction between news and commentary.

The *Baltimore Sun*, by contrast, was firmly wedded to its established responsibilities, to pulling its full weight in the trusted system of constitutional checks and balances, determined to report the truth and ferret out corruption, aghast at the notion of ever seeming lightweight, and totally committed to separating fact from opinion.

If the *Mail's* aim was to inform and entertain, to be the most popular of Britain's many newspapers, the *Sun's* was to educate and expose, to be Maryland's formal paper-of-record and watchdog.

The difference that was so striking to me almost half a century ago remains today. Writing in a recent edition of the British magazine, the *Spectator*, the columnist Toby Young, himself a former correspondent in America for a British newspaper, observed, "Our Yankee counterparts preen about, congratulating themselves on upholding the highest ideals of the fourth estate, whereas we focus on the bottom line and pride ourselves on keeping our papers afloat. For them, it's a profession and its members are expected to observe a highfalutin code of professional conduct. For us, it's a trade and, to be honest, it's more about not getting caught. If you said the word 'ethics' to most British hacks they'd think you were talking about the birthplace of Kelvin MacKenzie." (MacKenzie, a notoriously irreverent tabloid editor, was born in the English county of Essex.)

The reason for the unlikely and unexpected change in my life and location was simple enough: in 1971, the *Daily Mail* was taken over by a sister paper, and most of the *Mail's* employees were laid off. I, with a wife and three children, was out of a job after eleven years' service.

I was, at the time, the Rome correspondent of the *Daily Mail*. Previously, I had been the Moscow correspondent. In both places, I had met, worked, and become friends with the *Sun's* correspondents. One of these, on hearing of my unemployment, brought it to the attention of the editors in Baltimore, and as a result I was offered a job. I had never been to America, but the attraction for me was the number of foreign bureaus the *Sun* operated. Ironically, my main aim in coming to Baltimore was to leave it as soon as possible, resuming my career overseas and indulging my well-grounded belief that happiness is measured by the number of miles from the head office.

Arriving from Rome, the beautiful Eternal City, into Baltimore on a hot and humid August evening, into a city still reeling from the race riots of three years before, only strengthened my determination to make my sojourn as brief as possible.

The transatlantic clash of media cultures was immediately made clear through the *Sun's* inflexible induction system. I was an experienced international correspondent, but I was put on the night police beat in Baltimore. In 1971, this was how every recruit to the *Sun*, novice or veteran, started. After the police beat, the next way point was writing obits. There was a logic to this progression: learn the geography of the city by working the police precincts; absorb the style of the paper by writing to format.

Each step along the entry pipeline had its purpose. But the system also reflected the *Sun's* inability, or unwillingness, to be flexible: for Paul Banker, the managing editor at the time, the way it always had been was the way it always would be. Banker explained to me, honestly enough, "The *Sun* is like a ship-of-state—slow to turn."

I told him of my ambition to be posted overseas. He looked at me for a while, smiled, and said, "You can aspire to any foreign bureau of the *Sun*, but I will never send a Brit to London." The reason: the *Sun* had employed a local

Indian journalist as its correspondent in the New Delhi bureau, and when the Indian government declared a state of emergency, the restrictions on the press applied to him as a citizen, effectively silencing him. Had he been an American reporter, he would have been freer to circumvent the edict. Banker was not about to repeat that mistake, so he put London beyond my ambitions as a Brit.

A legislative session in Annapolis and a spell covering the Maryland congressional delegation out of the *Sun's* Washington bureau completed my programmed induction.

In 1973, Banker sent me to Paris. It had taken just two years, a transition speedy enough to reflect perhaps the *Sun's* greatest strength: its ready embrace of new talent, albeit immigrant (a Scot and a Finn were already working for the *Sun* when I arrived). After Paris, I did eventually become the paper's London correspondent, but by then Banker had left the paper, and the old ways had given way to the new. My foreign reporting days ended almost three decades later with a three-year tour in Johannesburg, itself a reflection of how far and wide the *Baltimore Sun* was willing to base its reporters.

Once overseas, another difference between American and English journalism became quickly obvious: foreign correspondents for the *Daily Mail* were in daily receipt of ideas, instructions, demands, and reaction from the editors in London. For the *Sun*, they worked with virtually no direction or reaction from Baltimore. During three years in Paris, I received no more than two phone calls from Baltimore, and one was to alert me to the likelihood of conflict in the Middle East. I asked if I should head there. I was told to use my own best judgment, which would never have happened on the *Daily Mail*. The London editors would have told me which flight I was already booked on. As it was, I went immediately to the airport and caught the last flight from Paris to Tel Aviv before the Arab–Israeli Yom Kippur War broke out on October 6, 1973, ending all flights into Israel.

There was also little editing of the stories filed to Baltimore, a far cry from the hands-on approach of editors in London. Editors in Baltimore would inform you, almost apologetically, of any changes they proposed to your copy. No such courtesy was ever extended in London.

All a *Baltimore Sun* correspondent received every morning was a brief list of how each foreign story had been displayed in the paper. Happy enough were the days when the reporters learned from the terse report that his or her story was on the front page in Baltimore. Happier, though, were the days when the foreign editor of the *Daily Mail* cabled the personal accolade, "Today you best in Fleet Street" (traditional home of British newspapers). On other days, of course, the word from London was not so welcome.

Again, there was a logic to the *Sun's* comparative restraint: the paper's editors felt the correspondent, chosen because he or she was trusted to do the job, should not routinely be second-guessed from thousands of miles away. In addition to understanding Baltimore as a result of having worked there, the correspondent was on the spot, and, therefore, better able than the editors back in North Calvert Street to judge what would interest the *Sun's* readers. The correspondent who fell short of that expectation would eventually be brought back to Baltimore to be given a job that mutely but effectively reflected his disappointing performance abroad.

Maintaining foreign bureaus was an expensive business. To enable the paper to avoid the risk of costly failures, I repeatedly tried to convince Paul Banker to create a full-time foreign staff of correspondents of proven reliability, who could be transferred with confidence between the overseas capitals. This was the system on many major papers. But he rejected the idea for one very good reason: the foreign bureaus were a magnet for young talent, and the magnet's strength relied on steady rotation of the overseas assignments. Certainly the *Sun* did attract some of the best over the years, and many were sent abroad to help make it the outstanding paper it was for so long. Polls showed that its foreign reporting was particularly appreciated by its readers. In its heyday, with nine overseas bureaus, the *Sun's* commitment to foreign news was literally unrivalled—globally!—by any general-readership, metropolitan newspaper with a similar circulation.

Just how far and wide the *Sun's* journalism could stretch became clear the day I was summoned from the Washington bureau to the head office in Baltimore for a meeting with John S. Carroll, the executive editor. With him were William K. Marimow, the managing editor, and G. Jefferson Price III, the foreign editor.

Carroll opened the meeting with a simply stunning sentence: "We want you to go to Sudan and buy a slave."

On his drive to work one day Carroll had heard a radio report of a United Nations agency accusing the Sudanese government of condoning chattel slavery in southern Sudan. The government in Khartoum robustly denied the accusation. It was not the first such report. Indeed, it turned out that almost every major human rights agency had condemned government condoned slavery in Sudan.

"If there is slavery in Sudan, we should be able to prove it by buying a slave," reasoned Carroll.

He said the assignment would be dangerous as there was an enduring civil war between the Muslim north of the country and the animist/Christian south, which was fighting to gain its independence. But sometimes journalists had to take risks to get the story, he said. I told him I would be the judge of how dangerous it might be and whether the risk was worth taking. Carroll had decided that Gregory Kane, an African American columnist for the paper, should join me on the assignment to give his perspective as the descendant of slaves (figure 12.1).

In researching how we might approach the story, it became obvious that we could not go into the north of the country where the government would do everything to prevent us from exposing the existence of slavery. We would have to go into the south, to the frontline of the civil war, where the African slaves were captured by Muslim militias operating on the government side. I discovered Christian Solidarity International, a Swiss organization which engaged in buying the freedom of slaves and reuniting them with their families, usually members of the Dinka people.

We arranged to join one of the CSI missions in May 1996, and ended up buying for $1,000 the freedom of two young Dinka brothers who had been captured by an Arab militia and forced to work, unpaid, in a northern Sudanese cattle ranch.

The *Sun's* series on Sudanese slavery attracted worldwide attention, garnered a slew of prizes, and earned a Pulitzer Prize nomination. (And sold for a small fortune to, of all papers, the *Mail on Sunday*.) But, unfortunately, it did nothing to end the slavery.

Figure 12.1. *Sun* **reporters Gilbert Lewthwaite (center) and Gregory Kane interview freed slaves in Sudan, 1996.**

That the paper would undertake such a distant, expensive, and risky enterprise to illuminate a dark corner of human experience lends truth to the motto which graces its front page every day: "Light for All."

It was not unusual for the *Sun*, in its heyday, to double-team a big overseas story. In the case of the Yom Kippur War, we triple-teamed it, with me in Israel, Stephen J. Lynton in Lebanon, and Gene Oishi in Egypt, sent from the Bonn bureau. The idea of having a reporter on each side in the war, of course, was to ensure a balanced account of events. The only problem was that access to the military action and diplomatic dealings was much easier in Israel than on the Arab side, so inevitably the flow of information was skewed, a propaganda coup from which the Israelis have benefitted over the years of conflict with their neighbors, and which even the *Sun*, with the best of intentions, could not completely counter.

When the United States intervened in Haiti in 1994 in "Operation Uphold Democracy" to end military dictatorship and restore democracy in the poorest nation in the Western Hemisphere, Bill Glauber flew from Baltimore to join me in Port-au-Prince. Here the aim of double-teaming was not so much balance but a wider perspective of the action, its background, and its ramifications. Glauber, with his particular talent for spotting the small detail that illuminated the larger picture, wrote daily features while I reported the news, ensuring that the *Sun's* readers once again were kept both interested and informed.

Clearly, if the cause was right, the *Sun* would spare no effort or cost to get the story. In 1989, I was dispatched from the London bureau to Czechoslovakia to cover what became known as "the Velvet Revolution." It was the early days of information technology, and I arrived with a computer the size of a small suitcase and an unwieldy modem into which a phone was plugged to send the copy to Baltimore.

Unfortunately, the modem quickly broke down. After a couple of difficult days of borrowing hardware from rival reporters, I suggested to Baltimore that my colleague in the London bureau, Judy Anderson, should fly out to Prague with a new modem. The *Sun* readily agreed, and once Judy arrived, the editors decided that she should stay to broaden the coverage, again treating the readers in Baltimore to an engaging array of stories of how communism was defeated in Czechoslovakia without a shot being fired, and how Vaclav Havel, a poet and playwright with a political vision as clear as it was democratic, became the country's freely elected president.

To help us get the news and understand the political developments, we had the translation services of Martin Mikulas, a young Czech physical education student who had been a volunteer bodyguard for Vaclav Havel as he set out to lead his country to freedom from decades of Soviet domination. So wedded to the cause of revolution was Martin that he refused to accept any payment, though he worked with us day and night. He was, he said, only too happy to work for the revolution. When I finally got home, I suggested that the *Sun* should reward Martin by flying him to London now that the strict Soviet-era restrictions on foreign travel movement had been lifted. Appreciative of his efforts, the editors agreed immediately to give him his first outing to the West.

The editors themselves, it should be noted, were not averse to taking their own outings north, south, east, and west. Having correspondents around the world meant the owners, publisher, and editors could expect a royal welcome on their travels: a limousine at the airport; the best suite in the best hotel in town; and perhaps a meeting with a president or prime minister. Such personal perks did nothing to detract from the serious professional intent of maintaining an extensive foreign news operation.

Whatever the imperatives behind the paper's impressive overseas reach, the *Baltimore Sun's* coverage of the world made a major contribution to the paper's reputation that extended far beyond the city it served. At its best, in the mid-to-late twentieth century, the *Sun* was widely recognized, inside and outside America, as one of the world's great newspapers.

13

The Op-Ed Page

Stephens Broening

The one thing that most immediately brings back the pleasure of running the *Sun's* Op-Ed page is the memory of Andrei Codrescu showing up unannounced at my office door. It was in the distant prelapsarian time when anyone could walk into the newspaper and state his business to a reporter or an editor. Codrescu stated his in dark Carpathian consonants. "I am Codrescu," he said. "I want to be a columnist." I thought to myself, "People in hell want ice water, too."

Codrescu was carrying a book of his poetry, as a sort of passport, I guess. As I remember it he was smoking a cigarette that sagged beneath a full dark mustache. He may have been wearing a leather jacket, though don't hold me to it. As I tried to restrain his hopes of becoming a columnist, he observed me through thick glasses with a bright ironic gaze. I told him I welcomed essays of 750 to 1,000 words by outside contributors, on practically any subject. Wouldn't he like to try his hand?

He would. In a couple of days I received in the mail from him a manuscript that needed very little attention. It turned out he was Romanian, or had been, which accounted for his accent. It also turned out that he wrote English with remarkable flair. And so began his run of rich deposits into the *Sun's* treasury—more on that later.

In Baltimore, things tend to occur with some delay. (If you hear the world is about to end, you might want to head to Charm City.) So it was with the Op-Ed page, an abbreviation of the term "Opposite Editorial," or the page opposite the editorial page. In its present form, it began at the *New York Times* in 1970 with Harrison Salisbury as its editor. It was to be a forum for sensible opinion that didn't necessarily coincide with the paper's institutional views. The *Sun's* Op-Ed page was launched seven years later, on September 19, 1977, with me as the editor.

For its inauguration, we were able to enlist as a contributor President Jimmy Carter, thanks to the efforts of the Washington bureau. Carter had been in the White House for just eight months and seemed to be still feeling his way, but he was comfortable talking about human rights. That's what he chose to instruct us.

The president said his administration was seeking "to weave a due regard for these rights into our foreign policy." Most fundamental, he said, was "the right of the integrity of the person" which "is the irreducible basis of the social contract, and a regime that systematically and repeatedly violates it ultimately forfeits its own legitimacy." This was clearly aimed at the Soviets, though he judiciously didn't name his target. (We were six years away from Ronald Reagan's blistering denunciation of the Soviet Union as an "evil empire.") With Moscow still in mind, Carter cautioned that, for all their importance to Americans, "human rights cannot be the only goal of our foreign policy—not in a world in which peace is literally a matter of survival."

He concluded with an expression of bland optimism that although "changes will not come quickly . . . they will surely come." It so happened he was right.

Carter's article got us off to a respectable start.

We imagined a page of worthy commentary and analysis tied to the news. Equally important were essays on subjects outside that realm. We wanted to refresh the harried reader with pieces that offered wit or graceful writing. We hoped the page would complete the paper.

On a typical day, we printed four essays: two by columnists and two from outside writers. The columns came to us from press syndicates—such as the Washington Post Writers Group, the Universal Syndicate, or the Los Angeles Times Syndicate—to whom the *Sun* paid a subscription fee. Individual columnists were scheduled by the syndicates for use twice or three times a week. We could publish them or not as we pleased. The choice was mine.

I might find a column tedious, or poorly reasoned, or too similar to something we had already run, so it was spiked. Or a group of essays by outside writers might take up most of the page, reducing space for the columnists. The usual practice at the *Washington Post* or the *Times* was to adhere strictly to a publication schedule. I favored variety—surprise when possible.

On occasion, I devoted the entire page to a single subject, sidelining the columnists altogether. This was notable in the case of Judith Banister, a China expert and demographer who was chief of the China Branch of the US Bureau of the Census.

At a conference in Beijing in March 1984, Banister had presented a paper that was newsworthy both for its startling conclusions and for the fact that the Chinese authorities had allowed it. I called Banister as a result of a story about it I read in *Le Monde*. I had seen nothing in the American press.

Banister had solved a mystery at the center of Mao Zedong's worst blunder: How many Chinese had died during the Great Leap Forward? This was the period between 1958 and 1961 when Mao forced the Chinese peasantry into communes, then caused them to starve through forced grain procurements. Mao and a few men around him became aware of the rough extent of the disaster, but suppressed the information. When Mao eventually abandoned the experiment, the human cost of it was added to the growing store of official secrets.

After Mao's death in 1976, some Chinese officials began to acknowledge privately that many, perhaps millions, had starved to death. By analyzing information from the 1953 and 1964 censuses, not released until 1982, and comparing it to age-structure data from the 1982 census and a new fertility survey, Banister was able to put a figure on it.

Her estimate, now generally accepted by Chinese officials as a baseline, was that about thirty million Chinese died in Mao's man-made famine.

By that measure, the Great Leap Forward was the worst catastrophe of the twentieth century. More Chinese died during a four-year span than soldiers in all the battles of World War I, or Jews in the Holocaust, or peasants in Stalin's collectivization. Deaths due to the Great Leap Forward were nearly double the battlefield losses of all countries in World War II.

Banister carefully and modestly spelled out her conclusions in a long Q and A on the page April 26, 1984. We had a scoop that justified shelving the columnists.

The syndicated columnists we used on a regular basis in the beginning included Joseph Kraft, Mary McGrory, James J. Kilpatrick, Neal Peirce, Garry Wills, Ellen Goodman, the tandem of Jack Germond and Jules Witcover, and George F. Will. To these I eventually added the Asia specialist Stanley Karnow, the *Harper's* magazine editor Lewis H. Lapham, and the *New Yorker* writer William Pfaff as well as TRB from the *New Republic* and Calvin Trillin from *The Nation*. We also published regular columns by the elegant Peter A. Jay (a former *Washington Post* reporter and small town Maryland publisher who had turned to farming); Ernest B. Furgurson, the *Sun's* longtime Washington bureau chief; and Fred Barnes, chief political reporter in the bureau.

Almost all of the columnists were good, solid journalists. The only one to cause me heartburn was George Will, who became ensnared in a matter of deontological delinquency.

Before the only pre-election debate Carter and Reagan would conduct in the 1980 presidential campaign, the Reagan camp came into possession of President Carter's briefing papers for the debate, which Reagan's handlers used to prepare their candidate. Will, it turned out, took part in the preparations. Right after the debate, on the popular ABC *Nightline* program where he was a regular, Will judged that his pupil had done splendidly. "Quite a thoroughbred under pressure," is how he put it. He disclosed nothing of his part in schooling the Republican candidate.

A mild flutter in the commentariat ensued when Will's pre-debate coaching was revealed a couple years afterward. Will, I concluded, should be publicly examined to assure *Sun* readers we were not displaying soiled goods. So I set up an interview with Will at his Chevy Chase home. The resulting, sometimes testy, Q and A took up three-quarters of the page on July 15, 1983.

Will was by turns evasive, combative, and finally grudgingly repentant. He had no specific memory of what the purloined Carter papers contained, and he could not recall how many questions he had asked Reagan during mock debates, nor which days he had attended the prep sessions. He did not disclose his role because it would have "appeared distasteful" to "say I know all about this man because what? Because I was coaching Ronald Reagan?"

At one point we had this exchange:

Q: If a columnist does become perceived as a sort of press agent for the political power, what then?

A: Well, then, I think he's—his usefulness to his readers is severely compromised. They wouldn't want to read him any more.

At the end I asked if he conceded that he made a mistake. "I think that's a—well, I think—yes. . . ."

That was good enough. Will could stay.

The most rewarding part of my job was selecting and shaping material for the heart of the enterprise, the original writing I hoped would not disappoint readers turning to us for opinion and commentary.

The sources were basically twofold.

A steady flow of copy came unsolicited, most of it in the mail. Some of it—as in the case of Carl Pohlner Jr., which I will get to in a while—was perfectly publishable. Much of it was not, and was returned with polite regrets that it did not suit our immediate needs. Rejections were not unknown in-house. I turned down a piece by John R. (Reg) Murphy not long after he became publisher of the *Sun* in 1981. For some reason, he wanted to use a pseudonym. I told him the policy was to do so only if it was necessary to protect the writer from harm. He got the *Evening Sun* to run it. My judgment was occasionally lax, as in rejecting a couple of pieces by Alice Steinbach, who was then, I think, working in public relations at the Baltimore Museum of Art. My sense at the time was that she just wasn't a good enough writer. Steinbach later joined the *Sun* as a feature writer and won a Pulitzer in 1985.

Figure 13.1. Raising a schooner of Arrow beer, H. L. Mencken celebrates the end of Prohibition with friends at the Rennert Hotel, April 7, 1933.

The bulk of the best material came from writers I sought out.

I knew some of them from earlier in my career. One example was Jacob Beam, who was ambassador to Moscow when I was a correspondent there. Another was Robert W. Tucker, the international relations theorist who had been my adviser at Johns Hopkins. Most memorable for me in this class of contributors was Alexander I. Solzhenitsyn, the Nobel laureate who had been expelled from the Soviet Union.

Following a visit I paid him during his exile in Vermont, Solzhenitsyn sent me an article which asked Russian émigrés for personal reminiscences to stock a library of memoirs he intended to set up in Russia "as soon as conditions permit." He was already counting on the downfall of the communist regime.

His request was directed at the generations that had experienced the 1920s, 1930s, and the German–Soviet war. He appealed for memoirs—short or long—that "bear upon the history of Russia in the twentieth century . . . so that our sorrow and our suffering may not vanish without a trace, but that it may remain in the memory of our people and serve as a warning for the future." He said the documents would be gathered and held for "a time when it will no longer be a criminal offense in our country to remember our history."

More typical contributors to the page were the kinds of experts quoted in newspaper stories, or newsmakers themselves: politicians, advocates, and, in one case, the longtime third baseman of the Baltimore Orioles who was marked for baseball's Hall of Fame—Brooks Robinson.

When he retired in 1977 at forty years of age, I asked Robinson to write a piece about leaving the game. He later called to say his article was ready. Would I mind coming to Memorial Stadium to get it?

I had been watching him practically since the time in 1955 when the parent club brought him up from Rochester. So familiar to me were his moves on the diamond that I could almost mimic them, though not with his predatory quickness. We had never met, but I would have recognized him in a snowstorm. When we did, he extended his hand and said, as if I wouldn't know, "Hi. I'm Brooks Robinson."

The article he gave me was handwritten, and, like everything about him, authentic, understated. He said that up to mid-season he had intended to play ball indefinitely, but his body was starting to let him down, and it was clear he could no longer do things that had come so naturally before. He played in only twenty-four games in 1977, batting a pitiful .149. All the same, the decision to quit was hard. "Bodies may change and weaken in some ways, but the desire to play the game is much more difficult to relinquish than anyone who hasn't played can imagine," he wrote. This from the man who won sixteen straight Gold Gloves for being the best fielder at his position, and was an all-star for fifteen consecutive seasons. He was voted the most valuable player in the American League in 1964, and chosen the MVP in the 1970 World Series.

I was glad to drive to the stadium to fetch Brooks's piece. I wouldn't have missed it. The fact is, I didn't have much choice. When Robinson handed me his article, he was dealing with the entire staff of the *Sun's* Op-Ed page.

Being on my own had one great benefit. In the peculiar culture of the *Sun* it meant plenty of freedom. I do not remember ever being second-guessed by my editor or the publisher; the almost total absence of interference let me imagine I was putting out my own daily newspaper. I went to work cheerfully.

Still, doing alone what the *New York Times* employed six people to do (an editor, a deputy editor, two staff editors, one copy editor, and a news assistant) imposed on me a fairly strict editorial economy.

A routine work day began about 7:30, when I would read the *Times* and the *Post* (I would have already read the *Sun* over breakfast), and scan the Associated Press and Reuters wires for story ideas. Cull the mail for articles. Telephone potentials. Give rejects to the department secretary to return with regrets (don't forget Alice Steinbach). Edit copy that had been entered into the computer overnight by converted linotype operators (we were in the cold type era, but before the Internet). Re-edit copy (maybe after a talk with an author). Edit articles a third time. Draft a layout for the page. Take art to photoengraving to be veloxed. Set the articles in type. Write and set heads. Pick up art and take with page layout to composing room. Go over it with the printer. Make calls to canvass contributors (fixing subject, length, and deadline). Call a freelance artist (often the gifted Amy Salganik) to pick up a manuscript for illustration. Scan the wires. Check with composing room for problems. Get page proofs. Proofread. Set corrections (if any). Choose copy for the next day (columnists and outside writers). Take it to the composing room for overnight entry. Catch up on magazines and opinion journals for story leads or excerpt possibilities. Browse the wires to make sure the page hadn't been overrun by events. If lucky, make more calls for new articles. Go home.

In competing with other major papers, the critical component was time. With little of it left after all the chores, I had to use it nimbly if I was to get writers who mattered, on subjects that counted. As I went along, I was able to gather a group of contributors who could produce expert analysis on pretty short notice—in reaction to the news or anticipating it. The longer I was on the job, the better my Rolodex became.

Because of the *Sun's* reputation, I had no trouble engaging the people I approached; it didn't hurt that the paper was widely read by policymakers in Washington. Nor do I remember ever being turned down because of what we paid (a hundred dollars an article). The subject seldom came up.

Along with timeliness, we strove for accuracy. As I was preparing this chapter, I noted smugly that the *Times* Op-Ed page had to publish yet another correction, this time for a David Brooks article which referred to the late French existentialist as John Paul Sartre. Try as I might, I couldn't recall us having to run a correction. Then, in reviewing old pages, I saw that I had once used a piece referring to George Shultz, the future secretary of state, as George Schultz. I had simply missed the error—twice. It was no consolation that a State Department publication later made the same mistake. I find it interesting that I have never seen Zbigniew Brzezinski's name misspelled.

Almost as bad as being wrong was being boring. Thanks to writers such as Andrei Codrescu, we sometimes avoided that bog.

"I lived for some time in a town that burned down every winter," was how he memorably began one article, my candidate for best lede of 1979.

"The Romanian government just banned typewriters," he wrote a few years later. "Persons with a record and especially persons suspected of distributing unauthorized literary material cannot now own one of those things I am furiously pounding. This strange bit of news came to me at a fine ironic juncture. I am shopping for a word processor."

In a piece I headlined "Treasure," Codrescu observed, "My mother has had a dream of riches ever since she came to America. This is, of course, the dream of many immigrants because, as my grandmother used to say, 'In America dogs walk around with pretzels on their tails.'"

Eugene McCarthy had been a Democratic senator from Minnesota. His insurgent candidacy in the 1968 presidential primaries had a lot to do with Lyndon Johnson's renouncing a second term in the White House. McCarthy's real love was poetry, though, not politics. I don't remember why, but in early 1980 I tracked him down to write an article about poetry.

"Poets are not prosecuted in the United States as they are in some other countries, they are not imprisoned for their poetry," McCarthy said in his essay. "They suffer what is, for poets, a worse fate. They are ignored."

This prompted Codrescu to respond some time later: "Poetry, the most sublime of arts, is also the cheapest to produce. All you need is a pencil stub and a wall. Or a razor blade and a rock face. The pay is likely to buy these materials, but not much more. Between the cheap tools needed to make a poem and the miserly reward stands the poem itself: a magnificent and priceless object."

"Utopia," he would write at another moment, "comes from the Greek word meaning Nowhere, and that is still where you are likely to find it."

Another of my favorite contributors was Carl Pohlner Jr., whose first article came in over the transom. Dozens of delightful pieces followed. Pohlner was an English teacher in Bel Air, a town not far from Baltimore, which I suppose is what led to these lines: "The book I'm checking now says that Samuel Johnson would eat tripe at a cookshop and wipe his hands on a dog. But I had always thought that it was oysters that Dr. Johnson favored and that he wiped his hands on a cat."

Daniel Mark Epstein, the Baltimore poet, agreed to try his hand at prose, and I'm glad he did. Once, ruminating on the mysteries of the internal combustion engine, Epstein remarked, "The car starts or it doesn't. Mechanics in faraway villages diagnose my car, tinker with its innards and bill me what they will. I am defenseless. A Hagerstown mechanic might replace my engine with a cage of hyenas and I would not know where the laughter was coming from."

I was also lucky to attract the attention of Josephine Jacobsen, the Baltimore poet and short story writer, who, in one of her lovely pieces, had this to say about flying on an airplane:

> The arms of transportation . . . affect me with insensate optimism. This explains, I suppose, why a plane's takeoff has a miraculous excitement; its descent a taint of disappointment as the flying object sprouts wheels and bumps on tarmac. I know nothing quite like that first transformation:

what seems at first the stealthy movement across the thick glass of the plane, the gathering speed as the wheels thunder along, the defiance of gravity as the huge weight climbs and lifts into the air, and the *chock* that signifies that wheel has given up its function, wheel is wing. Beyond the glass is a world of great curling crests, clouds and turrets of cloud terrain; a world of lovely, unreliable shapes. Nothing stales its variety, not even the bored, conscientious stewardess, gesturing toward the exits, hauling out the oxygen mask. Even the whistle, provided me "to attract attention" should I be plunged into the February Atlantic waters, cannot dim me. Shall I envision myself, like a frantic doorman, shrilly hailing taxis at dinner hour? No, I have what I want. At the moment earth left below, destination in abeyance, I am, in every sense transported.

So are we, Josephine Jacobsen, so are we.

14

The Shadow Government

C. Fraser Smith

A lot of good stories get started by pulling on a loose string. In this case, the thread was attached to the Peale Museum, a building I passed almost every day on my way to City Hall. It was Baltimore's official city museum, founded by the nineteenth-century American painter Rembrandt Peale, and it housed city artifacts. I had never been inside and was only mildly curious about its contents. I usually had more immediate things to worry about: the City Council, the mayor's many projects, the mayor's unhappiness with something or someone, including me.

Then one day, a matter of expenses incurred by the Peale came before the Board of Estimates, the city's bill-paying and contracting body with the authority "to formulate and execute the fiscal policy of the City," according to the City Charter. The mayor controlled this powerful panel. His vote and those of two of his appointees gave him a built-in majority of the five members.

The agenda for the Wednesday meetings was typically bare bones. There was little public discussion of the items, the board's deliberations—and its decisions—having been concluded at a private session beforehand.

So it was when the museum expenditure turned up on a quiet day. The Peale? No drama here, I thought, no big money involved; just something to check for the record, maybe a short for the next day's paper. A quick phone call and I would move on to something important.

I called the museum, told whoever answered I was the *Sun's* City Hall reporter and I asked about the Board of Estimates item. The response basically was "get lost." The museum, I was informed, was not a city facility, therefore its managers were under no obligation to answer my question. What?

"You *are* a city facility," I said, calmly offering what I thought would have to be accepted eventually. "You're the city museum. What goes on there is public business."

"No, we are *not* a city facility," I was told.

"What are you then?" I asked.

"A quasi-governmental agency," I was instructed.

I started asking around: What else was quasi-governmental in Baltimore? It turned out there were a couple dozen or so of what we in the newsroom started to call "quasis"—some of them with a whole lot more heft than the Peale Museum. In addition to the quasi-governmental agencies were a number of quasi-corporations.

Quasis were "not quites," or "almosts," or "half and halfs," part public, part private. They were governmental when official was important and private when private was important. The list included a development agency and several others that I had thought of as purely city departments.

For a time, I felt I was falling down the rabbit hole, trying to get my bearings in a world conducted in a different language. What followed was a five-month investigation by me and the newspaper. At the end, I wrote a series of twenty-two articles spread over eight days—from April 13 to April 20, 1980—under the heading "Baltimore's Shadow Government."

The *Sun's* city editor, Steven M. Luxenberg, was enthusiastic about the project at the outset and became even more invested in it as we went along. He remembers thinking at the time: "This is it. This is the one to go after. This is a whole new culture we're uncovering."

The city, I eventually wrote, had quietly built a parallel government—established stealthily over the previous three and a half years—to create greater "speed and flexibility," which Mayor William Donald Schaefer demanded in his determination to reverse Baltimore's decline.

Central to the parallel government were two "trustees" appointed by the Board of Estimates as directors of what was basically a development bank of last resort, intended to promote projects commercial banks might consider too risky. The formal name of the enterprise, I found out, was the Loan and Guarantee Program of Baltimore City.

The trustees conducted their business out of public view. By the time I started looking, they had established what was in effect a city-run development bank with $100 million to lend. (For a sense of proportion, it is useful to recall that the city's total operating budget at the time was about $1 billion.) For their aims, the trustees routinely used the quasis pretty much as they and the mayor saw fit.

Some of the money the trustees lent out started as federal grants. Another portion—the largest—originated in municipal bonds, money the city had borrowed. A smaller part came from the city's general fund. By the time I began looking into the program, the trustees had managed to earn for the city some $7 million in interest from the funds in their care. These "profits" went back into the development operation.

It was not all gravy, though. At one point, the trustees withdrew $2.75 million prematurely from a federal block grant, invested it in federal treasury notes and earned $209,000 in interest for the city. The feds made them pay it back. The trustees would eventually lose $1,499,000 in their backing of the Maryland Glass Corporation, which went bankrupt in 1981. The trustees had lent money to Maryland Glass in an effort to keep a major employer in the city.

There were some notable successes, such as the enormously popular National Aquarium in the Inner Harbor, a project overseen by the quasi Baltimore Aquarium, Inc. The Hyatt Regency Hotel and the Baltimore Convention Center were developed under the auspices of the quasi Constellation Management Corporation. Charles Center-Inner Harbor Management, Inc., an early quasi, had a hand in the landmark Harborplace project.

Much of the out-of-sight government had passed through the regular processes of city government. But the regular process had been used to create what amounted to a secret one. The entire sprawling enterprise was hiding in plain sight. Obscure items having to do with the "trustees" sometimes appeared on the Board of Estimates agenda, approved by the requisite number of votes—but never publicly discussed or actually seen for what they became.

Behind the trustees was a fast and loose team of problem-solvers that included a skilled lawyer and a tax expert, the city treasurer, and the finance director. One of their favorite devices was a sale and leaseback scheme.

Here's how that worked.

The "buyer" of a city building would borrow the purchase price at the market rate from a public authority—which had borrowed the money at the lower tax-exempt interest rate. In a sale and leaseback, the city pocketed the sale price and then rented back the building, which it was still occupying. In addition to assured income from the rents, the "buyer" used the transaction as a tax shelter by deducting the depreciation of the building from his federal tax bill. Proceeds from the sale went into the trustees' account for use in other development projects. And the city not only made money on the interest it charged the "buyer"; under the terms of the agreement it regained full ownership of the property once the lease expired.

The unelected director of schemes such as this one was the city finance director, Charles L. Benton Jr., one of the two trustees and a shrewd financial manager. He had a desk in the nether reaches of City Hall where he worked by the light of a green-shaded Tiffany lamp. He spoke to hardly anyone. When he did, he was likely to be giving an order to equally secretive men.

His chief action man was Arthur McHugh, who for reasons known only to him carried a knife strapped to his leg. I found that McHugh had an unusual system for keeping records: his files were strewn all over the floor of his office. He was responsible for keeping the sales and leases on track. (No doubt as a result of the series, Schaefer brought in an outside accounting firm, Coopers & Lybrand, to audit the trustees' books.)

The other trustee, City Treasurer Lawrence B. Daley, was beginning to grow restive. He disliked the whole sale and leaseback business. He called it a "double whammy"—delivered at the expense of the federal treasury.

To sort all this out, I had to build a raft of sources. I talked to local bankers about bonds. I talked to the head of a quasi who, I had heard, didn't like the operation either. Treasurer Daley helped. As his trustee work grew, he had trouble keeping up with his basic responsibilities. The law department, too, was under stress. The City Council's chief adviser had always thought Benton cared little for what she called the rules of the road. Troubled deals—areas where the city had problems—led me to some of the businesses and businessmen involved with trustee projects. I also talked to urban affairs specialists and lawyers, among others.

I was learning all this in the midst of what Baltimore proudly called a renaissance. Mayor Schaefer thrilled the business community and others by making his motto—"Do It Now!"—a command eagerly obeyed by a city worried about many of its deep problems and basically counting on His Honor to solve them.

And now here came the *Sun* apparently threatening a system that, as far as anyone knew, was working well for the city's benefit.

What we found was antidemocratic and risky—if not illegal, then certainly outside the procedures expected of open, accountable government. Not only was the new system cloaked in secrecy, there was also the possibility that the city and its taxpayers might be on the hook for repayment of loans if developers defaulted on any of the trustees' projects, as would happen in the case of Maryland Glass. This concern raised serious questions: Was the city's "full faith and credit" in play? Would the taxpayers—the ultimate backstop—be at great risk for something they had known nothing about? Until we did the series these questions had not arisen in public.

Before the articles were published, I had a long interview with Mayor Schaefer—the cranky, constant-motion machine of a man who even then had become a sort of folk idol in Baltimore. In the newsroom we called him "Mayor Annoyed," after headlines proclaiming that he was unhappy—annoyed about something or other.

Schaefer argued that with the urgency of restoration, his administration had created the tools that were necessary. "That's one of the reasons the city of Baltimore is known for its innovative ideas. We move. And the time to move is now, not two or three or five years from now."

At the conclusion of our interview, Schaefer stated that the city government was an "industry" devoted to the progress of Baltimore.

"But you're not an industry," I protested. "You're a government."

"Oh, we're an industry. Don't fool yourself. We're as much of an industry as you are. [Apparently, meaning the *Sun* newspaper.] We are as much of an industry and we're a corporation the way you are. Only, our clients are you," the mayor replied.

After the series, Schaefer reverted to the usual dodges. The straw man defense was first: we had accused him of stealing, he thundered. We had not. We were always against him. Always negative. In truth, the newspaper favored almost everything he did. He insisted on 100 percent.

We reported that the city's new go-go government gave unelected private citizens an outsized place in making public policy. We said it tended to weaken the role of other city agencies, including the City Council—many of

Figure 14.1.   Mayor William Donald Schaefer as "The Shadow."
Tom Flannery, courtesy of Baltimore Sun Media Group, all rights reserved.

whose members said they had known nothing of the Shadow Government. And, of course, the voters had been kept in the dark. Schaefer and his men were making an end run around democracy.

We had pulled on the string, not knowing what we would find. If we were crusading, in the final analysis it was for transparency, adherence to accepted democratic process.

An instinctively good politician, Schaefer guessed the general public would think the newspaper had something more in mind. Process was too abstract. So he started making himself the long-suffering object of what many would think was true—a typical newspaper smear job.

Within days of the last installment of the series, the Greater Baltimore Committee—a chamber of commerce of sorts—held its annual dinner. As the guests were finishing their dessert, there was a kind of a drumroll. A masked man in a wide-brimmed black hat and black cape stepped from behind a curtain near the head table. It was Schaefer (figure 14.1).

He said nothing. He didn't need to. People got it immediately. Laughter built and surged through the banquet room. He was doing his version of the old radio drama: *The Shadow,* unmistakably evoking the title of the newspaper series. (The radio program began: "Who knows what evil lurks in the hearts of men? . . . The Shadow knows.")

Following the paper's reporting, there was a momentary stirring of interest in reform of the City Charter to prevent further experiments in Shadow Government, but it didn't go much beyond that. Prominent among proponents of charter revision was Walter S. Orlinsky, who, as president of the City Council, was the titular chairman of the Board of Estimates, the body that had created the trustees.

Orlinsky observed, "What we have really done is create a government within a government because the institutional framework, namely the charter, and to some extent the state constitution and the general laws of the city are no longer able to shape and control an efficient, modern government." He favored a major change so that government is not "choking on its own red tape." Of the trustees' bank, he noted, "It is sinful to have to resort to these kinds of mechanisms."

The movement for charter revision never gained much traction. For one thing—a very important thing—the mayor opposed it. His influence was enormous.

A widespread feeling in the city was that Baltimore's revival and Baltimoreans' renewed pride in their metropolis were largely due to the efforts of William Donald Schaefer. A few years later, in 1985, in his fourth term as mayor, a public opinion poll measured his approval rating at above 70 percent. Schaefer as a politician was "godlike," in the view of Keith Haller, a polltaker and consultant.

With its lack of checks and balances, the parallel government could easily have been vulnerable to abuse and corruption, but neither materialized. No stain of misconduct or venality ever touched Schaefer or his trustees, who retained their reputation for probity.

The system could only have worked as well as it did under the guidance of honest men. No doubt Schaefer understood this. As he contemplated a run for governor, he arranged for the legal termination of the Loan and Guarantee Program of Baltimore City as of June 30, 1986. By the time the trustees closed up shop, they had spent $426 million. Schaefer's successor would have no Shadow Government at his disposal.

Schaefer was elected governor in 1986 and served two terms, all the law allowed. After that, he served two terms as Maryland comptroller.

15

The Conflict

Robert Ruby

Short wars may produce unanimity but long, seemingly endless wars lead to bitter dissension.

—Amos Elon, *The Pity of It All*

The *Sun's* Jerusalem office was in a government-owned office building, Beit Agron, the "House of Agron," on Hillel Street, across from an unkempt park. The office, with its telex machine and a long wall of books, anchored one end of the building's top floor. None of us needed to travel far to find colleagues and competitors. Nine other papers, a wire service, and the BBC were down the hall. Two other papers resided one floor down.

None of the papers put much stock in parachutists, the reporters who excitedly dropped in during crises. The economics and competitive self-interest of newspapers, for a long time, supported a straightforward theory: if a long-running story mattered, then reporters needed to live where the story was. To know the cast of characters and grinding fault lines of the Middle East, a reporter should live under its blindingly white sky. Everyone on the hallway was his newspaper's khedive, reporting on a large unruly province.

The editors in Baltimore paid more attention day to day to Israel than anywhere other than Baltimore or Washington. Among the foreign bureaus, Moscow mattered a great deal because it was one-half of the meta conflict that colored everything red or not-red. The Middle East developed a toxic dynamic of its own. If both Palestinians and Israelis were involved, you could write about a traffic accident that occurred in Tel Aviv and see the story on the front page in Baltimore. And editors pressed for that story. Correspondents did not file dispatches like that from Moscow. All of the other reporters in Beit Agron wrote the traffic accident story, too.

In Israel and the West Bank and Gaza, we wrote about the conflict and "The Conflict." Each side—Israeli and Palestinian—cited reasons why it was entirely in the right. There were claims of perfect rectitude based on the contents of holy books, on who inhabited a place first, and on use of force. You could pore over maps that showed the movements of armies or where especially horrifying events occurred. It hardly mattered when the map was made. The parties' grievances were based on the Israeli invasion of Lebanon in 2006 or in 1982; the Arab-Israeli War of 1973 or of 1967. Some of those fighting wanted to readjudicate 1948, when Israel became a state; others wanted to include in the balance sheet violence that occurred in 1929. I wrote about battles being fought for the second or hundredth time.

Even when it was exhausting, the day-to-day reporting was in important ways not hard. In Israel, almost everyone would willingly talk at length, whether a government minister, a military officer, or residents of any community, to an extent nearly unimaginable elsewhere in the region. Because American support was vital to Israel, American newspapers greatly mattered to Israeli officials, who had a keen sense of hierarchy among the papers. The *Sun* mattered enough, just enough, to make access relatively easy. I could reach any given cabinet minister as easily as a reporter on Calvert Street could reach the head of the Baltimore Department of Public Works. The Palestinian leadership was badly fractured, energetically undermined by both itself and Israel, but no less keenly aware of the United States' importance, and thus was nearly as attentive to the American press. Israelis and Palestinians indulged almost equally in lectures and cant, but you could see and talk with almost everyone, a degree of access impossible in Moscow or in Washington.

Yasir Arafat, the Palestinian leader, was a special case, especially before his return from exile in 1994. Security worries and habit made his whereabouts unpredictable and any announced schedule meaningless. He conducted much of his business at night, and his entourage seemed harried even when waiting was the main activity. It took hours and hours even to reach an outer office. I never saw him on my own. During the years of exile, his lieutenants, among them Mahmoud Abbas, the present leader of the Palestinian authority, would knowledgeably ask about fine points of Israeli policies or actions and defend the chairman's strategy. I had to settle for hurrying down hallways with other reporters in Arafat's wake on the off chance of hearing a few words.

Arafat countenanced great violence during part of his career and made catastrophic errors. More tragic, Israel and the Palestine Liberation Organization learned to mimic the worst of each other: obstinacy; fluency in instilling fear; a misplaced determination to exploit loopholes; engagement in ever more pitiless cycles of violence. But, for good reason, Palestinians believed Arafat was wholly dedicated to their cause. Many—most, I believe—would have accepted any terms that he and Israel agreed upon, if only he and his Israeli counterparts had fully lived up to them.

For good reason, the Palestinian leadership was more opaque for us. Israel arrested would-be public figures as soon as their stature became noticeable. It drove many intelligent, thoughtful Palestinians underground and radicalized others. The ostensible leadership was caught by surprise as much as the Israelis were by the marches and stone throwing that became the first Palestinian uprising. The intifada began in December 1987 after an Israeli truck in the Gaza Strip accidentally crashed into two vans and killed four Palestinians. It was literally a traffic accident, then a wave of increasingly violent protests. They were unplanned. Israel responded with mass arrests and then violence by the army.

After the first several weeks of turmoil, a small number of Palestinians in East Jerusalem and the West Bank drafted fourteen political demands. They were approved by most of the underground factions and became a first attempt to give the uprising concrete goals.

Everyone from Beit Agron, plus Palestinian and Israeli reporters, crowded into a poorly lit ballroom at the National Hotel on Salah el Din

Figure 15.1. The Conflict.
Courtesy of KAL.

Street, the tatty Broadway of East Jerusalem, for the public announcement of the fourteen points. It was a chaotic scene; Israel had threatened to arrest the Palestinians who attended, and the speakers could not be heard over the shouted questions. A besieged aide handed out typed copies of the fourteen points, a radical document for the time and guaranteed to land the authors in jail if Israeli authorities could ever identify them.

We speculated even more about who was behind "The Unified Command," which emerged at about the same time. It issued a leaflet on the ninth of each month, and demonstrators regarded each leaflet's themes and instructions as their orders. Sari Nusseibeh, an Oxford- and Harvard-educated philosophy professor, was one of the Palestinians I asked about the people behind the leaflets and the Unified Command. "No idea," he said. Years later I learned that the coordinator of the Unified Command and the author of many of its leaflets was Nusseibeh.

None of the demands contained in the fourteen points now seem radical in any way: direct negotiations between the Palestine Liberation Organization (PLO) and Israel, withdrawal of the Israeli army from Palestinian cities, free municipal elections in Palestinian cities, fairer allocation of underground water resources, and more equitable use of taxes collected from Palestinian workers. Nevertheless, such thinking was a guarantee of arrest. During a series of detentions and interrogations by the Shin Bet, Israel's domestic secret police, Nusseibeh was pressured to go into exile to avoid imprisonment. He would eventually be detained for three months on fantastical charges of spying for Iraq; no trial was ever held.

Looking closely, you could find seeds of the future. An important sign of change was a series of attacks by Palestinians against Gaza's liquor stores. More women began keeping their heads covered and gave up Western-style dress. Young couples began to favor weddings in a more traditional style. Students at Gaza's Islamic University enrolled in Islamic law courses, in classes segregated by sex. Rashid al-Shawa, an aristocratic former mayor of Gaza, removed from office twice by Israel, described the early tremblers in 1987: "People are using religion to express their political views and it is gaining ground very, very quickly. If I feel such a movement is going to help me get rid of the occupation, I'm quite willing to follow it."

Israel saw religion as a counterweight to the PLO and allowed Saudi Arabia to pay for new mosques in Gaza. Religion hardened into a substitute nationalism. Hamas, introducing a virulent strain of Islamic fundamentalism, was a fast-growing infant. Like Amal and then Hezbollah in Lebanon, Hamas and religion filled the void of ideology created by the failures of Arab nationalism and the PLO's guerilla war. Israel grew so inured to one set of combatants and so confident of its existing networks of informants that it failed to appreciate the importance of the changes. Most of the press made the same mistake.

* * *

You learned from everyone on the Beit Agron hallway: we ate together, endlessly gossiped, fiercely competed, traveled together, and knew each other better than anyone outside of romance. After Iraq's invasion of Kuwait in 1990, three of us flew from Amman to Baghdad as soon as our visas came through. We were the *Miami Herald*, the *Washington Post*, and the *Sun*. In Baghdad, we went straight to the hotel room of the *Los Angeles Times*, already in town for several days. It was an oven-hot Saturday afternoon, plenty of time to file for Sunday.

The day was stone dead, the *LAT* said. No news, really.

"You don't understand," the *Washington Post* said. "We're in town now and we told our desks last night we were coming. We're going to file. We're here." If you reached Baghdad, by definition there was news. But the possibilities for reporting at that time and place were limited. The story at that early stage was about the mirage of diplomacy; the armies remained in the wings. Iraqi officials were unavailable for any type of interview and in Saddam Hussein's Iraq would always be unavailable. No one outside the government could discuss politics safely. Out of necessity, Iraqis silently accommodated themselves to their government even when it seemed unhinged. Hussein's birthday was a national holiday. People praised the president more than their children. The government insisted that fear was love.

April Glaspie, the American ambassador, having recently assured her government that Iraq had only peaceful intentions, was out of the country when the invasion of Kuwait occurred; she would not be returning. Joseph Wilson, the senior remaining American, told the Marine guard to let us come inside the embassy. It was a large townhouse that appeared to have expanded without benefit of an architect. In this era before suicide vests, it was set back a half dozen steps from the sidewalk along a narrow tree-lined street. Wilson lit a cigar and gave us enough scraps for a story. Since we were there, it was on the Sunday front page.

A lot was about to change in how news came to us and to newspapers. Correspondents and foreign desks were early victims of the change, which forced, or should have forced, a rethinking of what correspondents did. The still future Internet had nothing to do with the initial revolution; cell phones were even further in the future; "social media" a nonsensical phrase. The Gulf War, in terms of press, was CNN's. Because of CNN, with its digital cameras and satellite phones, editors no longer needed to read the wires, much less wait for us to file to know the day's headlines, even the hour's.

The build-up of armies and ships gradually took over from the diplomats before the one-sided fighting began. I started my coverage of the war from a refitted Navy battleship that launched cruise missiles. I then moved to Dhahran, one of the jumping off points for the US military and reporters, and headquarters for the Saudi national oil company Aramco. When Saddam Hussein fired Scud missiles against Israel and Saudi Arabia—America's allies—he targeted Dhahran. The first time the air raid siren sounded there, I walked down a staircase to the basement shelter. The second time, my phone rang within a few seconds. "I see a Scud is heading your way," an editor said on the line from Baltimore. A newsroom TV was audible in the background. I heard the siren sounding in Dhahran and on television in Baltimore via the telephone. Then a short deep thud that was felt, then heard. I could have watched it on TV or heard it again with a slight lag by phone. The desk saw more than I did, in some sense knew more, which was not a problem—far from it—if we trusted and valued correspondents reporting and writing stories that were truly our own. That is, if we let CNN (and later the Internet) liberate us from "reporting" what was already well-known. Instead of writing "the war," we could focus on what we discovered ourselves. Every *Sun* subscriber knew the war story—and the daily developments of every subsequent war—long before the paper was delivered.

I should have understood and acted on its impact earlier, as the paper should have, too. I became foreign editor a few weeks before 9/11. Our resources for coverage were neither paltry nor limitless. The foreign desk had the liberty of using them largely as we chose. I was never told during the conflicts in Afghanistan and Iraq to hold down spending or meet a budget, which was a praiseworthy silence.

No one had to be coaxed into reporting from dangerous places. The Moscow correspondent traveled to Tajikistan before crossing into northern Afghanistan. A second reporter reached Kabul. The Beijing correspondent went to Islamabad and Quetta, a fourth to jittery Peshawar and then Afghanistan. The Johannesburg correspondent repeated the Islamabad–Quetta journey. When the United States invaded Iraq in 2003, a reporter and a photographer traveled to Baghdad from Kuwait with the Marines; the officer assigned to watch over them was killed along the way. A member of the metro staff went to Baghdad and then north to Mosul. A second photographer went to Baghdad. The Moscow correspondent went to Turkey and then, perilously, into northern Iraq. The London correspondent traveled almost everywhere, including around Baghdad by municipal bus. Doug Birch, Scott Calvert, Will Englund, Dan Fesperman, Frank Langfitt, John Makely, Liz Malby, John Murphy, Todd Richissin: they demonstrated that the greater the freedom to report, write, and photograph what only they could see, the richer, the more *true* the story.

When publishers began shrinking the newsroom staff, the presumed extravagance of the foreign budget became a focus of discontent. But even before the first bureaus were shuttered, the foreign budget was a pittance, however you measured it: per bureau, per story, or by lump sum; not including salaries of the correspondents (less than a million dollars overall), that paid the cost of airplane tickets, cars, hotels, the bare bones support staff some bureaus employed, office rent (where there were offices), computers, the electric bills, telephones, and every meal put on an expense account. It also paid for most of the front page (also, some of the work and careers likely to inspire younger colleagues). Our salaries, as best as I could determine on my own behalf, were for a long time generally second-lowest among the papers with overseas correspondents. The *Christian Science Monitor* was the one serious competitor in that dismal contest; in later years, the *Sun* prevailed, unfortunately. There was never a windfall from the foreign bureaus for the newsroom to inherit, none. Great events made for great reporters, the saying went, and some great events occurred beyond Maryland.

* * *

Everyone who became the paper's Jerusalem correspondent felt, eventually, a deep fatigue about "The Conflict" and varying levels of disgust about the combatants. We saw the limits of both force and diplomacy, even when leaders in the region did not. Whatever was gained here solely by force always crumbled away. The landscape included examples more than three thousand years old—Hazor, Jericho, and Megiddo among them.

Tel Hazor is a high grassy mound that flatbed Israeli army trucks carrying tanks and artillery pass as they climb the last hills toward the border with Lebanon. Hazor has partially excavated remains of a once powerful city where the Canaanites and then their conquerors kept watch over trade routes linking their kingdoms south to Egypt and east to Babylon. As many as twenty thousand people lived there before the Canaanite city, sometime after 1200 BC, was violently destroyed. An Israelite city that eventually replaced it was burned to the ground by the Assyrians in 732 BC, the residents killed or deported.

More recent lessons about force were Gaza and southern Lebanon. So was Iraq. With the best-equipped military in the world, the United States could not impose stability in Iraq. Israeli commanders cited their own chastening experiences in Gaza. Israel failed to find political allies or support an economy that might have tempted Gazans away from resistance, during an occupation that lasted more than thirty years. Israel's failure was not for lack of superior weaponry or inventive tactics, assassinations of gifted bomb makers, bulldozing of border areas, mass arrests, destruction of ministries, and suspected barracks. Hamas and other factions in Gaza were no less creative and at least as pitiless. They relied on suicide bombings, kidnappings, would-be attacks by sea, and never put Israeli civilians off limits.

Retired Israeli commanders admitted that military gains could be only short-term. "You cannot achieve peace only by using the Israeli army, but you can gain time," Ori Orr, a retired general who had served as deputy defense minister, told me.

Orr was captain of a reconnaissance unit during the six-day Arab–Israeli war of 1967. Israel defeated the armies of Egypt, Syria, and Jordan, gained control of Gaza, the West Bank, and East Jerusalem, and seemed a super-power. "I wrote my wife," Orr said, "'This is the last war.'"

Usually the tragedies were not large enough to command lasting attention. They were our traffic reports. But the expectation and fear of violence stunted millions of lives. The refugee camps stood as monuments to the failures of every party. In *The Yellow Wind*, a prescient account of Israel's near blindness to the effects of its policies, the Israeli author David Grossman called the camps "ruins of ruins." Israelis and Palestinians shared a profound unease.

Sari Nusseibeh, the Palestinian philosopher, told me in 1990, "We are entering one of the worst chapters in our history."

"What fighting does," Shlomo Brom, a retired Israeli general told me in 2006, "is prepare the background for a diplomatic solution."

The Conflict would not be resolved by adding up examples of brutality or forgiveness and awarding the prize to whoever had the better score. Everyone had points. Almost everyone knew on some level that the land in some way would need to be shared. I took seriously the absolutists on both sides—Israelis who wholly rejected creation of a Palestinian state or wanted to deport Israeli Arabs; Palestinians who rejected Israel's right to exist or favored violence over all else. They were always minorities, however, even when the violence was at its worst. Israelis and Palestinians wanted what others want: a good education for their children, economic opportunities for their families, and security for their communities. Wholesale violence and total defeat of "The Other" are not parts of the majority's wish list on either side.

In the early 1990s, I heard an Israeli politician describe an analogy for relations between Israelis and Palestinians, and an appealing solution to their conflict. His model was relations between Germany and France, countries that mercilessly fought each other during the nineteenth and twentieth centuries. The border province Alsace-Lorraine changed hands several times. "They killed each other over Alsace-Lorraine for, what, a hundred years? Three, four major, horrible wars. Now everything's peaceful, and there's an open border and tourism. The French and Germans can't stand each other, and it's paradise."

For Israelis and Palestinians, it should be possible.

16

Nightcops

David Simon

Behold, a prince of my city, or so I imagine myself, resting next to Ettlin and before the algae-green glow of the Harris terminal, dialing through the long-call list of Maryland State Police barracks and city districts, hunting down the brutalities and miscalculations of a reckless, teeming metropolis.

"State Police, Glen Burnie barracks . . ."

"Hey, how're ya? Simon from the *Sun*. Anything going on?"

"Nope. Quiet."

Right then. Next call.

"State Police, Waterloo . . ."

"Afternoon. Simon from the *Sun*. Anything up?"

"Quiet today."

Quiet. Okay, next.

"State Police, Annapolis . . ."

The long-call sheet—sixty-some-odd numbers for damn near every police agency operating in the Old Line State—wasn't even on my desk at that point. No, I had all the numbers memorized, not as a parlor trick, but simply because I'd called every night police desk from Cumberland to Ocean City two or three times a shift for nearly two years at that point.

Is it a testament to the power of human memory that, to this day, I can still tell you that the state police barracks in Hagerstown is 301-739-2101, or that the Coast Guard marine safety office in Baltimore was then 962-5105? Is it worth describing the recurring dreams suffered well into my fifth decade, in which I slow dial the entire list on one of the newsroom's early 1980s-era rotary phones, waking in a sweat only after reaching the last entry in the long column, the Ocean City Fire Department, and then beginning anew with the Baltimore police com center? Is it any wonder that for years, to better sustain the pleasure of a sexual partner, I would not—as Woody Allen once wryly remarked—lay abed focused on baseball, wondering whether to steal Alou or have McCovey hit away? No, whatever restraint came to me was gleaned from imagining a full round of *Baltimore Sun* cop calls. Being chivalrous, I would sometimes even imagine myself taking info for a two-car fatal from the Salisbury barracks, trying not to moan in the darkness about a westbound vehicle crossing the center line on Route 50.

I did this five shifts a week as the *Sun*'s night police reporter—my nights off, for the love of God, were Monday and Tuesday—harvesting death, dismemberment, and criminality, and then reducing most of it to bite-sized morsels for the "Maryland In Brief" feature, deep inside the metro section.

On a good night, something approximating real news would happen, and the night police reporter would work the phones, calling neighbors and detectives or even rushing over to one of the city districts to pry the incident report from a reluctant desk sergeant. If the story was especially notable, he might roll out of the newsroom, pen and notepad in hand, ready to wash up on the 1400 block of North Dallas Street or the 1800 block of West Lombard to gather some actual humanity and color on whatever brutality might be written to the front of metro, or perhaps, on some sacred and improbable night, the bottom of a front page largely reserved for the national and foreign desks, or perhaps, the more substantive and official happenings of government and politics in Maryland and Baltimore.

Such moments could never be conjured; they were elusive and decidedly random. For the night police reporter to find purchase on a front page, whole city blocks would need to catch fire, cops or firefighters would have to die, or, of course, upstanding white people would have to be killed in the right zip code. Otherwise, the great, insatiable maw of "Maryland In Brief" beckoned:

"A twenty-four-year-old West Baltimore man was shot to death . . ."

"Two Gambrills men were killed and a third injured in a three-car collision on Route 2 that police said . . ."

"A two-alarm rowhouse fire proved fatal to an elderly Curtis Bay woman . . ."

No, reportorial immortality was seldom to be found in the long-call list on ordinary nights. Young *Baltimore Sun* reporters harboring the most lurid and secret ambitions for their careers could go a week or more without a byline when working cops on a four-to-twelve shift. By the time they arrived in late afternoon, the metro editors were already meeting, their news budgets more or less cemented. And the daycops reporter, Twigg or LoLordo or Prewitt, had by then picked clean the police blotters of most everything from overnight to well past midday. Even the late-breaking stuff from the two afternoon papers had been gathered up and reprocessed. Certainly, any happenstance that a hungry nightshift reporter might slice and dice into enough column inches to rate a byline was no longer hanging low from any civic branch. Best a young fellow could do was sit at his desk and begin to make fresh calls . . .

"Homicide."

"Simon from the *Sun*. Anything happening?"

"Simon from the sun! Kurth from Earth!"

Charlie fucking Kurth. Every call to homicide, twice a night, the same goddamn joke. It made a cop reporter pray aloud for Worden or Kincaid to answer the goddamn phone.

Once, quite early in what at that point could only be generously referred to as my career, I came upon a remarkable coincidence that seemed to promise at least eight inches of copy and a byline somewhere in the bowels of the metro section. I took the discovery to the weekend night editor.

"Bill, I have two shootings on the same city block. Only an hour apart."

I showed him my notes: two human beings hit by gunfire on the same, solitary block of Baltimore, Maryland, on the same night, only an hour apart. My breath in my throat, I wondered secretly whether it might just be necessary to remake the metro front for the final.

The night editor pushed up his reading glasses, squinting at my ballpoint scrawl, then frowned.

"The eight hundred block of George Street is the Murphy Homes," he explained, almost sympathetically. "When you don't have a shooting there, it's news."

Oh, the reckless, teeming city.

In time, I learned the margins and even managed to get off a decent story or two. A gas truck caught fire and took a block of Pimlico rowhouses with it, and while the other reporters were at phone booths, dumping impressionistic quotes about leaping flames and acrid smoke, I managed to call the late Sunday rewrite, Jane Smith, with the actual cause of the fire and quotes from a battalion chief, earning the front-page byline. An undercover narcotics detective was shot to death after the double-dot deadline in a buy-bust on Frederick Road, and I managed to make the final with twenty inches and a photo. A Hopkins undergraduate was found murdered in her Charles Village apartment—a beautiful young woman, white, slain in a neighborhood that mattered. Bottom of the front, with a photo, in time for double-dot and then re-topped for the final.

But mostly, no. Mostly, the life of a twenty-something *Sun* acolyte, hired out of college and consigned to the night desk, was lived in four-paragraph installments, the kind that either ended in an acknowledgment that homicide detectives had no witnesses or suspects, or that the rear passenger in the second car was treated and released at an area hospital.

The written formula itself was an affront to the human spirit, so much so that Dave Ettlin, the late rewrite man who raised young pups relentlessly in the *Sun* way, once deigned to show me his lede for the apocalypse, composed so that it would fly without debate past the night editor and the copy desk slotman:

> Life as we know it ended in Baltimore yesterday, as the dead rose in every city cemetery and demon spawn from hell were seen wreaking havoc throughout central Maryland, police said.

The "police said" made it perfect, we both agreed, with Ettlin assuring me that attribution is always key.

In desperation, after almost a year in the existential nightmare that was night police reporting—if a drug dealer falls in West Baltimore and no one reports it, does he make a sound?—I handled the problem in part by learning to write a feature story.

My first attempt was the last early morning of the city wholesale fish market, an old but epic wreck of a building just off East Baltimore Street. The market was to be pushed out of the city for redevelopment, with the fishmongers decamping to modern facilities in Jessup. Slipping the surly bonds of police reporting, my lede on that piece had something about unseeing scrod staring one-eyed and uncomprehending at the cavernous old building one last time. Seriously.

Bob Benjamin, a veteran reporter with the dignified beat of higher education, sought me out the morning that the fish market piece ran off the front.

"Well, well," he said, trying, I suppose, for some facsimile of a compliment. "I'm reading my paper this morning, and I had to take note: Simon actually wrote something."

But the next day, the fish market was closed forever, and what remained for me, shift after shift, was more crime-blotter jetsam from a reckless, teeming, and wholly repetitive metropolis.

"Homicide."

"Hey, Simon from the *Sun*, Anyth . . ."

"Simon from the sun! It's Kurth from Earth!"

"Fuck you, Charlie. Fuck you and the whole Kurth family and everything on God's green fucking earth that you stand for . . ."

The occasional feature story, coupled with the fact that I was quick and clean on breaking cop stuff, resulted in only one modest enhancement in my status. On Sunday and Monday nights, the off days for Ettlin, I was given a rewrite shift.

The new duties offered only slightly more dignity and gravitas than night police reporting, in that you got a chance to boss around and abuse the nightcops scribe. But it was at least an acknowledgment that, in the eyes of those making up the work schedule, your copy was fast, clean, and accurate. In his own legendary memoir of life at the *Sun*, Russell Baker described a good rewrite man, more or less accurately, as a soul entirely capable of stringing an endless series of newspaper clichés together at the highest possible rate of speed. Baker shortchanges some of the nuance for the sake of humor, but mostly, he's on the money. Night after night, I got better at reducing the moral foibles and grievous tragedies of Baltimore, Maryland, to crisp, clear formula.

These heady days of instantaneous tweeting and perpetual, real-time digital information have made the very style of news writing—if not spelling and punctuation—almost a presumption. And the job of quickly writing and rewriting cogent, readable newspaper copy for three editions a night is now about as useful to humanity as that of a celluloid projectionist or typewriter repairman. But I can still give you twenty clean inches on a three-alarm warehouse fire in ten minutes. It may not count for much in the world as she now spins, but I can do it.

The other thing that rewrite taught me is that only a portion of those laboring with me at the *Sun* were of a temperament to accept the actual terms of engagement.

Simply put, I was ready and willing to insert myself into the tragedy of other people's lives, to stand there on a doorstep talking, begging, until the broken mother or shocked widow invited me inside. I would get the quotes. I would ask for the photo. I would watch other reporters get sent away and then I would ring the doorbell, convinced that my pitch was better, that I would not be denied.

A less honest soul would attribute this to a hunger for the story, or more shamelessly, the public's right to know. But no, sorry, it's just good old sociopathy that luckily finds some utilitarian purpose in the obscure craft of police reporting. Even wrapping this skill set in as much human warmth as I might, I knew it to be some cold shit, and the best I can say for myself is that I never lied to anyone, and I treated the words and experiences that I acquired with as much respect as the job allowed.

Others in my tribe had no stomach for it.

Once, when I was working weekend rewrite, we caught a story about an assault on an infant in the neonatal unit at Franklin Square Hospital in Baltimore County, a twisted little incident in which some wreck of a teenager had wandered from the psychiatry wing and, finding the door to the delivery ward open, had proceeded to batter a random infant in the nursery.

The cops reporter that evening was a kid, earnest and virginal, fresh from the *Sun*'s internship program. He came to me with nearly enough to write up a brief, but this was more than that.

"You have the baby's name and address," I told him. Use the criss-cross directory and call the parents. We have twenty minutes until the double-dot."

He looked at me, stricken.

"Call them." I repeated.

"I don't think that's right."

"*Right?*"

"They've been through a lot here. I don't think we should bother them tonight with this."

I used the criss-cross myself, found the home number and put it in front of the poor kid.

"This is the job. Call."

He let the phone ring twice, then hung up the receiver in a rush. I saw it and he knew I saw it, and there was nothing else I could do but walk over again, check the number, dial, and let it ring. A voice picked up, and after I indentified myself, a father screamed in the phone for about thirty seconds, calling me everything from a parasite to a son of a bitch. I replied that I was sorry to bother him at the late hour, but asked again if he was sure that he didn't want to take a moment and reflect on the incident. The father screamed some more and hung up. The kid, looking up at me, was self-satisfied.

"See?" he said, after I replaced the receiver.

"See what?"

"He didn't want to talk."

"We know that *now*. And you know what else we know? That he probably won't be talking to Jayne Miller on the eleven o'clock news, or to anyone from the *Evening Sun* early tomorrow."

A good, clean writer and a smart hire, he was entirely unconvinced. And in that moment, I like to believe, his career as a sports columnist was born.

No, ambulance-chasing and widow-consoling wasn't for everyone in newspapering, but at the *Sun*, it was for even fewer when the terrain was the inner city, where the carnage was largely confined to black lives.

In truth, police reporting in Baltimore, I came to understand, was a balancing act between the cynicism and self-interest of the police sources on which you relied, and the voices in the street that were, in my city anyway, very different from those I had known. I was a suburban kid, a child of New Deal Democrats and liberal, but nonetheless suburban, and the world being policed in Baltimore was elusive and angry. In my first year of police reporting, I had somehow accomplished something without giving it much thought at all: I had acquired an ear, an interest, and a patience not only for the banter of Irish and Italian detectives and desk sergeants, but for what was coming at me from the largely African American street. The *Sun* had put me here, and to do the job I needed to listen to voices and cadences and arguments not my own. I found that I was willing to appear ignorant, to ask a stupid question, to be the fool. Most of all, I was willing to listen to anybody and everybody, and more than that, I was not simply humoring them to get facts for the next day's edition. Not entirely, anyway. I was actually learning.

Inside the newsroom, of course, such lessons were of little practical importance, if they were acknowledged at all. At a predominantly white newspaper that had institutionally devalued black life in Baltimore for much of its existence—as a cynical and diminutive cue to white readers, black crime victims and suspects were routinely identified in the paper as "Negro" until 1961—my deepening curiosity, I later came to understand, was improbable, maybe even self-defeating. These were crimes that to society did not matter, in communities that did not matter.

Decades later, after I'd written a couple non-fiction narratives and some television dramas, a Baltimore detective I had come to regard not merely as good police but as an intellect would credit me with this much only. Most of my copy, in Terry McLarney's eyes, was the usual dilettante's from-on-high bullshit, albeit a little more amusing to him at a few odd points. But, he told me, before *Homicide* and *The Corner*, and before *The Wire* as well, "all of these ghetto murders didn't rate. They were invisible. Not because everyone couldn't see them, but because no one inside or outside the police department gave a shit. To get our attention in Baltimore, you had to kill a white person."

The city might be reckless and teeming, but much of it was apparently not meant to be glimpsed as more than a Maryland Digest brief in the verdant sinecures of Roland Park and Mount Washington. Ill-dressed and inconstant in his newsroom demeanor, Mr. Simon had apparently misspent his first years at the *Sun* undertaking an awkward, vaguely inappropriate embrace of the city's demimonde. After a year or so on the beat, he could actually find his way to Whatcoat Street or Lemmon Alley without so much as consulting a city map book.

This was not entirely a good thing in the eyes of some, so much so that some of my editors began to wonder just how long I was going to continue to slum on a split schedule of rewrite and police reporting. The way of the *Sun* was to quickly demonstrate a basic and rote competence on obituaries or nightcops, and then graduate to a couple years manning a county bureau in Columbia or Towson, showing the powers-that-be that school board politics or a circuit courthouse was manageable. With that much experience, the chance to be the third or fourth man in Annapolis during the legislative session was now a possibility. Cover yourself with honor in that assignment and, perhaps, the Washington bureau or a foreign assignment beckoned.

My career inertia was noted. When the Howard County reporter went on vacation for two weeks in the spring, I was offered to the county editor as a temporary replacement, but it was made clear to me that this first loan-out from the city desk was a harbinger.

"See how you like it," the metro editor said cryptically, banishing me for a fortnight from the downtown newsroom on Calvert Street.

How I like it? Like *what*? Getting my police information through a wire-mesh window rather than at the bar at Kavanagh's? Parsing a zoning board agenda as if it was some intricate Talmudic tract? Listening to the county scanner channels in the hopes that a wing of the mall might burn to the ground, or that county detectives might be rushing to one of the seven or eight annual homicides in a planned community where the subdivisions were named Hobbit's Glen and Harper's Farm?

"Bring me home," I begged the city editor. "I'll do anything you ask, including babysitting and window treatments."

And she did.

Which leaves me, of course, opposite Ettlin, who is now simultaneously eating his lunch and taking dictation from Jeff Price in Jerusalem—a real newspaperman with a real expense account covering real world events—while I climb the blank walls of the same rote, repetitive purgatory.

"Anne Arundel fire . . ."

"Simon from the *Sun*. Still quiet tonight?"

"Yup. Still quiet."

Ettlin watches me finish out the long-call list, and after cleaning up Price's copy and sending it on to the foreign desk, he's talking about setting up the Scrabble board for an early round of humiliating, triple-word-score dominance. At a penny a point, I am into the son of a bitch for more than ten dollars this month.

And I can't bear it. When the last of the phone numbers yields nothing so much as a brief, I grab notepad and car keys, rise and stare down at the rewrite desk and the prospect of another wasted shift.

"I'm gonna run the districts."

Ettlin raises an eyebrow. Run the districts?

Not since the days of hot type and Mergenthaler have day police reporters volunteered to run the nine Baltimore police districts, visiting desk sergeants and perusing arrest and incident logs. Why bother? You've already called the city com center and homicide, as well as traffic investigation. Other than street robberies and purse-snatches, what is there to be gleaned from showing up at the Southwestern or Western Districts, presenting a press card to the desk man, and being handed the useless and inconsequential dross of a quiet news day, the stuff of which newspaper columns are never made.

"Why?" Ettlin asks.

"Because they're there."

But at the Southern, there's only some shoplifting and a prostitution arrest on the books, and at the Southwestern, someone robbed a Korean carryout of twenty-two dollars with either a gun or a finger in the pocket of a hooded sweatshirt. The Western yields some penny-ante drug arrests, and the Northwestern has two minors arrested for joy-riding an AMC Gremlin.

In the car on the way to the Northern, it all seems so empty, so utterly valueless as the instrument by which the great men of journalism might be sifted out and exalted. Here I am, cycling like a fool through police districts, and doing so after calling fifty-odd other places, looking for some fresh, creative, and fascinating manifestation of man's inhumanity to man. And Baltimore is just not up to the task.

At the Northern, the desk sergeant refuses to let me see the incident book, as desk sergeants at the Northern always seem to do. The shift lieutenant is called, and he eventually arrives and hands me the clipboard as if it is a holy relic. One residential burglary from lower Hampden: taken, a purse with eight dollars and change.

"This is what you didn't want to show me?"

The desk sergeant shrugs.

I'm thinking of skipping the Northeastern District. Nothing happens out there. Ever. In Mencken's memoir of newspapering, his first assignment as a police reporter is the Northeast and, as a wide-eyed apprentice, he asks his editor how far out he should go looking for news.

"Until you see the Philadelphia reporters walking toward you," he is told.

But now I am standing at the Northeastern desk, running through the scant pickings on the incident sheet, telling myself that Howard County might not be so bad, that any idiot can manage ten or twelve bylined inches every day on the school board or the county council agenda. I am barely listening to the squawk of the district channel on the deskman's radio.

". . . in a tree, two youths . . ."

"What's your twenty?"

"Herring Run. South end."

"Ten-four. Has fire been called?"

"Ten-four. Waiting on 'em now."

What, I ask, was that about a tree?

Five minutes later, I am down in Herring Run Park, watching Baltimore firefighters rescue two fifteen-year-old prodigies from a tall oak. They had skipped a day of middle school, climbed to an upper perch, and then proceeded to freak out about the risks of returning earthwards. There are two young girls on the ground as well, teasing them for their cowardice, giving what is known in this business as good quote.

One of the firefighters starts up the tree, while his partner waits below, holding an axe.

"Hey, man, what's the axe for?" asks one kid.

"That's if you don't want to come down," replies the Northeastern patrolman, dry as dirt.

And why they were up a tree in early afternoon, it being a school day and all? "Let's say we took a vacation," explains the other kid, nodding at my notepad, "but please don't print that."

Once aground, both of them regain their composure, if not their bravado, eyeing the girls and even bumming cigarettes from the patrolman.

I fill about ten notepad pages and race back to the newsroom just in time to give the city editor a budget line for the four o'clock meeting.

"How long?" Rebecca asks.

"Twenty, twenty-five . . . ?"

She looks at me, dubious.

"It writes itself," I assure her.

An hour later, she reads my stuff, and Paul, doing makeup, begins dummying my story for the front of metro. It runs to twenty-five inches.

"If we had art, telegraph would have taken it," my editor tells me. "Did you think to call photo on it?"

The front page—immortality, or at least the whispered margins of such. At the sound of Rebecca Corbett's words, my whole being puffs into a state of reportorial tumescence. For want of a photo, I might have made the front.

The next morning, Milford Prewitt, the daycops reporter, sits with his legs crossed atop Ettlin's desk, reading my righteous shit. Like me, Prewitt has lived and died with the long-call list, but he's done so for years now. He's sick of it, too, and will be gone in less than a year, moving on to something else, something beyond newspapering.

"Simon, you got twenty inches on kids in a tree."

Twenty-five, I correct him.

"You got twenty-five inches on kids in a tree in Baltimore. How in the hell . . ."

"I ran the districts and picked it up."

"You went to the Northeastern District and got twenty-five inches on kids in a tree on the front metro."

Milford folds the paper and laughs loudly, but not at my expense. Sometimes, the magic is there, waiting to be conjured. Sometimes not. But yesterday, I had a good story.

"You're gonna be alright, Simon," he says, still laughing, beginning his own long-call round, his second of the day. "Two kids in a tree."

Oh, my reckless and teeming city.

17

Covering the Gipper

Robert Timberg

Covering the White House was not the most enjoyable newspaper job I ever had. That was the Maryland politics beat, when I was a local reporter for the *Baltimore Evening Sun*, the *Sun's* sister paper.

But the White House beat was the most important. Why? Because, as I quickly learned, every national or international story that mattered managed to find its way to 1600 Pennsylvania Avenue. It made no difference if the story was foreign, domestic, military, diplomatic, economic, or political. Eventually, they all came banging on the door of the White House. And as the *Sun's* primary reporter covering the place from 1983 to 1988, I got more than a taste of all of them.

This was one of the first, perhaps for me the most painful.

I was just waking up on Sunday, October 23, 1983, to the first reports of the terrorist truck bombing of the Marine barracks at Beirut International Airport.

Ronald Reagan, in 1982, had deployed some 1,200 American troops to Lebanon as part of a multinational peacekeeping force, a muddle-headed decision in the view of many.

Strategically, it may have made sense at some point, but that reasoning never caught up with the reality on the ground. By the end of that day, a day that has haunted the Marine Corps ever since, reality translated into 241 dead American servicemen, 220 of them Marines.

For me, the ghastly toll was personal as well as professional. I was a Marine veteran of the Vietnam War and thought of all Marines as brothers. But I now had a far different role, and my job as a reporter was to tell the readers of the *Baltimore Sun* what had happened and why.

For the next several weeks that's what I tried to do: a job that became all the more complex two days later when American forces invaded the tiny Caribbean island nation of Grenada.

Fortunately for a rookie on the beat, I did not have to take on the job alone. The *Sun's* Washington bureau was not the largest in the capital. The *New York Times* and the *Los Angeles Times* had more reporters. So, of course, did the *Washington Post*, the hometown newspaper. But we were determined to cover the big stories ourselves—not just in Washington, but overseas as well, where we maintained a sizeable network of foreign bureaus, the only paper of our size that did so.

This meant that in my early, demanding days covering Ronald Reagan and the Beirut bombing, I could turn to veteran members of the *Sun* bureau to supplement what I was picking up at the White House.

On military matters, for example, there was Charles Corddry, our experienced, knowledgeable, and very plugged-in Pentagon correspondent. As for the foreign aspects of the story, I had Henry Trewhitt, our longtime diplomatic correspondent, to lean on, which of course I did.

There were big stories, yes, but there was also the man at the center of all of them—Ronald Reagan, one of the most fascinating, if unlikely, men to hold the presidency.

Reagan was an aging actor who came riding out of the West in 1980 and booted Jimmy Carter out of the Oval Office after one term. They called him "the Gipper," after George Gipp, the celebrated Notre Dame football star whom Reagan played in one of his movies.

Reagan lay claim to the presidency by asking voters a question that has since been proclaimed one of the most effective political messages ever crafted: "Are you better off today than you were four years ago?"

A majority of voters were not, or felt they were not. Turmoil in the Mideast pitted neighbor against neighbor, and gasoline became a scarce resource, leading to long, often unruly lines at the pump. Gas prices rose to levels previously unknown.

The nation, moreover, was in the grip of debilitating double-digit inflation. Reagan had a killer quote for that, too.

"Inflation," he said, "is as violent as a mugger, as frightening as an armed robber, and as deadly as a hit man."

On the international front, a revolution in Iran early in 1979 resulted in fifty-two American embassy personnel being taken hostage in Tehran. Under the approving gaze of Iran's revolutionary government, the American flag was routinely set afire by student militants, and the United States was denounced as "the Great Satan." Carter seemed helpless. One major television network headlined its nightly reports on the crisis "America Held Hostage," a label that screamed presidential impotence.

The hostages were still in the embassy on election day in 1980, effectively dooming Carter's reelection hopes. They were finally released on inauguration day, January 20, 1981, clearing Iranian airspace only after Reagan had taken the oath of office. The timing was widely viewed as the Iranians using the hostages to humiliate Carter one last time.

In his inaugural address, delivered from the West Front of the Capitol in a wintry chill, Reagan urged the American people to join him in beginning "an era of national renewal."

He also played on the themes of his successful campaign—the need for a sharp reduction in the size of government, lower taxes, and a stronger national defense.

He may have compromised from time to time on these, his bedrock issues, but his subalterns quickly learned not to push him too hard to give ground on such matters.

One evening in the Oval Office after a press conference, for example, aides took turns trying to persuade him that he had gone too far in ruling out a tax hike widely favored by many in Congress. His press secretary, Larry Speakes, who related the incident, drafted a short statement designed to give him some flexibility on the matter—wiggle room, as it's known in Washington. Reagan grabbed the draft from Speakes's hand so forcefully that the inkstand on the desk was knocked to the floor.

"Here's what I want to say," he fumed. With that he scrawled "No New Taxes" on the draft and thrust it back at the wide-eyed Speakes.

* * *

Someone once described the *Sun's* Washington bureau as having a champagne taste on a beer budget.

There was some truth to that—maybe a lot of truth. But I never heard anyone use that as an excuse for getting beaten on a story. Making excuses was not in our DNA.

Still, even if we were loath to admit it, we couldn't do everything. But what we did do we did quite well, to my mind as well as anyone and better than most.

Teamwork was so often the key. My first night on the White House beat, a few months before the Beirut bombing, one of the major policy initiatives of the Reagan years came flying at me. Officially, it was called the Strategic Defense Initiative (SDI). Its detractors ridiculed it as "Star Wars," and the name stuck (figure 17.1). SDI, as it turned out, was abandoned by the Pentagon in 1993, its feasibility unproven.

The White House press corps, which now included me, was briefed on the initiative an hour or so before Reagan announced it in a televised speech to the nation.

Figure 17.1.   President Ronald Reagan proposed in 1983 a space-based missile defense system known as "Star Wars."
Mike Lane; courtesy of Baltimore Sun Media Group, all rights reserved.

I had trouble understanding what the briefers were talking about. There was a lot of discussion of the 1972 Anti-Ballistic Missile Treaty between the United States and the Soviets, first-strike capability, and a bunch of exotic weapons programs I had never heard of. Brilliant Pebbles? The central point, I gathered, was that the president wanted to establish a space-based system to intercept Soviet intercontinental ballistic missiles aimed at the United States.

My head was spinning as I walked the three blocks from the White House where the briefing had taken place back to our bureau. I was nearly hit by cars twice as I carelessly crossed streets. I was expected to write a story about Reagan's speech and SDI, on deadline no less. And I had only a vague understanding of what he was talking about.

But Charlie Corddry was there. Our Pentagon correspondent—I'm tempted to say our sainted Pentagon correspondent—was still at the office. He had heard through his sources that Reagan's speech related to military matters so, rather than go home, he had remained in the bureau to watch it on TV and help out if need be.

Thank the Lord. I stumbled into the bureau, saw Corddry, and blurted out, "Charlie, do you know anything about the Anti-Ballistic Missile Treaty?"

Of course he did. He understood everything Reagan had been talking about and quickly realized as well that I had no clue. So he sat me down and patiently explained it to me (or tried to explain it to me). When he finished I went to my desk and over the next twenty or so minutes wrote a story that I hoped covered the ground. Then I passed the story to Charlie. I'd like to say he fixed a few things here and there, but my recollection is that he performed major surgery on it. All I know for sure is that the story I sent to Baltimore read smoothly, made sense, and resembled—if only remotely—the story I had shipped to Charlie several minutes earlier. And when I read it the next morning under my byline on the *Sun's* front page, it looked like I knew what I was talking about.

* * *

Reagan may have been death on taxes, but he was no less relentless when it came to the Soviet Union. In early March 1983, a day or so after I took over the White House beat, I found myself on the press plane that always accompanied Air Force One on its travels.

Our destination that day was Epcot Center, part of Disney World in Orlando, where the president was to address the annual convention of the National Association of Evangelicals.

Considering the audience, I fully expected Reagan's speech to be on such hot button social issues as abortion and prayer in school. I was in for a big surprise.

Reagan's subject that day turned out to be the Soviet Union. It was, he told the gathering of conservative clerics, "an evil empire," nothing less than "the focus of evil in the modern world."

There was no question that Reagan's words reflected his deep-seated hostility toward communism in general and the Soviet Union in particular. That made it all the more fascinating to me to see that hard-edged antipathy erode over the next couple of years.

The reason for this evolution, my reporting revealed, was Mikhail Gorbachev. To my mind, Reagan came to view the new Soviet leader over time not just as a man with whom he could do business, as Prime Minister Margaret Thatcher of Britain had described him, but as someone with whom he enjoyed matching wits.

* * *

During my five years at the White House, I covered three US–Soviet summit meetings. One was in Washington, but the first two, in Geneva and Reykjavik, Iceland, were the most exciting. There was a historic quality to all three, coinciding as they did with the emergence of Gorbachev as a new kind of Soviet leader and fresh evidence of cracks in the Iron Curtain.

Relations between the two superpowers had been frosty for years. Reagan did not meet with a Soviet leader during his first term. When pressed for a reason, he said, "They keep dying on me." In fact, Gorbachev's two predecessors had died during those years, but I, along with other Reagan watchers, believed that for a long time he simply saw no value in such a meeting.

Little things often signal major developments. On the first day of the Geneva summit, Reagan was waiting outside the chateau where the two men were to meet. A black limousine appeared, came to a stop, and Gorbachev stepped out. As he did, I remember him theatrically whisking his fedora from his head before striding up to Reagan and grasping his right hand. It struck me as a kind of salute, and I reacted to it by thinking a new day in US–Soviet relations just might be beckoning. And it was.

There is always a lot of deadly blather at diplomatic events, but the US–Soviet summit in Geneva in November 1985 was anything but boring. The two men startled observers the first day when they took an impromptu stroll on the banks of Lake Geneva to a lakeside pool house. Inside, joined only by their translators, they continued their discussions while warming themselves before a blazing fire.

The White House, as was its style, did what it could to dampen expectations for any breakthrough in superpower relations out of fear the high-profile meeting might be judged a failure. But the summit ended with an important achievement. The leaders agreed to two more meetings, the first in Washington, the second in Moscow. It seemed the two most powerful men in the world wanted to talk some more.

Reagan loyalists, even many individuals less philosophically close to him, maintain that the impromptu summit that followed Geneva, the one in Reykjavik in October 1986, set in motion events that led to the collapse of the Soviet Union a few years later. The issue has been debated ever since, and the argument shows no signs of abating.

I don't know the answer, but I was there, and I have a sense that I witnessed something historic.

The two-day meeting was called a "snap summit" because it was set up quickly with very little time between the announcement and the start of discussions in Iceland's capital. And, as usual, the White House warned the press against expecting anything momentous to result from the talks.

The first indication that something of consequence was transpiring in Hofdi House, the modest home in which the talks were taking place and whose guests had included the Queen of England and Winston Churchill, came when the meeting was extended a second day amid hints that a breakthrough of some sort was possible.

Both men left the morning meeting the next day smiling. But at the conclusion of final talks lasting three hours and forty-two minutes the president looked unusually grim and Gorbachev's goodbye wave seemed limp, his smile forced.

Following the departure of the two leaders, the president's aides, who included Secretary of State George P. Shultz and a platoon of arms control experts, entered the briefing room where the press was gathered. They seemed devastated, their faces drained of color, as if something of great value had been in their grasp, then snatched away just as they were tightening their grip on it.

Over the next hour or so, my colleagues and I did some heavy-duty reporting, first struggling to figure out what had occurred, then reducing what we learned to story form.

My story began:

REYKJAVIK, Iceland—Tentative superpower accords on a broad range of issues, including a 50 percent reduction in all strategic nuclear weapons within five years and the total elimination of ballistic missiles within ten years, fell apart yesterday when President Reagan balked at Soviet leader Mikhail S. Gorbachev's demand that he kill his space-based "Star Wars" defense plan, U.S. officials said.

The two leaders, it turned out, had reached agreements on a number of issues that stood to vastly reduce the global nuclear threat. Reagan was momentarily thrilled. Then Gorbachev sprang his trap, as many have since described it. Everything he had agreed to, he told Reagan, depended on the president accepting language that eviscerated his beloved Strategic Defense Initiative, the program he had unveiled my first week as White House correspondent.

Reagan said no, refusing to give ground then or ever. But if major arms agreements did not emerge at Reykjavik, they did a year later at a follow-on summit, this one in Washington. But the role of SDI in bringing about the collapse of the Soviet state remains in debate.

One side, the Reagan side, says the threat of SDI and the vast amount of money the economically strapped Soviet Union realized would be needed to match it caused the Soviets to scale back their nuclear arsenal. The other side says the collapse of the Soviet Union was inevitable, sooner rather than later, because of a variety of internal weaknesses and, above all, due to the reforms Gorbachev initiated.

The *Sun* took a back seat to no one in coverage of those summits. In fact, we won a prestigious award from the White House Correspondents Association for our work in Geneva. But we had a team of correspondents reporting on those meetings that to my mind lit up the journalistic firmament. It included Stephens Broening, Antero Pietila, Robert Ruby, and Scott Shane. Directing our efforts was Richard O'Mara, the foreign editor, a man of keen judgment and calming leadership.

* * *

Some of my experiences covering Ronald Reagan do not fit neatly into any category. His May 1985 journey to a World War II German military cemetery at Bitburg and the Bergen-Belsen concentration camp cannot easily be labeled.

The visit to Bitburg was to be little more than a side trip, a twenty-minute drop-by during the gathering of leaders of major industrial nations at their annual economic summit.

Bonn, the West German capital, was the site of that year's summit. During the planning stages Reagan's aides came up with what was promised to be a great photo opportunity at what of one of them called "a lovely little cemetery" in the nearby town of Bitburg.

The script called for the president and Helmut Kohl, the German chancellor, to walk together through the cemetery to a granite war memorial against which would be resting two brightly colored floral wreaths. The men were then to place their hands on the wreaths, signifying reconciliation between the two wartime enemies.

What Reagan's advance team didn't realize until much too late was that among the approximately two thousand German soldiers buried in the cemetery were the graves of forty-nine members of Hitler's dreaded Waffen SS.

Reports that the president was going to pay his respects at a cemetery in which SS troops were buried ignited a firestorm of protest from Jews, many of them concentration camp survivors, veterans, politicians including both houses of Congress, and much of the general public.

Efforts were made to get Reagan to cancel the Bitburg visit, but he refused. Aides said he had made a commitment to Chancellor Kohl and was not going to renege on it.

Before the controversy erupted, Reagan had ruled out going to a former Nazi concentration camp, but Bitburg changed that.

Thus, in the morning of the day he was to visit Bitburg, the president, along with his wife, Nancy, found themselves at the gates of Bergen-Belsen. An estimated fifty thousand men, women, and children had died at the camp, among them Anne Frank, perhaps the most enduring symbol of the Holocaust.

And in one of the most emotional professional moments of my life, I was very close to the Reagans as I was the pool reporter, essentially the stand-in for the rest of the press corps, tasked with passing on everything I saw or heard to my fellow reporters.

The Reagans, walking hand-in-hand, and I were surrounded by death, more precisely mass murder. All around us sat flat-topped rectangular mounds, about shoulder height, covered with heather.

Each mound bore a plaque. As the Reagans turned up a path toward one of the mounds, Mrs. Reagan appeared to stiffen, as if suddenly confronting an unspeakable horror. The plaque they paused at read, "*Hier ruhen 5,000 tote.*" The translation: "Here rest 5,000 dead."

My story the next day began:

> In a day of jarring contrasts, President Reagan laid a wreath of reconcilia-tion at a cemetery for German war dead yesterday just hours after speak-ing to a silent, unprotesting crowd of thousands of Nazi victims huddled together in death beneath a blanket of heather.

Much of the following is a product of my overheated imagination and never made it into print. But when I think of my time amid the mounds, this is how I remember it:

> As the Reagans, hand-in-hand, turned up the path toward the mound under which lay 5,000 of their fellow human beings, they seemed to enter a force field, one driving them back. They gamely pushed on, but the force field distorted their features, elongating them so that their eyes broadened to twice their size, their cheeks were pulled back behind their ears, and their noses all but disappeared.

* * *

All roads did indeed lead to the White House: congressional battles, usually over budgets and taxes; US–Soviet relations; the hijacking by Middle East terrorists of the *Achille Lauro*, an Italian cruise ship with many Americans on board; the bombing of Tripoli by American warplanes in response to the Libyan bombing of a club in Germany frequented by American servicemen.

Then there was the Iran–Contra affair, which for a time threatened the Reagan presidency. The convoluted episode gained the status of scandal after it was learned that high administration officials had secretly facilitated the sale of arms to Iran to ransom Americans held hostage by radicals in Leba-non. Doing so violated both an arms embargo against Iran and administra-tion policy against negotiating with terrorists. A second shoe dropped with the disclosure that profits from the arms sales, along with funds from other secret sources, were provided to a right-wing guerrilla insurgency (the Con-tras) in Nicaragua despite a congressional ban on such action.

But covering the White House was not always serious. Occasionally, there were moments of comic relief.

One came when the bureau had a private interview with President Reagan in the Oval Office. Four of us took part and we came well prepared with questions. The interview went very well, and I knew we would get least four stories out of it.

I asked several serious questions, as did the other bureau reporters, but I had a lighter one squirreled away that I hoped to ask if we had time at the end. And we did.

"Mr. President," I said, "do you ever send out for Chinese food in this place?"

I was hoping for a humanizing answer, or a funny one, something like, "Well, I sometimes want to. I love chop suey, egg rolls, moo goo gai pan, fried rice, though I always pick out the peas. But Nancy always vetoes it. She says eating from cardboard boxes is unpresidential."

Sadly, the president said nothing like that. Instead, he said, "No. I just eat what they put in front of me."

· 18 ·

Mandela Saves the Day

Jerelyn Eddings

On February 11, 1990, the world watched in excitement as Nelson Mandela walked to freedom after twenty-seven years in South African prisons. He was the most famous political prisoner in the world and had become the rallying point for a global movement to end the system of racial oppression known as apartheid.

I saw the event unfold on television from the comfort of my apartment on Federal Hill overlooking the Baltimore harbor. I was still waiting for my visa to be approved so that I could travel to South Africa and take up my post as the *Baltimore Sun's* Johannesburg bureau chief.

Three months later, with the visa stamped in my passport, I boarded a flight to what would become the most remarkable news story I would ever cover. I had missed Mandela's first steps of freedom, but over the next three years, I would witness the transition from the old South Africa of segregation and brutality to a new South Africa filled with hope for a better future.

I was replacing a talented South African journalist named Peter Honey who was hired as bureau chief after I failed to get a visa three years earlier, the first time the *Sun* offered me this assignment. I had jumped at the chance for the foreign posting in 1987, even though the end of apartheid was not yet in sight. There were early signs that change could come—student protests at American universities and growing pressure for corporations and governments to disinvest in South Africa and increase its isolation in the global community.

Inside South Africa, there was a determined antiapartheid movement of activists who kept up a steady campaign of protests and confrontations with authorities while their counterparts around the world pressed their cause. South Africa was a big news story, and the *Sun* was giving me a chance to see it close up.

Besides the obvious attraction of being a foreign correspondent, a rarefied post at any newspaper or broadcast network, I had a personal reason for wanting the assignment. It would give me the distinction of becoming the *Sun's* first African American bureau chief and, I believe, the first resident black correspondent from any foreign paper.

But in 1987, the South African authorities were still clinging to apartheid and to the belief that they could define the way the world viewed them. They retained the illusion that they could control the news stories coming out of their country by refusing entry to journalists they deemed unfriendly. Serge Schmemann, a veteran *New York Times* reporter, was denied a visa that same year. For me, to be in his company was a badge of honor.

I neither knew nor sought to know how the South Africans reached their judgment about other journalists, but I had certainly given them enough evidence that I was against apartheid. Growing up in South Carolina in the 1950s, I had endured my own system of racial injustice, the Jim Crow South, where everything was segregated by race—schools, churches, housing, lunch counters, toilets, and most of all, opportunity.

For many children of the South in my generation, the solution was to get out—to go North or anywhere else. I ended up in Washington, then Baltimore, not as far north as many others ventured, but in cities where I had better opportunities to work as a journalist. When *Sun* editors tapped me to go to South Africa, I was on the newspaper's editorial staff, writing daily opinion pieces and a weekly column on the Op-Ed page. The injustice of apartheid had been my topic more than once.

Now, three years after I was first assigned to go, and with the approval of a new white government which was admitting more Western journalists, I would see that system firsthand, working as a correspondent for one of America's most respected newspapers.

By the middle of 1990, change was in the air across South Africa. Frederik W. de Klerk had been elected president the preceding year, and he was determined to change his country's status as a global pariah and usher in a new era. In his first few months in office, he began to undo the most repressive laws that had been used by his predecessors, led by President Pieter W. Botha, to enforce apartheid and crush the antiapartheid movement.

On February 2, 1990, in his first major speech to Parliament, de Klerk surprised the nation and the world by announcing that his government would lift restrictions on antiapartheid groups that had long been banned, including Mandela's organization, the African National Congress (ANC), that been outlawed for thirty years.

"The well-being of all in this country is linked inextricably to the ability of the leaders to come to terms with one another on a new dispensation. No-one can escape this simple truth," he said.

Figure 18.1.
Courtesy of KAL.

On de Klerk's initiative, men who had been locked up for a generation were released from prison; Mandela was the most prominent among them. But there were others in their sixties, seventies, and eighties who had spent much of their lives imprisoned for fighting apartheid. Some, like Mandela, who was seventy-one, had been sentenced to life imprisonment and were never expected to experience freedom again.

Exiles were returning after decades outside of the country. Entertainers such as the trumpeter Hugh Masekela and the singer Miriam Makeba, both of whom had settled in the United States, were welcomed home by jubilant crowds who knew their music but had never seen them in person. Young men and women returned from military camps in Zambia, Tanzania, and Zimbabwe, countries that had offered support for the ANC and the other major antiapartheid group, the Pan Africanist Congress.

Oliver Tambo, the ANC president in exile, returned from London with his family. Thabo Mbeki, who had represented the ANC at the United Nations, came home from New York. Barbara Masekela, who had represented the ANC in Paris, returned and would soon take up a post as Mandela's top aide. Hundreds of Western-educated exiles were joining countrymen who had stayed behind to face government pressures.

As a new correspondent, I covered this flood of returnees who were reshaping the country's political life as much as de Klerk was reshaping it through policies that had opened the door for them. In this emerging new South Africa, I was welcomed by the government's press officers, who helped me with the required credentials when I arrived, and who eagerly responded when I had requests for information. South Africa had a positive story to tell, at last, and the government wanted it told.

In the early 1990s, the story out of South Africa had two main focal points—political negotiations and violence. No one could predict which would win the day. Corporations were considering whether to pull out before the inevitable explosion. And nervous whites were beginning to emigrate—to the United States, England, Australia, and elsewhere—as blacks moved out of their old roles of invisibility and servitude.

Except for the ubiquitous maids who lived on white estates in tiny rooms away from the main house, black workers were confined to living in townships on the outskirts of the cities or in rural areas known as black "homelands."

The largest black township in the country was Soweto, a sprawling bedroom community southwest of Johannesburg, where Mandela and his then-wife Winnie lived both before and after his imprisonment. Soweto had been the launching pad for antiapartheid protests for decades and was the home of many black leaders. A student uprising in 1976 against the compulsory teaching of the Afrikaans language in schools had ended in hundreds of deaths at the hands of police and had sparked an international outcry.

Blacks who didn't live in townships generally resided in one of ten tribal "homelands" established by the government, originally in an attempt to deny the residents formal citizenship in white South Africa and to identify them instead as visitors who required travel and work permits to be in white areas. The largest homeland was KwaZulu, led by the Zulu chief Mangosuthu Buthelezi, who emerged as the African National Congress's main black adversary in the negotiations for a new South Africa.

The rivalry spawned violence between urban blacks and Zulu migrant workers who had come from their homeland to work in mines around Johannesburg and who lived in large compounds isolated from the permanent township residents. Hundreds were killed or injured in clashes that erupted from time to time during this period, threatening to engulf the region.

When I first went to South Africa, I thought my skin color would be an advantage, allowing me to move freely and without notice through black communities and to blend in at gatherings of Africans. I thought I would be privy to a side of black South Africa that my white colleagues would never see. In fact, the reality sometimes turned out to be very different.

During the clashes between black rival groups, I traveled to urban townships, to rural homelands, and to migrant worker hostels. But instead of blending in, I was often greeted with suspicion by residents who wondered if I might be aligned with a rival group. I could not speak Zulu among Zulus, or Xhosa among Xhosas. So while the skin color might get me in the door, my lack of fluency in tribal languages marked me as a stranger.

At these times, I would quickly produce my press badge and identify myself as an American, in the loudest, most American voice I could muster. This often led to surreal conversations in the midst of tension and conflict. "Do you know Eddie Murphy?" one young man asked me at a street protest in Soweto, referring to the popular African American comedian. The young man's face had lit up at the prospect of meeting a black American in person after seeing us only on television. "I always wanted to meet a nigger," another chimed in happily. We wound up having a brief conversation about racial epithets. In South Africa, the epithet for blacks was "kaffir," an ugly word that would make the blood of even the most mild-mannered African boil. The dialogue over racial slurs forged a new bond between us.

In the 1990s, before the South African television industry created its own array of black stars to entertain the new democratic nation, the state broadcaster—the South African Broadcasting Corporation—carried American shows purchased as part of a package of programming. Black stars such as Bill Cosby, who played a cosmopolitan doctor married to a beautiful lawyer with five adorable children, were familiar faces in homes across the racially divided country.

I never expected to have an advantage in covering white South Africa, but I had peculiar experiences that were worth recording for the *Sun*. Afrikaners, like de Klerk and his predecessors, were the creators of apartheid. They ran the government after wresting it from British South Africans in a 1948 election. But they had first arrived in South Africa as farmers from Holland in the seventeenth century, and three hundred years later, they dominated politics as well as agriculture. In fact, they were commonly known as Boers, which literally translated to "farmers" in the Afrikaans language.

I traveled to the Orange Free State, a farming province south of Johannesburg, in the company of a veteran Afrikaner journalist named Hennie Serfontein to meet Afrikaner farm families. Hennie had arranged for us to interview a middle-aged couple in their home, a quaint residence with doilies on the tabletops and frilly curtains. It was much the same as you'd find in a rural American home. This particular couple, Manie and Louisa van Niekerk, were Conservative Party members who opposed President de Klerk's changes.

Mrs. van Niekerk served us tea, and her husband proceeded to explain why blacks and whites needed to be separated: because the "Africans" had to be allowed to develop at their own pace and required the protection of the more advanced whites. He said I might find this hard to understand because American blacks had been removed from Africa so long ago and had become educated and assimilated. We were not like their blacks. "They are very slow people," his wife added. "Even if they want to go fast, I don't think they can cope with it."

"What about Nelson Mandela?" I asked, using the most prominent example of a black African who had developed beyond many whites, since he was a lawyer, the president of a major political movement, and an internationally respected figure. He, too, was different, Mr. van Niekirk explained. He was "de-tribalized." It was the first time I'd heard the term for a black person who had been cut off from his roots. In fact, it wasn't accurate. Nelson Mandela was honored among his Xhosa kinsmen, and although he had moved to Johannesburg as a young man, he respected the Xhosa tribal traditions.

I wrote about the interview, which provided a striking glimpse into the thinking of simple, decent whites who wanted to preserve a status quo that put them on a higher plane and gave them many advantages over their black countrymen.

On May 26, 1990, I encountered right wing Afrikaners in a different way. There was no tea. No polite conversation. Instead, I had a serious brush with injury or possibly death had the situation turned bad.

President de Klerk's political changes had infuriated right wing whites. The most radical among them, a militant group of khaki-clad Boers called the Afrikaner Weerstandsbeweging (AWB), or African Resistance Movement. Their leader, Eugene Terreblanche, was determined to oppose the changes by any means necessary, and since the group was heavily armed, that meant through violence.

On this bright Sunday in 1990, hundreds of conservative whites gathered at the Voortrekker Monument on a hillside outside of Pretoria to express their opposition to the new South Africa taking shape. The monument was the Afrikaner shrine, a carved granite monolith that celebrated the Boers' flight from their own British oppressors in the 1830s and 1840s, a trek from the Cape Colony to the inland provinces where they settled and farmed.

The Conservative Party had organized the rally, and its politicians were out in full force bellowing their opposition to change. I went to cover the rally along with three white colleagues—reporters from the *New York Times*, the

Figure 18.2.   *Sun* correspondent Jerelyn Eddings and Nelson Mandela chatting at the foreign correspondents dinner in Johannesburg, June 1990. Mandela, released from prison in February 1990, was president of South Africa from 1994 to 1999.
Courtesy of Ms. Eddings.

Detroit Free Press, and Southam Newspapers of Canada. Any thought we had about safety in numbers was soon proved wrong.

While politicians made speeches from the monument steps, a rowdier crowd hugged the edge of the rally. Many had been drinking. Many were heavily armed. Some wore the khaki uniforms of the AWB. We would need to pass through this gauntlet to hear what the politicians were saying up front. So we moved slowly forward, attracting stares, frowns, and soon afterward harsh remarks. "You're in the wrong place," someone said. "The ANC rally is in Mamelodi," referring to a township near Pretoria where blacks were rallying on the same day.

To the crowd, my skin color acted like oil on a flame, igniting anger and prompting threats of injury and death. My three white colleagues seemed to give equal offense for being in my company—or perhaps they were blamed for bringing me, since the whites, in the minds in this crowd, were always in charge.

I saw only two other blacks at the rally that day—a man selling ice cream from a cart who didn't seem to give offense, and a lone black female reporter who headed toward our little group the moment she caught sight of us.

Her name was Sylvia Vollenhoven, and she was there covering the rally for *The Star*, a large daily newspaper based in Johannesburg. She also was a correspondent for *Expressen*, a Swedish paper, covering the antiapartheid movement.

She had the advantage of speaking Afrikaans, having grown up in Cape Town as a "colored," the official designation for mixed-race people. Afrikaans was their first language, as it was for the Boers. But Sylvia kept her mouth shut as members of the crowd moved in on us. We all identified ourselves as foreign correspondents for American and European newspapers, hoping that would give us some measure of protection.

"But you're black," one man said to me, as if that was all that counted. Never mind Bill Cosby on South African television every week.

Someone in the crowd caught hold of Christopher Wren, the *Times* correspondent, and twisted his hand behind his back. It appeared we were about to be force-marched away from the monument to a fate unknown. Sylvia later said that some were shouting in Afrikaans that they should shoot us. But fortunately for us, two uniformed police officers turned up to see what was amiss.

They dispersed the crowd and explained to us that we had the right to stay if we chose but they wouldn't advise it. We agreed. As they watched, we made our way down the hill and away from the Afrikaner shrine. We then went to the black rally in Mamelodi.

What followed in South Africa was three years of negotiation, tension, public protests both for and against change, and violence between different factions whose leaders were jostling for advantage. Mandela emerged as the clear leader of the country, a ramrod straight, clear-thinking man of high principle and steely determination. He was an undisputed hero.

Near the end of my assignment in Johannesburg, I witnessed the remarkable moment when Mandela distinguished himself as the new leader. He put out a flame that threatened to consume his country.

On April 10, 1993, Chris Hani, a gregarious and charismatic figure often mentioned as a possible successor to Mandela, was shot to death in the driveway of his home in a racially mixed neighborhood called Dawn Park. Hani had bought a house in this pleasant new community established after President de Klerk scrapped the Separate Amenities Act that segregated housing. It seemed a nice, safe place after a long exile. Hani's wife Dimpho was away from home, he had given his bodyguard the afternoon off, and Hani was scheduled to take his teenage daughter to the hairdresser. She was there in the driveway when he was murdered by a right wing Polish immigrant named Janusz Walus.

Black South Africa erupted in anger. Riots broke out, much as they had in 1968 America after the assassination of Martin Luther King Jr. And there was the threat of more violence, especially against whites since the assassin was white and the attack on Hani was seen by many as an attack on the entire antiapartheid movement. Hani, the chairman of South Africa's Communist Party with a lifelong history of fighting apartheid, was a special favorite of radical young activists.

I had been working on a profile of Hani when he was killed and had accompanied him on visits to urban townships and rural villages. One week before the murder, I interviewed him at his home about his vision for a new South Africa and had enjoyed lunch on the patio with him and Dimpho. He bade me farewell, standing in the same driveway where he was to die. When I arrived after learning of the shooting, his body lay there in a pool of blood. A crowd of neighbors, supporters, and reporters had gathered.

The country's white leaders were paralyzed, unsure how to respond to this latest, awful twist on the road to a negotiated settlement. It was Mandela who made a nationally televised address appealing for calm. In fact, he saved the day.

"Tonight I am reaching out to every single South African, black and white, from the very depths of my being," he said, in his formal, staccato delivery. "A white man, full of prejudice and hate, came to our country and committed a deed so foul that our whole nation now teeters on the brink of disaster. A white woman, of Afrikaner origin, risked her life so that we may know, and bring to justice, this assassin," referring to a Hani neighbor who followed the shooter and wrote down his license tag number.

"The cold-blooded murder of Chris Hani has sent shock waves throughout the country and the world. Now is the time for all South Africans to stand together against those who, from any quarter, wish to destroy what Chris Hani gave his life for—the freedom of all of us."

It was an incredible feat of political foresight and skill, and it brought the needed calm. Soon afterward, the government and the African National Congress, which had been bickering and unable to find common ground, agreed that democratic elections would take place on April 27, 1994, a year after Hani's death.

Mandela was elected the first president of a democratic South Africa. He took the oath of office on May 10, 1994.

• *19* •

Drawing Contempt

The Art of the Editorial Cartoonist

Kevin Kallaugher

I always thought that becoming a cartoonist would be difficult. I was wrong. Starting out is easy. Anybody can do it. Find a joke, draw a few people, use your very best penmanship to write a caption, and presto! You're a cartoonist!

Now try drawing another cartoon . . . then another. You soon discover, as I did, that becoming a cartoonist is easy. The hard part is keeping it up and getting paid for it. Harder still, in a climate where the profession is shrinking so rapidly, is to retire as a newspaper cartoonist.

At the start of the last century, there were about two thousand full-time editorial cartoonists in the United States. The number had withered to just above two hundred in the 1980s, and by 2015 there were fewer than forty.

I've been pretty fortunate. I estimate that I will have drawn as many as ten thousand original cartoons by the time I retire, due in large part to the nearly four thousand drawings I produced in my sixteen years as the daily cartoonist for the *Baltimore Sun*.

I joined the *Sun* in late 1988 after an eleven-year stint working as a cartoonist in England. American by birth, I had left the United States after graduating from Harvard to lead a bicycle tour of teenagers to the United Kingdom. I ended up staying longer, working first as a semi-professional basketball player and later as a street performer/caricaturist. In 1978, nine months after arriving, I landed my first job as a staff artist for the *Economist*. Over the course of the next decade, I built a substantial portfolio of cartoons which had been published in London for the *Economist* and other English dailies and periodicals, including the *Observer, Today,* and the *Sunday Tele-graph.*

In 1987, on the advice of a colleague, I sent my portfolio to Joseph Sterne, editorial page editor at the *Sun*. While happy raising a young family in England, I was curious about working in the United States. When the *Sun's* long-serving cartoonist Tom Flannery retired in 1988, Joe asked me to join his team.

I accepted the job on one condition: that I could continue to do my weekly cartoons for the *Economist*.

In 1988, the Internet was new, and, though no other artist may have tried, the *Economist's* art director, Aurobind Patel, was eager to use this new technology to deliver my artwork from across the globe. After some initial technical bumps, we eventually were able to build a system making me, I believe, the first artist to regularly use the web as a transmission vehicle. I would deliver two drawings to the *Economist* each week. At that time, I was creating five cartoons a week for the *Sun*.

How does an editorial cartoonist work? Let me describe a typical day.

I normally started my daily search for inspiration just after midnight. Tucked away in a studio at home, I used the Internet to check any late breaking news stories before I went to bed. CNN and C-SPAN also act as nocturnal cartoon subject advisors—and snooze inducers.

As I drifted off to sleep, I found that there was a fertile moment of clarity between the time when I was conscious and comatose. A surprising number of cartoon ideas come to me then. What is not surprising is that I rarely remember any of them.

My radio alarm goes off at 6:50 am. It's fixed to the news on National Public Radio (NPR). Despite its jarring early morning attack on my senses, NPR radio has become an indispensable friend in the morning.

It allowed me to get on with things—shaving, ironing, preparing breakfast, browbeating the children—while still learning about the world's happenings. I had NPR on in the car with my children as I drove them to school. They, too, had special feelings about its educational prowess. "Change the station!" they'd blurt. "Put some good music on!"

I would arrive at the office before 10 am and have until late afternoon to come up with a cartoon for the next day's paper. The morning hours were spent reading newspapers and periodicals, talking to colleagues, answering phone calls and letters, and, in between, desperately searching for some inspiration.

Letters from readers ranged from outrageous to the outlandish. A good 85 percent of the reaction to my cartoons was negative, and understandably so. If readers liked what they saw in the newspaper, they would not take the time to express their satisfaction. Yet if there was something in the paper that upset them, you were more likely to hear about it.

In Baltimore, pretty much every cartoon I drew would manage to annoy someone. Some of the letters I received posed intelligent counterpoints to

1. TAKE IN INFORMATION

Figure 19.1.   Four steps on how to draw cartoons.
Courtesy of KAL.

2. LOOK FOR IDEAS

Figure 19.2.
Courtesy of KAL.

my cartoons. But most were agitated, emotional, and often unsigned. I was attacked as too liberal by some, too conservative by others.

Some readers took the time to send me altered versions of my cartoons with personalized, sometimes obscene embellishments. My favorite letter remains one sent to my editor. I was away on vacation and the paper used a substitute cartoonist in my spot with a caption underneath announcing, "Kal is on vacation." The letter writer kept it brief: "I hope Kal is enjoying his vacation as much as we are."

National politicians rarely responded directly by letter or phone to the cartoons. Sometimes I would hear from an aide that the politician wanted the original of a cartoon to hang in his or her office. Some politicians

3. SKETCH OUT IDEAS

Figure 19.3.
Courtesy of KAL.

4. APPLY INK TO DRAWING

Figure 19.4.
Courtesy of KAL.

(Al Gore comes to mind) kept a collection of cartoons. No matter how roughly you might treat these public officials in your cartoons, they wanted to display it on their walls.

After Steve Forbes withdrew from the presidential race in 1996, he instructed the Forbes library to buy seventy-five less-than-flattering cartoon originals about him.

My daily searches for a cartoon idea would, at first, seem deceptively easy. I only had to look at the front page to find a host of subjects for comment. The trick was finding a compelling angle which would expose the irony or hypocrisy of a situation.

When searching for hypocrisy, I needed to look no further than our nation's politicians. Hypocrisy, dishonesty, and egotistic idiocy were a part of the everyday life in the White House, Congress, the State House, or City Hall. I may have been one of the few Americans who believed that my hard-earned taxes were being wisely spent when our elected representatives acted like members of Ringling Bros. and Barnum and Bailey Circus. Their continued antics provided me with a living.

Yet, despite the bountiful nonsense on display in the world of politics, I was not looking for a story with humorous potential when I scanned the newswires.

That's because unlike most cartoonists, the editorial cartoonist's job is not to make you laugh but to make you *think*. We use humor, but we use it as a vehicle for a message. The editorial cartoonist is really a visual columnist, using drawing, caricature, and satire to drive home a point.

So my search for subject material was primarily focused on finding vital stories to comment on. I also used other guidelines to help narrow my search.

I would try to keep a good mix of local, national, and international cartoons. I would also look to balance the temperament of the cartoons over the course of a week. One day I might deal with some serious weighty topic, then the next day leaven the mix with a lighter subject (the insanity of war one day, the inanity of weather, the next).

As I regarded each cartoon as one sentence in a long conversation with my readers, I felt it imperative to keep the conversation sparkling by supplying cartoons that were interesting, varied, and unpredictable. There were times when such guidelines failed, such as in the aftermath of 9/11 when a single subject gripped the news, the nation, and the cartoons for a prolonged period.

By late morning of a typical day, I should have decided on a subject and contrived an angle to tackle it. It would now be time to draw.

This stage of the process was both exhilarating and daunting. I started with a pad and a 2B pencil in front of me. I brainstormed on the paper often in small thumbnail sketches. To the untrained observer, the images would look like some indecipherable hieroglyphic. But to me these were finely honed, insightful, and inspired.

While I was sketching, I was thinking of the different forms of humor—overstatement, understatement, allegory, farce, etc.—and how I could employ them to deliver my message.

I was also thinking about caricature, perhaps the most powerful weapon at the disposal of an editorial cartoonist. A successful caricature was part portrait and part poison with an ability to tar a politician in a way no written word can.

Mastering the caricature of a politician was to me one of the most enjoyable challenges of my job. It was a curious process that has fascinated me for over thirty years.

Figure 19.5.   President Clinton's truth problem.
Courtesy of KAL.

JUST A NORMAL DAY AT THE NATION'S MOST IMPORTANT FINANCIAL INSTITUTION...

Figure 19.6.   A day at the Market.
Courtesy of KAL.

The first caricature I remember drawing was of a fifth-grade music teacher. She was an enthusiastic nun who had the habit of singing in utter rapture with her eyes firmly shut. One day while Sister was in full choral flow, I seized the moment to capture her on paper. I gave her a little button nose, curly hair, slits for eyes, and a mouth open wide enough to fit a battleship.

The cartoon was soon, surreptitiously, finding its way around the classroom. To my excitement, it was met with copious giggles and guffaws. The inevitable discovery of the offending drawing by the singing nun changed the mood of the class dramatically.

I was summarily marched down to the boy's lavatory by the teacher. There, she stood over me and ordered me to take a bite out of a bar of soap.

"Don't you ever draw another cartoon like that again!" she bellowed.

I've been drawing them ever since.

When drawing personalities for the *Baltimore Sun*, I didn't often get as close to my target as I did in fifth-grade music class. Occasionally, political leaders would come visit the editorial board at the paper and I would position myself across the table from them and sketch as they bloviated. But largely, I'd have to rely on photographs, television and, more importantly, the Internet, to supply me with the images from which I could gain inspiration.

The early caricatures of a new political figure are quite tame, often closely resembling the photographs. But over time, the caricatures became increasingly daring, distorted, and ridiculous. In some cases, the cartoons became so over-exaggerated that if you placed a photograph of a personality next to his or her caricature, you would be hard-pressed to see a resemblance. However, standing on its own, the caricature was widely recognized as being that of the intended target.

This was because the cartoon audience had learned over time what cartoon features symbolize which politician: Richard Nixon's heavy brow and ski slope nose, Bill Clinton's jutting chin and bulbous nose, and George W. Bush's big ears and baffled look.

By mid-afternoon, the pencil drawing of the day's cartoon would be in full flow. This stage would take approximately two to three hours.

This time was spent developing a thumbnail sketch of the chosen idea into a larger detailed pencil drawing. With the aid of a light box, I would do copious sketches and designs, experimenting with different compositions and concepts and perfecting caricatures. Over time, I would continue to refine the composite elements and assemble them into a completed pencil drawing that I would trace onto a high quality piece of smooth one-hundred-pound bond paper.

With completed sketch in hand, I would make the dutiful march to my editor's office for the official blessing.

During my time at the *Sun*, I was fortunate to have editors and publishers who granted me a great deal of freedom in my editorial commentaries. Part of this freedom was established in my original agreement with the paper in 1988, which granted me independence from the editorial position of the paper.

But with freedom comes responsibility. I took my responsibilities seriously. My meetings with my editors were routinely brief and professional. Ninety percent of my cartoon sketches would get the green light without a problem. Another 8 percent would receive constructive comments, often regarding text edits, spelling errors, and added elements. Approximately 2 percent of the time we'd have a longer discussion. If my bosses said, "We think you can do better," they were probably right.

With the editor's blessing, I could now move onto to the final chapter.

I would now spend the next three hours applying black India ink to the pencil artwork to make it fit for reproduction in the newspaper. As I inked, my emphasis shifted from being a journalist and commentator to being an artist. I had other considerations now—shading, texture, and calligraphy. Using century-old pen nibs, I dedicated myself to the lonely pursuit of applying ink to the cartoon. For hours I scratched, scratched, and scratched closer to the 6:30 pm deadline.

Near deadline, the drawing would soon be finished—well, not really finished. There was no drawing that couldn't be improved with twenty-four more hours spent working on it. So the drawing was not really finished, just stopped. I escorted it down to the composing room to be scanned for the next day's paper. When I looked at it, I saw nothing but the mistakes I had made and the lessons I could learn for my next cartoon.

On the way home in my car, my old friend NPR would be talking to me. I would look at my watch. Now 7:00 pm. I've just finished work and it's already time to start again—time to start working on tomorrow's cartoon.

With such a fulfilling job, I have always felt like I was awarded every day I came to the paper. Still, I have been doubly blessed over the years to receive recognition for my cartoons from outside organizations. I have won a number of awards in the United States and abroad, including the 1999, 2002, 2005, and 2014 Thomas Nast Award presented by the Overseas Press Club of America. In 2015, I was a finalist for the Pulitzer Prize in editorial cartooning. Also in 2015, I was honored to receive the Herblock Prize for Editorial Cartoonist of the year in the United States for a portfolio of cartoons for both the *Sun* and the *Economist*, which address quite different audiences.

The *Economist* is read worldwide by people I have no contact with. When I do a cartoon on a local subject for the *Sun*, you can pretty much guarantee the target of the ridicule will read the cartoon—and react to it.

William Donald Schaefer, who was mayor of Baltimore and then governor of Maryland, had a particularly thin skin when it came to criticism in general and cartoons in particular. After being lampooned for eight years as governor, he surprised me one day with a written request.

He sent me a letter asking for a cartoon for his personal collection. He wrote, "As you charge for these depressing monstrosities, I enclose herewith the value I place upon it." He taped a penny to the letter, and wrote "Overpaid" on the top of it.

Meanwhile, former Mayor Kurt Schmoke once had an entirely different response to one of my cartoons.

He recently told me that a cartoon I drew in 1991 actually changed public policy in Baltimore. The mayor was ready to take steps to dismember our city's unsavory red-light district better known as the Block. When I did a cartoon pointing out some of the flaws in his plan, the mayor took notice. He said the cartoon changed his mind. He scrapped his policy initiatives to blot out the Block.

I can now die happy knowing my gravestone will read: "Here lies *the idiot* who saved the Block." Actually, as a person who has a bad habit of tardiness (except cartoon deadlines), the inscription will more likely read: "Here lies the *late* Kevin Kallaugher."

Of the mass of cartoons I produced over the decades, a few stand out as favorites that still tickle me today.

The first is a classic on the insanity of Wall Street—often dubbed the "Buy! Sell!" cartoon (figure 19.6). It appeared in the *Sun* after the "Black Friday" minicrash of the stock market on October 13, 1989, sent investors reeling. The cartoon was an immediate hit and soon appeared in papers around the globe. Today, I continue to get regular requests to reuse the cartoon in books, periodicals, coffee mugs, prints . . . you name it.

My next favorite is a series of drawings I created in the 1990s called "Kaptain Keno." These cartoons appeared sporadically over several years and featured Governor Schaefer as a bumbling superhero championing a gambling game, Keno. The governor naturally hated it with a passion but readers embraced it.

Though I repeated my daily routine thousands of times, I never tired of it. I felt a distinct exhilaration every time I opened the newspaper and saw my handiwork on display.

Today, I get the same sense of excitement when I see my cartoons appear on my laptop, iPad, or smartphone. The home for cartoons is emigrating, and more people are viewing them than ever before.

In addition, a new generation of visual satirists is turning its skills toward visual commentary. These tech-savvy lampooners are not employing the ink and pen tools of past masters. Instead they are using animation, film, and pixels as their tools. I am very excited about the new prospects. As the opportunities shrink on paper, the doors are opening on the web.

We will see many more people around the globe confronting the vital issues of the day through the art of visual satire. New formats, platforms, and software will unleash new possibilities for creative critics to harness. In the same way that the technology of the printing press gave us the cartoon of today, these new technologies will shape the cartoon of tomorrow.

I welcome the prospect of a new generation of online cartoonists. I wish them good luck and Godspeed as they start their long challenging careers. They will need it.

As I know, starting out as a cartoonist is easy. Retiring as one is the hard part.

20

Just North of Pleasant

Laura Lippman

Although I am and will always be a Baltimorean, there came a time in my life when my husband and I also became part-time citizens of New Orleans. Once, asked to give directions to our home there, I said, "Oh, we live just one block from Harmony. In fact, that's going to be the memoir of our marriage: One Block from Harmony." My husband tried to top me: "And Two Blocks from Pleasant." Ah, but the second take is never as sharp as the first, something I am allowed to say because I was a second-generation *Sun* reporter. A chip off the old block, and the chip is always smaller than the block.

Baltimore has a Pleasant Street, too, and it happens that I met my husband just north of there, in the *Sun* newsroom. Between the *Sun* and Pleasant lies Bath Street, a one-block road that had no real purpose once the printing presses and loading docks were moved to Port Covington in the 1990s. Bath Street now has one of those red-and-white "honorary" street signs, for Eugene "Skid" Dailey, who died in 2011 from pancreatic cancer at the age of sixty. I'm sure that Mr. Dailey's long career with the city's transportation department is worthy of this tribute, but I wish Bath Street had been reserved for an employee of the Sunpapers, preferably my father, who worked there from 1965 through 1995.

If not my father, then maybe Johnny Ketchum, the editorial assistant for the *Evening Sun*, whose malapropisms so delighted the staff that we kept a running tally in a file slugged Ketchumisms. Or Vida Roberts, the *Evening Sun* fashion editor, who was cruised by Robert Mitchum when only fourteen and once confided that a certain *Sun* editor, while handsome in his youth, was the kind of man no woman ever dated twice. "Too boring," said Vida. Or—well, the list could go on and on, beyond the newsroom, beyond the dead, even beyond the list of people I actually like. But I would, of course, put my father first, and not just because he was my father. In my memory, the story of the *Sun* and my family begins on, is forever intertwined with Bath Street.

Theo Lippman Jr. took a job as an editorial writer at the *Sun* in 1965. He was the Washington correspondent for the *Atlanta Constitution* at the time. His decision landed, as I recall, with a kind of soap opera intensity at our dinner table in Alexandria, Virginia. My stoic mother cried. My older sister, Susan, took me aside and told me foreboding things about our future hometown. A few years later, I would read a wonderful children's book, in which a brother and sister learn they must spend the summer in Baltimore while their father has an operation at Johns Hopkins. The girl looks up the city's encyclopedia entry and reads: "The eighth largest city in the United States, population 859,100. Chief industries, iron and steel, straw hats et cetera. She . . . shut her eyes, seeing a sky flaming with the orange of many steel forges, while in the black iron foundries below, 859,100 dark figures labored, all wearing straw hats."

859,100—the book was published in 1956. Sometimes, living in Baltimore makes one feel a little like Gloria Swanson in *Sunset Boulevard*. It's the city that got small—the city and the newspaper.

Yet the Orleans Street viaduct, looming over Bath Street, seemed enormous then and enormous now. The first time I saw it, in August 1965, we had just visited my father's new office, a proper office with a door. That was a big deal in 1965. It would be a bigger deal now in the era of open space offices. We did not yet know where we were going to live, but we knew where my father was going to work. A freak summer storm swept through suddenly, the rain so heavy that my father did not dare drive. We sat snug on Bath Street, curtains of water streaming from the viaduct. It was glorious. Baltimore appeared magical to me, a place where you could sit out a storm, untouched by the raindrops.

At the time, it would never have occurred to me that I would report to work at the red brick building just north of Pleasant. I did not want to be a reporter, although I had already banged out my first story on my father's portable typewriter despite the handicap of knowing no word other than "pig." I wanted to be Supergirl. At night, I fell asleep while making up stories in which I had an array of super powers, including being blonde. I never learned to fly, but thirty-five years later I discovered that being blonde was actually a power available to almost any woman willing to pay for it. The gray hair that I covered at age forty was natural enough, a genetic inheritance on my mother's side. But the gray accelerated alarmingly when I turned forty-one and entered what would be my last year at the *Sun*. What else broke, deteriorated in that awful, final year? My teeth, stressed by grinding until my molars cracked and I spat them into my hand; my back, suddenly prone to going out; my first marriage, although that was not the paper's fault. To steal a joke from my second father-in-law: I spent twelve years at the *Sun*. They were eleven of the happiest years of my life.

But in 1965, this is what I knew about newspaper life and the Sunpapers: (1) it was a source of endless reams of copy paper, which my father brought home for my sister and me to draw on; (2) it had free long-distance, a so-called wide area telephone service (WATS) line, on which my father called his parents every Sunday; and (3) the boss was named Schmick. Once, when my mother drove past the building, I waved out the car, "You make a good beer, Mr. Schmick." Publisher Schmick, beer maker Schlitz—they sounded the same to my young ears.

I did not really understand what my father did when he was at 501 North Calvert. He was an editorial writer, but what is an editorial writer when you are a child? I told people that my father had a job in which he told others what to think. I was not particularly interested in the news unless it involved someone my age and/or murder. The murder of someone my age was the most intriguing story of all. I did not understand why my father followed politicians around or what happened at the political conventions he attended. I knew enough to hate Nixon and I understood why my father had to shave his beard the year he worked on the book about Spiro Agnew. With a beard, he would look like a "hippie," even in his seersucker suits.

As far as I knew, my father was happy in his job, or happy-ish. Maybe that's why, when it came time to think about college and career, I chose journalism. Because by then, I really did want to write and I couldn't see how else one made money writing full-time. I knew lots and lots of journalists. They came to our house, played poker with my father, smoked and laughed into the night. I did not know any novelists, although it was novels I was trying to write, even then.

So journalism was never a passion. It was a pragmatic decision, although the professors at Northwestern University's Medill School of Journalism immediately set out to disabuse me of this notion when I enrolled in 1977. "If every working journalist in the country died today," my adviser told the freshmen assigned to him, "there would be too many journalism majors in college to fill those jobs."

My parents were paying a lot of money for such pep talks, which continued for the next four years. And, perhaps because of that money, my father often despaired of the grades I brought home in my early years at Northwestern. The writing was on the wall. The writing was in my work. In journalism, I couldn't even scrape together a B average; my Medill classes pulled down what otherwise would have been a stellar GPA. Yet in my creative writing classes, where Professor Meredith Steinbach said she would give A's only to those who showed true professional promise, I earned straight A's.

Still, when graduation loomed, I did not consider pursuing an MFA in fiction. I wanted to make a living as a writer, not teach others to write. With much of the country in recession in 1981, I ended up at the *Waco Tribune-Herald*, an indirect beneficiary of nepotism; my previous summer internship at the *Atlanta Constitution* had been given to me solely because of my father's association with that paper. The *Tribune-Herald* hired me because it was owned by the same chain.

That would be the last time that my father's "connections" yielded anything for me, just for the record. Over the next eight years, whenever I applied to the *Sun*—and I applied almost every year—I was rebuffed. That is, I was rebuffed if anyone bothered to reply at all. There was one editor, no need to name him here, who kept assuring my father: "I'm going to call Laura back right now!" He never did. One day, he would be my boss. Surprise, surprise, I wasn't one of his favorites.

Finally, in the spring of 1988, a *Sun* editor gave me the courtesy of a return phone call. By then, I had seven years' experience under my belt, five in a truly competitive market in San Antonio, Texas. I had covered cops, general assignment, education, features, and politics. But I wasn't a good enough *writer* to work for the *Sun*, the editor explained to me. My style was not suitable. "What are you looking for?" I asked. "What characterizes the *Sun* style?" A *Sun* writer, I was told, could make a ho-hum event interesting primarily through his or her dazzling words.

"I read the *Sun* very closely whenever I'm home," I told the editor. "I have to say, I don't think you have many writers like that. Maybe Rafael Alvarez, or Sandy Banisky." (It would be a better story if I had invoked the name of the man who became my second husband, David Simon, but the truth is I didn't really notice him until he spilled coffee on my desk four years later.)

The editor was quick on his feet, I'll give him that. "That's why we need more of them," he replied.

Ah, well. I covered the 1988 presidential election, hating every minute of it. I received a grant to study Spanish in Mexico, which made sense for a reporter in San Antonio. I have no idea how John Fairhall of the *Evening Sun* persuaded the National Press Foundation that it also made sense for him, but I am always grateful it worked out that way. Because it was Fairhall who called me in the summer of 1989 to tell me that the *Evening Sun* had five openings, just like that. But the bosses were cheap, he said. They would never pay for my fare back to Baltimore for an interview. I should just fly home and pretend I was there on vacation.

I took his advice. It was my decision to cloak my identity. The metro desk at the *Evening Sun* wouldn't necessarily know I was the daughter of Theo Lippman Jr. I rolled the dice and charged a terrifyingly expensive plane ticket for a three-day weekend.

My father drove me to the interview, of course. Did we plan some ruse, part company a block or two out from Calvert Street so we would not be seen together? Did he let me out on Bath Street? I don't remember. I do remember sighing in the car: "Looking for a job is awful."

"Yes," said my father, who at that moment had held the same job for twenty-four years. "And if you don't mind my saying so, you go about it all wrong."

Why would anyone mind hearing *that* just minutes before a job interview? Yet I got the job. They figured out before it was over whose daughter I was—they were good newsmen, Mike Shultz and Ernie Imhoff—but that only heightened their respect for me. I started at the *Evening Sun* in August 1989. The *Evening Sun* would be subsumed into the *Sun* in 1991, gone forever by 1995, the year my father (and the man would become my second husband) took buyouts. I would end up working at the Sunpapers for twelve years. As I noted: eleven of the happiest years of my life.

The best years were at the *Evening Sun*—anarchic, tolerant of eccentric personalities as long as they met their deadlines. We had "wing parties," eating chicken wings after meeting the mid-day Friday deadline, our last of the week. We hired a stripper for Sue Miller on her eightieth birthday, bought a retirement cake for Peter Kumpa with the salutation, "So long, fascist," echoing his daily goodbye as he strolled through the newsroom. (Only a Hampden bakery spelled it "fascest," so Leslie Walker and I had to do some magic with a toothpick.) We consulted a Ouija board, asking H. L. Mencken when we would fold. "2 ED" the Ouija board foretold. "TWO EDITIONS!" we yelled in glee. The sage of Baltimore was not far wrong.

Staffs were merged, new editors arrived, and buyouts were used to avoid layoffs. On my eleventh anniversary, almost to the day, things went pear-shaped for me. I know that's a Britishism, one that a *Sun* copy editor would excise, but it's the best word here. I felt like a once-fit person who was suddenly flabby and potbellied. I was in the doghouse—the Baltimore County bureau had two kinds of reporters: young ones on their way up and middle-aged ones on their way out, and it was my burgeoning career as a novelist that had marked me as a target. The truth was out; I had outed it: fiction, not journalism, was my true passion. Maybe I shouldn't have told that one editor that I'd rather win an Edgar Award for mystery writing than a Pulitzer. (FYI: I did.)

My father said the math was irrefutable: "If you're doing something else, you're not giving them your all." But they did not pay for my "all." They paid for forty hours a week, with overtime mandated by the union contract. I prized my ability to do my job and do it well within the confines of the forty-hour week. I didn't understand why slower writers, duller writers, were more prized just because they were always *there*, sitting at their computers, obsessing over their copy. I, too, could have stayed late in the night, putting commas in, taking commas out. I preferred to leave on time and I didn't consider that a character flaw.

I also put in for overtime and invoked the contract when my rights were violated. Yeah, that made me really popular.

But, no, I wasn't passionate about my work. I wasn't a *natural*, only the daughter of one. Now that I'm married to a natural, a man whose nostrils quiver when there's smoke on the horizon, I get it. But I couldn't fake it then and I probably couldn't fake it now. I was a solid reporter. I was twice selected by *Baltimore* magazine as the *Sun's* best writer. On the rare occasions these days that I do some reporting, I am rigorous and thorough, well aware that it's harder than making stuff up in the privacy of my office. But I knew what I really wanted, and when the brass ring came looming into view—a contract for three novels that exceeded my annual *Sun* salary by almost 100 percent—I took it.

My father was terrified for me. "Stay," he said. "Memories are short, they don't have the discipline to be cruel to the same person forever." I fear he spoke from experience. Still, I leapt. It was 2001, just weeks after 9/11. In my timing, I was ridiculously, improbably lucky. Changes were coming, technological changes that would reduce paid circulation, gutting advertising in turn. The *Sun's* first layoffs were only a few years away. I predicted none of it. I just knew I wanted to be a full-time novelist.

My father, meanwhile, had been freelancing since his retirement in 1995, and suddenly saw his assignments dwindle, dwindle, dwindle. So many people were writing for free now. And he would not write for free. I love him for that. Did his diminishing assignments lead to his diminishing faculties? I don't know. But it didn't help. Yet he remained a newsman at heart, even as he found it harder and harder to read a newspaper. Almost literally until his dying day, his memory fogged, his wit still dry but not so quick, the one thing my father always asked me was: "What do you hear from Calvert Street?"

I understand now that my father was not always happy in his office at 501 North Calvert Street, even if he was always aware that the mere fact of having an office was a pretty cool thing. (He had a dartboard with Agnew's picture on it for a time, but they made him take it down because the copy boys were spending too much time in his office.) I know that anyone who puts together more than a few years in journalism will have a mix of good years and bad years. That's what all jobs are, a mixture of good and bad. But it's easier to take the bad if you genuinely love what you do.

When my father died in December 2014, a friend brought me old photos of an impromptu party in the *Sun's* editorial offices. There is my father, looking as gleeful as I've ever seen him, yet standing next to an absolute schmuck of a man he probably didn't like very much. My father was a grown-up in a way I never quite managed. I could not smile, standing next to the schmucks. And that, much as anything, ended my career at the *Sun*. The schmucks took over, inside the building and out, and I couldn't pretend to be happy about it.

When I was twenty-two, I made the opposite of a Faustian bargain. I kept my soul when I went into journalism, accepting that it was not my first love, but determined to do my best despite an absence of passion. In return, I was offered not much money, but a lot of fun. It was a life just north of Pleasant, you might say. That was the compact. When the compact was broken, when newspaper life became increasingly corporate and rigid, I left. Fiction is my true love and has enriched me more than I deserve, but I never forget that I was lucky enough to work in newspapers when it was *fun*. "The life of kings," as Mencken said. And queens, too, Mr. Mencken. We had our day as well.

Which reminds me of my favorite Ketchumism: the *Evening Sun* Society Editor, Sylvia Badger, was going to the ladies room, but she was much too proper to say it that way. Asked by Johnny where she was headed, she said with prim elegance: "I'm going where the queen goes alone."

Johnny said: "Where I live, the queens never go alone."

Oh, okay, I'll concede Bath Street to Ketchum.

* * *

My favorite among the regular editorial page columns my father wrote under the rubric *Notes & Comment* was this one, which appeared on December 19, 1981, with the headline "God on Trial." The column won him recognition by the American Society of Newspaper Editors as the best commentary writer of the year. It is reprinted here with permission from the *Baltimore Sun* (all rights reserved).

God on Trial

Judge: Call the next witness.

Bailiff: God!

ACLU Attorney: I object! God is not on trial here.

Arkansas Attorney General: He's an expert witness.

Bailiff: Do You swear to tell the truth, the whole truth and nothing but the truth so help me You?

God: Of course.

A.G.: Where were You in the beginning?

God: I was hovering over the void.

A.G.: And what did You do?

God: I separated light from darkness, created the firmament, earth, vegetation, the heavenly bodies, birds, fish, beast, and man.

A.G.: The latter in Your own image?

God: Yep.

A.G.: No further questions.

Judge: Cross-examination?

ACLU: Yes, your honor. You are the Supreme Being? the Creator? the First Cause?

God: Numero Uno, that's Me.

ACLU: So who created the void, which preceded You?

God: You don't create voids. Voids are, like, nothing. Formless. Chaos.

ACLU: But You said You were hovering over the void. How do You hover over nothing?

God: You're just playing with words. It's a question of semantics. Let's define our terms.

Judge: Get on with it.

ACLU: Okay, when You were listing Your accomplishments You were reading from something. What was it?

God: Genesis. I needed to jog My memory. It was a long time ago.

ACLU: Who wrote Genesis?

God: I dictated it to Moses.

ACLU: Did he get it exactly right?

God: Oh, close enough. This was before shorthand, you know.

ACLU: It says here creation took six days. It says You created sea creatures and birds one day, beasts and man the next. Is that correct? Man after the lower animals?

God: Oh, yes. That I remember very well.

ACLU: Was a day 24 hours, as it is now, or could it have been, say, a million years or more?

A.G.: I object!

Judge: Over-ruled.

God: I guess it could have been a million years. I'm not even sure I said "day," now that you mention it. That may have been Moses's word.

ACLU: Is it possible that what Genesis really says is that man evolved—

A.G.: Objection! Objection!

Judge Over-ruled.

ACLU: —from the lower creatures after a day of millions of years?

God: Well, again, it's a question of semantics. I guess you might put it that way.

ACLU: No further questions.

Judge: Re-direct?

A.G.: Are you now or have you ever been a secular humanist? . . .

—*Theo Lippman Jr.*

21

Doubling Up in Moscow

Kathy Lally

When the Soviet Union collapsed in 1991, sending seismic shifts through Russia, my family felt the reverberations. My husband Will Englund and I shared a job as *Sun* Moscow correspondent from 1991 to 1995 and again from 1997 to 2001, and our two daughters couldn't help but take personally the world-changing events we witnessed.

In October 1993, Russia was in the middle of a constitutional crisis. President Boris Yeltsin was struggling with the parliament, which was thwarting his plans for reform. After months of acrimony, Yeltsin dissolved the parliament and called elections. But some of the legislative leaders—including Speaker Ruslan Khasbulatov and Vice President Alexander Rutskoi—organized a vote to impeach Yeltsin and then holed up in the Russian White House, the seat of parliament, to defy him.

Yeltsin ordered tanks to surround the building, and when they noisily rolled past our apartment one night, seven-year-old Molly gazed out her bedroom window with a troubled look. "Mom," she said, turning to me, "does this mean no Halloween?"

We had arrived in Moscow in June 1991 to take over from Scott Shane and his family. Kate turned nine a few weeks later and Molly was five. The *Sun* Moscow bureau had a long history. The *Sun* was one of the first American papers to set up a permanent office not long after Stalin's death in 1953. The bureau was in the coveted building—restricted to journalists and diplomats—on Sadovaya-Samotechnaya Street, desirable because it had been built by German prisoners of war, assuring good workmanship rare in the city, and was just under two miles from the Kremlin. A subway stop was around the corner next to the Moscow Circus.

Our apartment was across the hall from the office—handy for dealing with the eight-hour time difference with Baltimore because you could file a story at midnight Moscow time and fall into bed a minute later. Our neighbors included the offices and families of the *New York Times*, *Los Angeles Times*, *Christian Science Monitor*, *Financial Times*, Reuters, BBC, and CBS. Soviets—and Russians—knew the *Sun* from hearing American-financed broadcasts penetrating the Iron Curtain and quoting *Sun* articles.

Scott and his wife Francie had turned over their lives to us—a mostly furnished apartment along with friends for us and our daughters, a car, and an office staffed as required by the Soviet authorities with an assistant/translator, a driver, and a housekeeper. We brought the kitchen sink with us—boxes of Ikea cabinets bought in Baltimore to remodel the aging kitchen with materials unavailable in Russia and too pricey for us to import from Scandinavia.

Our first big story was Yeltsin's inauguration July 10, 1991. We had studied Russian in a three-month immersion program in Monterey, California, and had diligently plowed through a reading list Scott had compiled for us. But if today's correspondent has access to oceans of information on the Internet, we had relatively tiny droplets to absorb. Our file cabinets bulged with newspaper clips from our predecessors (one favorite of mine—Michael Parks traveling to Tajikistan in the mid-1970s, where it was so hot he fried an egg on the sidewalk). We got feeds from the Telegraph Agency of the Soviet Union (TASS) and from Reuters, walking over to that office twice a day to pull carbon copies of news from their wires.

Not only were there no cell phones, but our fax machine had to be registered with the authorities, who also had records of the models and serial numbers of our computers. There were no direct-dial calls out of the country; a telephone call to Baltimore, London, or Helsinki had to be booked through an attentive Moscow operator. At least we didn't have to take copies of our stories to the main telegraph office for transmission to Baltimore as correspondents once had to do. Having finished writing a story, we punched out a tape that we then fed through our own telex, shipping our work off to the *Sun's* wire room in Baltimore.

There were few restaurants in Moscow in those days, so the US Embassy allowed us journalists to join their community association, giving us access to the cafeteria, where we would gather at lunchtime on Fridays to pick up our mail sent through the US Embassy in Helsinki, another privilege granted because of lack of any alternative.

One Friday I asked Fen Montaigne, the *Philadelphia Inquirer* correspondent, for advice on covering this impossibly enormous and opaque empire, stretching over eleven time zones. "Your big advantage," he said, "is your fresh eyes."

I repeated those words to myself as I wrote the story of Yeltsin's inauguration. The Soviet Union was still stumbling along, but its largest constituent,
the Russian Federation, had just chosen a president, the first freely elected
chief magistrate in Russia's long history.

I watched, and I wrote:

> Boris N. Yeltsin was inaugurated yesterday as president of a Russia that
> is creating itself day by day, a state still so unformed that there was no
> Supreme Court justice to administer the newly written oath of office and
> no official words for the new national anthem.
>
> As he sat in the crowd of people's deputies, awaiting his moment at
> the rostrum, he looked like a man fully aware of his moment in history, a
> man who felt the weight of the past and foresaw the dimensions of what
> lay ahead.
>
> He looked like a man who had not slept well the night before.
>
> He looked, even, like a man who half expected tanks to circle the Krem-
> lin while the KGB carried him off.

About ten weeks later, tanks were indeed circling the Kremlin—and the
Russian White House where Yeltsin presided over the Russian Federation.
He prevailed, and the head of the KGB was carried off to jail, not Yeltsin. At
the end of the year, the Soviet Union disintegrated.

The failed coup of August 1991 opened an extraordinary window for
journalists, and we tumbled through with open notebooks. The coup had
offered a lifetime of experience in three days as we watched Yeltsin climb
up on one of the tanks aimed at his White House, the tanks turning their
guns away later that night, thousands of Muscovites camping out around the
White House to protect it with their bodies, purposeful, for once believing
they could determine their own fate.

Of course, a few blocks away, life went on as usual. On the second day of
the coup, I watched in astonishment as a linebacker of a middle-aged woman
presiding over a nearby metro station grabbed a slight man whom she caught
ducking the five-kopeck fare. She held him and shouted for a cop while the
government teetered outside and history changed course.

Not only did we learn about people in those three days, we picked up the
geography of the city and its surroundings. Dodging roadblocks, we studied
the side streets. When I drove sixty miles south to Serpukhov to report on
the effect of the coup outside of Moscow, it took me three circles around
the Garden Ring before I could figure out how to get off the road and onto
the right exit. Our friend Andrei Mironov—introduced by Scott—sat beside
me offering little help. He had been a dissident, a courageous inmate of the
gulag who knew how to parry the KGB. But like so many other, he traveled
by subway and had no idea how to navigate above ground.

Figure 21.1.   Boris Yeltsin drives the Soviet Union to a breakup, frightening his passenger Mikhail Gorbachev.
Courtesy of KAL.

We got to Serpukhov to find that half the people we talked to had rushed into the Communist Party offices to pay their back dues and the other half had torn up their party cards. Some had no idea there had been a coup until it was over. Andrei himself had called us the first night of the coup. He asked us to take his address book and hide it. The KGB would be rounding him up, he was sure. He didn't want to incriminate his friends. Of course we agreed, full of fear at taking on the KGB so soon after our arrival. The coup failed before they had a chance to come for him, and Andrei became the closest of friends—steadfast, warm, insightful, the bravest of the brave. He fought every day of his life to make his country better, and he would die in the effort. He was killed in May 2014, hit by a shell, bearing witness to the Russian incursion in Ukraine.

Will and I had arrived in a country where foreign correspondents were required to get permission from the Foreign Ministry before they could travel to other parts of the Soviet Union. Many cities and roads were closed to them. For just a drive outside the city—beyond a twenty-four-mile limit—you had to file a detailed itinerary with the authorities. Now, our job sharing was an enormous advantage for the paper. The *Sun* had two correspondents in what had always been a one-person bureau. During the coup, we had page 1 bylines every single day for a few months, and multiple stories in the first days of the coup. (We started out each paid for about five-eighths of a job and eventually each got three-quarters.) And as the former Soviet Union was opening up, one of us could be on the road while the other was ready to cover news from Moscow.

We had begun sharing a job in 1983, an unusual arrangement for a rather conservative company. It hadn't been so many years earlier when the *Sun* expected a woman to leave the paper if she married someone on the staff.

I had been hired on the copy desk in 1975. Women were scattered around the newsroom then, but few were in a position of authority. One evening, the formidable Francis X. Whittie, the makeup editor who transmitted newsroom instructions to the composing room, was told to teach me the ropes so I could fill in on the job.

He marched me down a flight of stairs and into the center of the composing room, which still jangled with metal type. "All right, you animals," he roared. "See this woman? Don't even *think* of touching her."

I came to appreciate the men in the composing room. I never touched their type—an uncrossable line—and they kindly helped me do my job, offering to chip the metal tail off a comma to make a period if something didn't fit on the page, helping me read upside down and backwards. Once, when I went down to the composing room to get coffee, returning after four years in Moscow, one of the printers gave me a welcoming shout. "Where you been?" he called out. "On day work?"

From the copy desk, I went to a reporting job on the *Sun's* first suburban section—a weekly called Arundel Living—when it was created in 1977. From there, it was editor of the section, then weekend metro editor, Sunday features editor, and eventually assistant managing editor (AME) for features, the first woman AME at the paper.

Will and I had married in 1980, and after our first daughter was born in 1982, I planned to take a leave and return as AME. But once at home, I was conflicted. I didn't want to put in the long hours that consumed me on features. But I didn't want to quit, certain I would be forgotten as soon as I was gone and my career over.

We came up with a solution, proposing sharing a job as a metro reporter. The metro editor by then was Steven M. Luxenberg, who knew us and our work well and fought hard to make the job sharing happen.

There was a great deal of talk around the country about job sharing in those days, but not much actually happened. In our case, we ran into problems with the union. Management agreed to our arrangement, but didn't want to establish a policy. The Newspaper Guild argued that it should be open to anyone who qualified under whatever rules were set up. Eventually both sides agreed to let us try without setting a precedent. No one ever followed us. Dividing up benefits and responsibilities was too difficult if you weren't married.

Will and I both thought we would be heading off to the sidelines of our careers. Wrong. Wrong. Wrong. Covering education, one of us would work for about six weeks while the other would stay home; then we would switch. While working, we could stay as late as we had to without worrying about relieving a babysitter or neglecting our daughters. They were home with a parent. We could devote all of our energies to the job—and to the kids.

The paper got used to it quickly. We would switch when we felt the rhythm was right, as in not in the middle of a big breaking story or a project. All we had to do was tell Pat McLellan, the managing editor's assistant, that we were switching, and she would notify payroll.

The big disadvantage was living on a single paycheck, but we would fill in on other jobs from time to time—Will sometimes worked as weekend metro editor while I was working Monday through Friday, or one of us would fill in as editor of the Sunday Perspective section, which could be done nine to five in a babysitter-friendly way. The paper liked the available backup and we liked the periodic extra money.

We shared the education job for about eight years. It turned out we were in good position for the Moscow job. The Soviet Union could be a forbidding place for a spouse, with little opportunity to work and a partner who was always on the job. A job-sharing couple solved the problem.

Richard O'Mara, then the foreign editor, reflexively designated Will as the bureau chief. Scott Shane thought that was sexist and informed the Soviet authorities that I was the bureau chief. And so I was.

I never forgot that the *Sun* was an institution at the heart of a community and that I was writing primarily for its readers—our readers. I felt I understood what interested them. I also had a feeling as a reporter that they were looking over my shoulder as I tried to make sense of what was going on in the world and why they should care.

Our readers gave us our distinctive voice. When we went into KGB headquarters, or anywhere else, it seemed they were by our side.

August 1991:
   MOSCOW—All this coup business has the KGB rather put out. They'd been working tirelessly to improve their image, and then their boss gets himself arrested for overthrowing the government.

"I've worked for a year and a half to create a new image," Col. Vladimir Maslennikov, first deputy chief of the KGB press center, lamented yesterday. "Now, it's smashed—suddenly smashed. The coup has thrown the KGB back to 1953 or 1954."

The new public relations mood before the coup last week was so infectious that the inventive Moscow district office even came up with a beautiful Miss KGB.

Now every time the men of the Committee for State Security look out their front windows, they are reproached by a different image: the empty base of the statue of their founder, Felix Dzerzhinsky, who once proclaimed, "We stand for organized terror."

The huge, 14-ton statue of "Bloody Felix," standing in his greatcoat in the middle of the expansive square outside KGB headquarters, was unceremoniously pulled from its pedestal last Friday while thousands of Muscovites cheered.

We took *Baltimore Sun* readers to the frontlines of the Chechen war. They watched as an American company introduced pet food to Russia, as Yeltsin quit the presidency and turned it over to Vladimir Putin, as the well-connected divided up the wealth of the Soviet Union, as Russians lost faith in a better future.

The *Sun's* reach gave Baltimore standing. Ordinary citizens and public officials throughout the former republics of the Soviet Union would give us interviews because they wanted their voices heard in the United States, in Baltimore, in Maryland.

Once, in March 1993 when legislators were accusing Yeltsin of being drunk while addressing them, the Russian president surveyed the ornate hall, looking for a foreign reporter. His eye fell on me, and he marched up to assure me that he certainly was not drunk, only grief-stricken from his mother's death. Of course I passed the word on to my readers:

MOSCOW—Boris N. Yeltsin was missing his usual boisterousness yesterday when he walked into the dazzling gilt-and-white Kremlin hall built for czars.

But he wanted to make it clear he was not drunk.

He paused at the hall's magnificent gold doors that rise nearly fifty feet to the arched ceiling until his eye fell upon a Western reporter interviewing a member of the Russian Congress.

Mr. Yeltsin headed straight for the reporter, firmly shook her hand and stood expectantly, waiting for questions. The president of Russia was showing the world he was sober and in control, even if physically suffering both from days of abuse at the hands of an antagonistic legislature and from the anguish of his mother's death. . . .

"Do you see me?" Mr. Yeltsin said, in a clear, level voice. "Look at me. I'm speaking to you right after my speech. Look at me." The president looked steadily into the face before him, his eyes glistening slightly but unblinking and not at all red.

"I haven't slept for three nights," he said.

He spoke and walked slowly, almost stiffly, like a person who felt unwell, or had a bad headache—or hadn't slept for three days. . . .

"I was very close to my mother," he said yesterday. "We were friends. We survived the war together and we saw famine together and we lived in a barracks together, and that's why it's very difficult for me to get used to the idea I have lost her."

But as he stood in St. George Hall, Mr. Yeltsin seemed to gather strength from the very walls. A bas relief of St. George slaying the dragon loomed over his shoulder.

The hall was dedicated to czarist Russia's highest military decoration; gold-engraved marble slabs line the walls, summoning forth heroes who vanquished foes more terrible, even, than a Congress of People's Deputies.

"I will hold on," Mr. Yeltsin said. "I will stick to my point of view. My stand is firm, and I will not retreat."

He died in April 2007. At the end of that year, the *Sun* closed the Moscow bureau. Two eras had ended. Without its own reporters in place, news of the world was not an imperative in the pages of the *Sun*. A staff byline commanded attention and space on the news pages. A wire report of far-off events was always expendable.

The foreign bureaus were just one mark of the paper's ambition. In 1997, between our two tours in Russia for the *Sun*, Will devoted most of the year to investigating the shipbreaking industry, winning the 1998 Pulitzer Prize for investigative reporting.

We were traveling outside of Russia, on a springtime vacation to Ireland, just before the prizes were to be announced. John Carroll, the *Sun's* editor, called Will and told him to interrupt the trip and come to Baltimore. We were in the newsroom with our two daughters when the announcement came.

Later, Kate would tell my sister how her life had again been disrupted, like so so many times before, by the demands of the *Baltimore Sun*.

"I hate it when that happens," she said.

22

Balkan Road Trip

Dan Fesperman

At seven o'clock on a fine May morning along the Adriatic coast, the phone rings on the bedside table, signaling that it's time to go to war. You hesitate before picking up the receiver, because you know the caller is your traveling companion, a correspondent from Finland who will issue the day's first marching orders. After a mostly sleepless night, you're wondering if he shares your reluctance.

Finally, you say hello. He replies in a caffeinated rush of Nordic vowels.

"Hello Dan, it's Kalle. Are you ready to rock and roll?"

Well, that's one question answered.

"Sure. See you downstairs?"

"Half an hour."

Thus began my first journey into Bosnia in 1993, a road trip from the Croatian port city of Split, which, for all my reservations, led to one of the most memorable weeks of my life. Even at the time it felt remarkable, a sometimes spooky and often exhilarating procession through a land of dark wonders. It was also useful, a crash course on covering a patchwork war of irregular armies and shifting alliances. Each town and every mountain seemed to impart a valuable lesson on how to navigate in a world without order.

Only in retrospect have I realized how lucky I was to be there at all, poking around on someone else's dime as I witnessed small moments of history with the freedom to write about them however I chose. It was the tail end of an era in which the *Sun* still planted its flag in bureaus around the world. A little more than three years later, my bureau in Berlin was gone, as were the ones in Tokyo and Mexico City. By the end of 2007, they had all disappeared, and the paper's corporate overlords no longer had the money or inclination to send correspondents to places with baffling grudges and unpronounceable

Figure 22.1. *Sun* correspondent Dan Fesperman and teenage shepherd boys near Jalalabad, Afghanistan, November 18, 2001, just after witnessing a tense standoff between two mujahideen groups seeking to fill the vacuum of power left by the departure of Taliban forces. The next day, Fesperman and several colleagues just missed being ambushed by Taliban fighters who did seize the following two cars in a convoy of journalists and murdered four international reporters.
Courtesy of Michael Kamber, the *Village Voice*.

names. As with so much in life, timing was everything, and I'm nearly as grateful for that bit of good fortune as I am for having emerged unscathed.

A careworn Kummerly & Fry map survives from that trip. The cover is gone and the folds are tearing, but my blue ink scribbles of battlefronts and favored routes still mark its villages and mottled gray ridgelines. I need only trace a finger down the red and yellow roadways to be back on those narrow, twisting blacktops, creeping through a village of silent ruins while gunfire chatters in the distance; or approaching a checkpoint in the pines at the crest of a hill, stomach aflutter as I hope that the bearded, well-armed fellows looming just ahead are sober enough to let us pass without a hassle, bribe, or worse.

Also surviving are my tan reporter's notebooks, dated on the covers, the yellowing pages filled with my awful handwriting. By reading them, I can reenter that week and proceed hour by hour, page by page.

There is hardly anything in those notes about Kalle Koponen, the correspondent for Finland's largest newspaper, *Helsingin Sanomat*, whom I traveled with that week, but I remember him well: tall and rangy, with piercing blue-gray eyes and a blond brush cut; late twenties, but he smoked a pipe, which made him seem older. Or maybe it just felt that way because he was making his fourth trip into Bosnia. I leaned heavily on his experience, and he was generous in teaching me the rules of the road. We shared expenses, a translator, and his rental Lada Niva, a powder blue, Russian-made, off-road vehicle that creaked and groaned on every curve, its shock absorbers as worn as an old man's knees. His English was excellent. It had to be. Finding local translators who spoke my language was fairly easy. Finnish? Practically impossible.

Each of us had a flak vest, and on that morning in Split we stowed our bags next to jerry cans of gasoline and a pallet of bottled water. We were flush with cash—mostly Deutsche marks, which had become the coin of the realm along with Marlboros and other black market items, although some places still took the local currency.

Before departing, Kalle offered a word of warning.

"If we come under fire, open the door and jump into a ditch."

"Have you had to do that yet?" I asked, figuring his advice was probably like the stuff you learned in a school fire drill—nice to know, but never needed.

"Just once," he said.

Rock and roll, indeed. Fortunately, we never had to repeat the experience, and even on the first occasion, Kalle and the Lada had come through without a scratch.

The Bosnian border was only thirty-five miles away, but our planned destination was Vitez, a town smack in the middle of the country in the Lasva River valley. In the previous few months, Central Bosnia had become a very interesting place. While most of the world had continued to fixate on the besieged capital city of Sarajevo, where the blockaded citizens had been pinned down for more than a year by Serbian shellfire and snipers, out in the smaller hill-and-vale towns near Vitez the two-sided war had turned into a three-sided conflict. Out there, the Serbs were mostly just watching from remote hilltops while the enclosed populations of Bosnian Croats and Muslims fought it out from town to town, and street to street. Only a month earlier, a major offensive by Bosnian Croat troops had tried to kill or drive out every Muslim in the Lasva valley, with Vitez at the center of the action. Now the valley was chopped into competing zones of control between the Croats and Muslims (or Bosniaks, as the United Nations called them, mostly because in Bosnia "Muslim" has more historical than religious significance. The men drink plenty of plum brandy, and few women cover their hair. They're descended from locals who, for pragmatic reasons, converted to Islam long ago during the rule of the Ottoman Turks).

Journalistically speaking, my mission was blessedly simple, thanks to Jeff Price, my foreign editor: don't sweat the daily summary stories with their body counts and official briefings. Look for small but significant things that illustrate the bigger picture—telling details, extraordinary moments, interesting characters. Find them, and bring back their stories. For a writer setting off into unknown territory, that's about as good as it gets.

We reached the border quickly. The crossing offered a bit of comic relief. Some enterprising fellow had set up a "Bosnian Duty Free" shop inside a converted shipping container, with ample supplies of Marlboros and Johnny Walker. The roadway narrowed on its descent to Tomislavgrad. I must have been feeling that every detail was important at that point, because the first pages of my notebook are a model of precision:

> Fri—May 14. Dep. Split 7:58. Reach Tomislavgrad about 9:40, prob less than 5 miles from Serb lines (Brit engineers base is here). Villages along way display their political leanings in graffiti, w/many for far-rt. party & an occasional U for fascist Ustasha. . . . Countryside is a lot of rugged hills and broad, flat fertile valleys—black soil. Has been some Serb shelling earlier. Clotheslines strung with HVO (Bosnian Croat militia) dark camouflage uniforms. Red tile rooftops on homes of stone and plastered concrete block. Apple and plum trees are flowering.

The Ustasha was a Croatian fascist movement that worked hand in glove with Hitler during World War II, slaughtering hundreds of thousands of Serbs in the process. Displaying its symbol to a Serb is like waving a red flag before a bull, yet at an HVO checkpoint, a few militiamen had pridefully posted photos of the late Ustasha leader, Ante Pavelic.

Beyond Tomislavgrad, the main highway was no longer an option because it led to Serbian checkpoints which weren't allowing passage. British engineers had graded and bulldozed a dirt road for aid convoys and UN military vehicles that twisted across a mountain ridge to reveal a spectacular view of a lake and the crossroads town of Prozor. From here on, Kalle told me, we had to proceed with greater care, and I soon saw what he meant. Every subsequent village had been damaged by recent fighting, and our progress became a game of stops and starts. We paused outside each town to await a vehicle from the other direction. Usually it was an aid truck or a British armored vehicle. They also stopped because everyone wanted to know what conditions were like around the next bend.

"How are things in Prozor?" we asked an aid worker at the wheel of a white UN truck.

"Quiet today. But stay on the main road. Yesterday was terrible. How about up ahead?"

"All clear."

A thank-you and a nod, and both parties resumed their progress. We kept our windows open to listen for gunfire because conditions could change in an instant. Prozor had been almost entirely emptied of Muslims—or Bosniaks. Its few Serbs were also gone. The HVO militia was now in full control. Entering the town, I began to scribble:

> Several burned out houses and storefronts, former homes and businesses of Serbs and Muslims. One has a plaque commemorating the atrocities of 1943. Two HVOs sit on a wall, assault rifles slung on backs. A kid swings on a tree. Small grove of plum trees blooms in a small glen.

We moved on, climbing another mountain, back on paved road again as we headed deeper into the heart of the country. The next flashpoint was the town of Gorni Vakuf, where the HVO had been unable to dislodge the Bosniak half of the population. The town was now roughly split down the middle, and its center was a pockmarked ruin. The residents that day were moving about peacefully but keeping a wary eye on their enemy neighbors a few blocks away. We stopped on the Bosniak side of town to marvel at this bizarre coexistence while sipping cups of muddy Turkish coffee at a café with shattered windows. Our young waiter, a boy of about twelve, frowned when Kalle offered him Croatian currency.

"Ustasha money," he said, waving it away. We paid in Deutsche marks.

Finally arriving in Vitez, our base of operations for the week, we went looking for a local fixer-interpreter, and in doing so came upon the basis for my first story.

A lone Croat sniper had been been targeting a cluster of a dozen Bosniak homes from his perch on an overlooking hillside. He worked at all daylight hours, the residents said, firing off rounds morning, noon, and evening, his shots popping throughout the day like bacon in a skillet, a one-man "ethnic cleanser" with a deadly grudge against his former neighbors. It was the war in miniature, and we set about interviewing the residents of the beleaguered homes. Some had already moved away in exasperation. Others simply boarded up their windows, determined to stick it out.

That was the case at the home of Jasmina and Ferid Barupa, who had taken in five men displaced from homes elsewhere. In the backyard, the men had dug a small network of trenches about six feet deep to help defend the house and avoid gunfire. They carried AK-47s. A hand grenade hung by its pin from a peg on the basement wall.

Jasmina was fluent in English, and we hired her as our translator for the week, a bargain at 150 D-marks a day, especially given her courage in passing in and out of HVO areas where, now and then, one of her old neighbors recognized her.

She instantly made our work easier. She knew where to go for the passes and documentation needed to get through the various local checkpoints. One thing you learn in a hurry in a war zone is that you can spend more than half your time and energy attending to logistics. At that time, one twenty-mile stretch of the main road through the Lasva valley crossed six different lines of confrontation, and at every crossing you had to have the right papers.

Keeping yourself and your vehicle fed and watered was another daily chore. Another correspondent once told me that the two most dangerous things you ever did in a war zone were driving and eating. That line often gets a laugh, but the mirth hides grim truths. Six colleagues of mine have died while riding from one place to another. Michael Kelly, with whom I traveled in Saudi Arabia and Kuwait during the Gulf War, died in Iraq in 2003 when the armored personnel carrier he was riding in swerved off the road to avoid gunfire and overturned in a flooded ditch. Elizabeth Neuffer, with whom I shared an office in Berlin, died in Iraq the same year when her car hit a railing near Samarra. Four international colleagues riding in vehicles behind mine in a convoy in Afghanistan in 2001 were killed after being waylaid by thugs who ordered them out of their cars and shot them in the head.

As for food and drink, I've been felled for days at a time by one microbe or another, and there are few experiences as lonely as writhing on a sick bed in some filthy room without electricity or running water, and where the toilet is a grimy hole in the floor.

In Vitez, where, with Jasmina's help, we soon found lodging, our digs were comparatively soft. We rented rooms from a farmer. His family's rustic but spotless home was tucked among twenty or so other houses against a pretty green hillside. On a nice evening, you could write your story on a roughhewn table out front, where birds chirped, small boys led cows back from the pastures, bells clanking, and kerchiefed women from the neighborhood leaned across rail fences to gossip. The only disconcerting notes were the frequent snake's rattle of machine gun fire and the occasional thump of a mortar, echoing in the hills like summer thunder.

The best breakfast in town was available at the nearby base of the UN Protection Force, home to a British battalion that served up meals in a big mess tent. Visitors from the Fourth Estate were welcome, and for three dollars you could eat your fill of scrambled eggs, back bacon, baked beans, toast and marmalade, and tea or watery coffee. Not bad, until I later discovered that a French army mess just across the mountains came equipped with vats of all-you-could-drink red wine.

The other main local convenience was the British Army press center, where you could file stories from a satellite phone, paying by the minute. Nowadays, when a Wi-Fi connection is all you need to send entire manuscripts by e-mail attachment, it can be sobering to recall just how difficult it was to file copy even in 1993, when the laptop of choice was a Radio Shack TRS-80. Its nickname, Trash 80, offers a rough idea of what reporters thought of it. The narrow screen displayed only a few rows of text, and, if you were lucky, you'd get a clear enough connection to transmit your story by hooking it up to the phone with a pair of suction cups called acoustic couplers, which would have made excellent props in those silent comedies heavy on pratfalls and banana peels. Transmitting a lengthy story might take four or five minutes, a white-knuckle experience because you knew you'd have to do it again if the connection failed for even a second.

By the end of the war, the *Sun* had equipped me with a rudimentary satellite phone, a heavy contraption that came in a hard-shell briefcase. Its main advantage was that you could run it off your car battery if you needed to file from the road or while staying in a town without electricity. The disadvantage was that it wouldn't work at all with your laptop, meaning you had to dictate to Baltimore. Spelling out the vowel-deficient names of Bosnian people and places to the *Sun's* overworked rewrite staff was another exercise in low comedy. Doing so while standing on a snowy, moonlit highway with the hood of your car raised and the engine running, funnier still.

From our base camp in Vitez, Kalle and I wandered up and down the Lasva valley in search of stories. That sounds haphazard, but it's often serendipitous. The smalltime local sniper was one example, but we found an even better story the following morning while driving east.

Looming on our left was the burned-out village of Ahmici. Only a month earlier, Croat militias had massacred more than a hundred of its Bosniak residents, including thirty-two women and eleven children, some of them burned alive. Forewarned Croat residents had fled in advance. The place was desolate and still smelled like a drowned campfire. A dynamited minaret lay broken on its side next to a destroyed mosque.

Our story was waiting only a short way down the road from that grim site, at a deserted gasoline station chipped by gunfire. Standing in the parking lot on shards of broken glass were soldiers from rival sides. There was also a white UN vehicle with blue flags. Something was going on.

It was a local peace conference, and it was just getting under way. Hrustan Mckic, a brigade commander for the Bosniak side, had wheeled into the lot in a sleek gray Alfa-Romeo with his local battalion leader, Mirsad Smaka. Their Croat counterparts, Dusko Grubacic and Ante Juric, had arrived in a UN escort vehicle from HVO headquarters just up the road in Busovaca.

Presiding over their chat was Hendrik Morsink of the Netherlands, who had brought them together in his role as a war monitor for the European Union.

Morsink didn't seem to mind our presence. If anything, he was happy for another set of impartial observers, perhaps to help ensure that civility prevailed. It was a testy exchange, with the rival officers discussing various possibilities for ceasefires and prisoner exchanges. The atmosphere was that of a confab between rival street gangs, with heavily armed escorts slouching in the wings.

We ended up with a colorful story on the dynamics of local grudges. Even Jasmina seemed fascinated, although when we went to HVO headquarters the next day for follow-up interviews she was almost petrified with fear after recognizing one of the local officers as a former neighbor. She stared at the floor and wouldn't look up, although she bravely kept translating every spoken word.

Our good luck continued through most of the week. One afternoon, we ventured up a mountainside on a bumpy dirt road, following a Red Cross ambulance that had been dispatched to retrieve the body of an old man from a hamlet near the top of the hill. We arrived to find two clusters of farmhouses facing each other across a small meadow, abloom with dandelions and buttercups. Residents on each side—Bosniaks on one, Croats on the other—stood in their respective groves of trees, armed with AK-47s. One group had an ancient-looking tommy gun and an antiaircraft gun mounted on the bed of a pickup truck. Many of the men were toothless, bearded. The war vehicles were hay wagons and rusting pickups. It was a Balkan version of the Hatfields and McCoys, playing out among a few dozen people who lived miles from the nearest paved road.

We also journeyed across the hills to Travnik, which had become a refuge for a few thousand Bosniaks who'd been driven from their homes. The highway to Travnik ran through heavily contested territory, with neither side in control, which made the trip a bit of thrill ride. Kalle said it had become a popular shooting gallery for snipers. He floored it at every opportunity, with the Lada tossing us from side to side.

In Travnik, we met a pretty young woman, Amira Klipic, and her older sister, Mensura, who in their pressed skirts and blouses easily stood out from a grimy and disheveled crowd. They had put on makeup, too, in hopes that their family would arrive that day in a refugee convoy from the north. The two women had turned up a month earlier from the Serbian-held city of Banja Luka, but had not yet heard from their family even as reports of massacres filtered south. Three previous times they'd come here to await refugee convoys only to be disappointed. They were hoping the fourth time was the charm.

Kalle and I wished them luck and walked to the northern edge of town, where gun-shy locals directed us to nearby trenches, the main lines of defense against the Serbs. They took cover behind a wall as we moved off, and they mimed running motions with their hands, signaling that we had best move quickly.

In the trenches, a weary militiaman took us on a slow climb up a muddy hill, followed by a sprint to another trench further forward. A single soldier sat on a board inside an earthen bunker, peering out a narrow slit toward the enemy.

"Don't get too close to the opening," he said, grinning. "Sniper."

So this was what passed for the front. It was unprofessional, forlorn—the work of civilians, not soldiers. We made our way back downhill, where we heard that the refugee trucks had arrived, a dozen in all. We saw Amira and Mensura Klipic seated on a low stone wall. Amira was in tears. Her carefully applied makeup was streaked and smeared. Their family had not been aboard.

It was that kind of a week. Go almost anywhere and you found another human drama.

At week's end, Kalle decided to carry out an unusual equipment test. It was his final trip to Bosnia, and he wanted to find out if the flak vest he'd been wearing actually worked. We went to the small trench behind Jasmina's house, where Kalle took off his vest and placed it on the mud at the opposite end. He borrowed an AK-47 from one of the five men staying there, and we all stood clear while he chambered a round and then fired it into the vest from about fifteen feet away. The gunshot crackled into the hills. He handed back the gun and retrieved the vest. The bullet had made a deep bulge, but it hadn't broken though.

Kalle now felt reassured—as long as some sharpshooter didn't hit the same spot on our way out.

For me, there would be about a dozen more trips to Bosnia, and they would fill many more notebooks with similarly bizarre adventures and har-rowing accounts—a man in an ethnically mixed marriage whose wife hid him in their attic throughout the war; a village still littered with bodies following a brutal Serbian retreat; the exhumation of a reeking mass grave by gasping men with shovels; refugees being trucked into reconquered villages to stake new territorial claims; the brave residents of Sarajevo trying to live normally in their third year of siege.

After the Dayton peace accords took effect in 1996, a colleague and I even managed to try a little fly fishing. We instead became the catch of the day for a Bosnian Serb policeman, who arrested us and hauled us back to the station. He and his colleagues were still peeved about all the bad publicity they'd gotten during the war. Even that episode ended well. Within an hour or so, we were laughing and swapping fishing lies. They set us loose with a "tourist pass" in case we wanted to try again.

Most of my notebooks from those trips are long gone. But I'll always keep the ones from that first week. Flipping through them is powerfully evocative, a memory on every page from a time when being a foreign correspondent for the *Sun* was still something you could claim, and touch, and even be paid for.

23

No Such Agency

Scott Shane

It was September 1995, and I was surprised to find myself in Switzerland at the expense of the *Baltimore Sun*, working on an epic espionage detective story. For many years, there had been hints of a special relationship between the National Security Agency (NSA) and Crypto AG, a Swiss company which manufactured cryptographic equipment—the devices used by armies and embassies to send coded messages. If true, it would be one of the great intelligence sting operations of the Cold War. Crypto AG's customers included dozens of governments, including important targets of American intelligence such as Iran, Iraq, Libya, and Yugoslavia. If the NSA had rigged the machines, it might well mean that for decades the United States had read those countries' secret messages without effort, a huge coup for diplomacy and security. I was trying to prove or disprove the old rumors for a series I was writing with my colleague, Tom Bowman, about the NSA, a secret agency barely known even to its Maryland neighbors.

It had been a nerve-racking trip in some ways. I had hunted down former employees of the company, Crypto AG, and tried to persuade them to talk. I had confronted the company's executives at its headquarters in the town of Zug, near Zurich, awkwardly repaying their invitation to lunch with accusations that they had hoodwinked their customers for decades. But I recall several moments on that trip when I paused for a moment and felt that I was pulling off my own sting operation against my editors, or against life itself. I had been sent to Switzerland to work on a fabulous story. Tom and I were being given the greatest gift reporters on a difficult and important story could get: time—lots of time—to try to plumb the intricacies of the United States' largest, most secretive, and most expensive intelligence agency. It was enough to fully validate that H. L. Mencken quote on the wall of the *Sun's* lobby: "As I look back over a misspent life, I find myself more and more convinced that I had more fun doing news reporting than in any other enterprise. It is really the life of kings."

I'd been at the *Sun* for twelve years by then, having a grand time. I'd covered Baltimore County courts, and written a long investigative piece on an incompetent radiation therapist, sued so many times that his hospital was in financial jeopardy. I'd covered medicine, chronicling the early years of the AIDS epidemic, writing an explanatory series on schizophrenia, and following a little girl at Johns Hopkins Hospital through an astonishing operation in which half of her brain was removed to cure a seizure disorder. In 1988, I was sent to Moscow just as Mikhail Gorbachev's attempt to remake the Soviet Union was gathering steam, and I wrote a book on the Soviet collapse when I got back. Then, freshly shocked by the poverty, crime, drug addiction, and abandoned housing of Baltimore, I had been allowed to write series of stories on juvenile crime, guns, a drug corner, and a block of vacant rowhouses.

One proposal had languished on my story list for a few years. In Moscow, I had watched the KGB, the feared Soviet security service, dragged reluctantly into the light of day by reformers in the first elected parliament. When I got back to the United States, I realized with chagrin that I knew more about the KGB than I knew about the NSA, which was a short drive from the newsroom down the Baltimore–Washington Parkway. The only public glimpse of the agency had been James Bamford's book, *The Puzzle Palace*, a dogged piece of reporting that predated the Reagan-era spending boom on American intelligence. I suggested to the editors that we take a look at the sprawling, eavesdropping agency at Fort Meade.

A few years later, the *Sun's* top editor, John Carroll, independently heard some things about the NSA that got him interested. He liked big, consequential, challenging subjects, and this was one. My boss, Rebecca Corbett, had the patience and ambition to give reporters lots of running room when the material seemed worth it. She paired me up with Tom, the newspaper's skilled and eternally upbeat Pentagon correspondent, and let us loose on the agency. The NSA was among the largest employers in Maryland, but most of our readers confused it with the National Security Council and had no idea what it actually did, which was fine with the government. Edward Snowden, whose massive leak of NSA documents would one day ignite a global debate about the agency, was eleven years old.

If John Carroll had not initially realized what we were up against, he did soon. Tom and I had immediately called the NSA's public affairs office—a bit of an oxymoron at an agency whose initials were said to stand for "No Such Agency" or "Never Say Anything." We figured the agency would soon hear from employees and ex-employees we contacted, so we asked for whatever information the agency was willing to provide. The response came in the form of a breakfast invitation for John from Mike McConnell, the admiral serving as the agency's director. Recognizing a reporting opportunity, John said he'd gladly accept the invitation—but only if he could bring a reporter with him. So one morning John and I arrived at Fort Meade, the Army base that hosts the NSA, went through security, and rode an elevator up to what rank-and-file spies called "mahogany row," the executive office suites in one of the pair of glass towers built during the 1980s.

McConnell was cordial and relentlessly on message: we should abandon the project. The NSA was secret for good reasons, he said. Anything we managed to find out and print could only undermine national security. The agency would offer no interviews and no help with our research. Over scrambled eggs served in the director's private dining room by a discreet military aide, we fenced politely with the vice admiral, a brainy son of South Carolina. We argued that the public deserved to know something about this mammoth agency which was spending so much of their taxes and played such a central role in foreign affairs. Not permitted to take notes, I did my best to commit to memory what I had seen on my way into the building—the portraits and plaques along the corridors, the fine wire mesh over windows to defeat electronic spies. When we got back to John's car in the sprawling parking lot, I scribbled everything I could remember of McConnell's off-record remarks. John did not consider for a second dropping our project.

It was a classic encounter of a kind that I would experience many times in later years as a national security reporter. The intelligence bureaucrats wanted to keep everything secret; the culture of classification taught them that even the tiniest revelations might lead to bigger, more dangerous disclosures. As journalists, we saw the secrecy rules as a challenge, felt we were on a noble mission, and probably did not fully understand the fragility of NSA operations. McConnell was trying to keep us out of the agency's business. We were determined to find out its secrets and, within limits, publish them.

That may make the reporting sound straightforward. It was anything but. The NSA was an institution that then had some twenty thousand workers at the Maryland headquarters alone, and tens of thousands more doing eavesdropping overseas, mostly from military installations. Few would talk. Time after time, Tom and I would hear the click of the phone being hung up as soon as we said the words "reporter" or *Baltimore Sun.* (There was something comical, after all, about calling professional eavesdroppers *on the telephone* and assuring them that we would protect their identities.) On the old reporter's conviction that people are more willing to talk if approached in person, we did a lot of that, too. Some slammed the door angrily, while others smiled before closing it in our faces. A good share of NSA employees viewed the idea of writing a series on the agency's work as tantamount to treason. A friend's wife, who worked at the NSA, heard from her husband about our project and called me on the spot. She cheerfully informed me that she would not talk to me about the agency, period, and that her next call would be to the NSA security office, to report this first call. We realized that the frontal approach to reporting on the agency would not work, and we began to brainstorm side doors, tunnels, and peepholes that might give us a glimpse of its secret work.

One fruitful collection of sources turned out to be NSA's "customers," as they were called: the people who worked in the White House, the State Department, the Defense Department, the CIA—even the Commerce Department—who read and relied on the intelligence reports based on NSA intercepts. Not immersed in the agency's secret culture, some were quite willing to talk. Richard Allen, who had been Reagan's national security advisor, described vividly, on the record, sitting on the deck of his home in Arlington, Virginia, and listening on a secure phone to the NSA's moment-by-moment account of Israeli fighter jets' destruction of an Iraqi nuclear reactor in June 1981. The NSA was listening in on the pilots' radio chatter. "They kept us in real time," Allen told us. "NSA performed, in my view, absolutely invaluable services."

We got a little help from former NSA officials who were so senior that they had the confidence that they could talk without revealing damaging information. "It was the best job I ever had," said Bobby Ray Inman, who had run the NSA before becoming deputy director of the CIA. One of the curious features of NSA culture was that directors, always a general or an admiral, came and went every few years, while the civilian bureaucracy stayed in place. As a result, former directors were generally less paranoid than some NSA lifers about the dangers of describing the agency's work. Sometimes we took advantage of a reporter's friend: ego. Former officials were flattered to be asked about earlier years when they had been at the heart of crises in diplomacy and military affairs. Sometimes, thank God, they got just a bit carried away with remembering the details. One former director seemed to be in the early stage of dementia—which may well be why he agreed to talk. But we weren't sure we could rely on what he said.

To our surprise, even Louis Tordella, a legendary *éminence grise* in American intelligence, agreed to talk with us. He had served as the NSA's deputy director for a record sixteen years; colleagues said that when a new director arrived, Tordella would sometimes wait for months before deciding whether his new boss could be trusted with the details of the agency's most sensitive programs. He strongly defended the agency's eavesdropping on

American activists: "If Jane Fonda wanted to call Hanoi," he said, "I thought that it was legitimate to intercept it." Tordella also told us about the greed of the customers, who got used to timely deliveries from the NSA of transcripts of what foreign counterparts had said privately the day before. "I think it's fair to say that the demands on the agency approach infinity," he said. "Everybody wants to know everything about everything."

But as we worked the upper echelon, we also spent long hours working the lower ranks of the NSA—indeed, some who had been thrown out of the place altogether. Tom courted an attorney who had worked at the agency before going to law school and now had built a decent practice helping NSA workers sue the agency for discrimination and wrongful dismissal. He introduced us to his clientele, a colorful bunch. One high-strung fellow explained in a tone of outrage that he had been fired merely for bringing his MAC-10 pistol to work. His nickname, he told us, was "Animal." Another, a talented linguist, had been fired after his wife, amid contentious divorce proceedings, informed the agency that her husband had boxes of classified documents in the basement. By the time we found him, he was working at the only job he could find: as a state prison guard. Tom and I joked sometimes that you had to be crazy to talk to us about the NSA, which explained why so many of the people who talked to us seemed crazy. We had to be careful with what they told us, but over time, we learned to patiently listen to their sad stories while plucking out nuggets that illustrated how the agency operated.

Over time—a lot of time—we began to make progress. We heard about how the NSA had caught an agent for Airbus paying a bribe to a Saudi prince to steer a huge airline contract its way, and how US officials had used that knowledge to shame the Saudi government into reversing course and giving the deal to Boeing. We confirmed a story that had broken in Australia, where a brand-new Chinese embassy had been rigged by the NSA during construction with all kinds of listening devices. We learned about loopholes in the rules which supposedly protected Americans' privacy from the NSA. During training, for instance, eavesdroppers could practice on local phone lines as long as any records were destroyed "as soon as reasonably possible." One former NSA officer told us that during his training, "We listened to all the calls in and out of Washington," including "senators, representatives, government agencies, and housewives talking to their lovers."

Looking back two decades later, it seems that we were making steady progress. At the time, it seemed embarrassingly slow. I was glad to have Tom for company, as well as our demanding but encouraging editor, Rebecca, to whom we promptly reported every morsel of new information. Rebecca showed appreciation for whatever we unearthed—and then pushed us every day to keep digging.

After about nine months of reporting, in the spring of 1995, the three of us sat down with John Carroll to give him an update on how the project was going. Tom and I joked before the meeting that we might both be fired, and it was a joke that reflected real anxiety. Two reporters for a daily newspaper had been assigned to work on the NSA, and after all those months we felt we had distressingly little to show for it. Writing about the NSA, a fortress of mathematicians, codebreakers, computer programmers, radio technicians, and expert linguists, was a little like visiting an exotic country. It took a while to learn the lingo, understand the issues, and collect sources. (An old joke asked how you can tell an introvert from an extrovert at the agency. The answer: the extrovert looks at *your* shoes when he's talking to you.) But would John understand that? Nervously, we recounted to him what we had learned, gilding it a bit, and emphasizing all the obstacles. Rebecca vouched for our diligence, if not our productivity. John asked a few questions, then got quiet. We awaited our fate.

Finally he spoke. "Why don't you go out there for a few more months," he said, "and see what you come up with?"

We were as overjoyed as prisoners given a stay of execution. But looking back on that moment, I'm not sure we fully appreciated the extraordinary support we were getting. The newspaper industry was still in its profitable heyday. The *Baltimore Sun* had lavish resources, by comparison with later years. To take a serious look inside the NSA was an assignment of foolhardy ambition, surely nothing that would add to profitability. When I called Bobby Inman, the former NSA director, to try to arrange an interview, he said he could give us time if we would visit him at his mountain home in the ski town of Beaver Creek, Colorado. The newspaper agreed to pay for both of us to fly out to Colorado for a few days. When we realized that former President Gerald Ford lived in Beaver Creek, we typed up a letter at our hotel and asked for an interview with him, too. That didn't go so well; not only did we not get the interview, but when we walked up the driveway to his chalet to deliver the letter, a tense Secret Service guy appeared from the bushes, talking into his wrist. We felt fortunate he had decided to question us instead of shoot.

By the time news broke in March 1995 that a "communications technician" named Gary Durell had been killed, along with a secretary, when their van was machine-gunned on the way to their jobs at the US consulate in Karachi, Pakistan, we knew enough to start asking around. Soon we had established that Durell worked for a secret within a secret, a subagency called the Special Collection Service (SCS), jointly run by the NSA and CIA since the late 1970s. The SCS sent officers overseas under cover to do up-close eavesdropping of the kind that could not be conducted from the fleet of

NSA satellites and special aircraft. Working from cramped quarters on the top floors of American embassies and consulates, they listened in on local police and military radio, captured the car-phone chatter of local politicians, and sometimes planted listening devices in foreign offices. The SCS was all but unknown, barely mentioned in the media. We discovered that its original location had been in a windowless building hidden away in an industrial section of College Park, Maryland. But then the Washington Metro decided to open a subway stop a block away, so SCS had been packed up and moved to fancy new headquarters on a corner of the Department of Agriculture's research farm in Beltsville, Maryland. The complex was down a long driveway off a back road, and the sign at the entrance said "CSSG," a cover name that looked like one more anonymous tech company. When we drove in the driveway, however, we were turned around by very serious-looking, heavily armed Defense Department security officers who had nothing to offer about what, exactly, the complex was. When I traveled to Ohio and paid a visit to Gary Durell's widow and parents, however, they showed me letters of condolence from President Clinton, the acting director of the CIA, and McConnell, the NSA director. Two FBI agents had preceded me, making sure that Durell's family did not know too much about his work. "He was a good one for secret work," he mother told me, "because Gary never said anything."

But there was nothing we wanted to nail more than the Crypto AG story, which was why the editors had agreed to send me to Switzerland. I was scheduled to fly home from Zurich at midday, and I had been pressing one former Crypto AG engineer to search his home to see if, by chance, he had any documents which might shed light on the rumored secret relationship with the NSA. I called him one last time, and he told me to stop by his place before heading to the airport. He handed over a memo dated August 19–20, 1975, the minutes of a meeting between technicians for Crypto AG and one of its suppliers, Motorola, about the design of a new cipher machine. But there were two more people at the meeting who were not listed as employees of Crypto or Motorola, but as "IA." The names were Herb Frank and Nora Mackabee, and the retired engineer said they were the key to my quest—mysterious Americans who showed up in Zug periodically to talk about Crypto AG's designs and suggest certain changes.

I never found Herb Frank, who I came to believe was likely a CIA officer, perhaps using a cover name. But after a long and frustrating search for "Nora Mackabee," I finally got hold of a membership directory for the Phoenix Society, NSA's retiree organization. I eagerly turned to the M's and saw no Nora. But there was a Lester Mackebee, with a different spelling. I went to Maryland driver's license records and quickly established that Lester Mackebee's wife was named Nora. The 1975 minutes had misspelled her name. I found a number and called their house in a rural area an easy drive from NSA headquarters. Lester answered, and I explained that we were talking to retirees for some stories about the agency. We chatted, and he declined in a friendly way, but not before mentioning that his wife had worked at the agency, too. Might she be willing to talk? He said she was outside painting a fence, but I should try her later. When I called back, holding my breath, and Nora Mackebee answered, she turned down my interview request, too, apologizing but saying they really weren't allowed to talk about their work. The conversation was clearly coming to an end, so I had to take a shot. I said, "Oh, there's one specific thing I wanted to ask you. I wanted to talk to you about your work with Crypto AG." She was silent for a moment. "I can't say anything about that," she said. I thanked her and hung up, rejoicing that she had not had the presence of mind to pretend that she had never heard of Crypto AG and had no idea what I was talking about.

Our six-part series, with many sidebars, explanatory graphics, and photos, some shot from helicopters, ran in December 1995. A few days before we went to print, Mike McConnell called John Carroll with one more request that he kill our series. When that failed, he sent a memo to all NSA employees, reminding them of their secrecy obligations, and saying that they should be careful not to comment in any way on what we wrote, for fear of inadvertently confirming something classified. Part 1 was an introductory story describing what the agency did. Part 2 was about what it was like to work at the NSA, including the variety of jobs and lore from retirees. Part 3 was about the Special Collection Service, giving the first detailed, public description of what this super-secret organization did. Part 4, titled "Rigging the Game," gave our account of the relationship between the NSA and Crypto AG; we printed the 1975 memo that I had retrieved from Switzerland. Part 5 was about the potential threat the agency posed to Americans' privacy. Part 6 was about the agency's evolution after the end of the Cold War, as it fended off budget cuts by finding new targets, including terrorist groups, drug cartels, and high-tech hackers. In all, the *Sun* gave us more than sixteen full pages of space to explain this institution.

The reaction was gratifying and unnerving. There was plenty of praise for the work, including gratitude from Marylanders whose fathers, wives, or sons went off to Fort Meade every day and never said a word about what they did there. And there were many angry calls and letters about the series, mostly from devoted agency employees who sincerely believed that we had put the nation in grave danger. A number of the agency's defenders left phone messages overnight suggesting that we should be put on trial for betraying our country or, better, summarily shot. The newspaper decided to do a broadsheet reprint, which it sold for $6.95. It sold eleven thousand copies before, we were told, the printing plates were lost, ending the sales well before the demand was exhausted. Many of the buyers were relatives of NSA veterans. But I recall seeing a list of orders, and was a little taken aback to see that the Chinese embassy had purchased a few copies.

We had waited anxiously for the reaction of Crypto AG, whose executives had assured me that the company had never had anything to do with the NSA. When I had told them about the 1975 memo and the Nora Mackebee connection, they said no one at the company remembered her. When I asked whether they could imagine any legitimate reason that a NSA cryptographer might have attended a company design discussion, they said they could not.

After the series ran, we received a cordial letter faxed from one of the executives I had met. It made no complaint about the series, wished me a good Christmas, and asked if I could send a few copies of the story. Two weeks later, the company issued a denial to the Reuters bureau chief in Zurich, saying that the *Baltimore Sun* had dug up and repeated some "old hearsay" that was "nothing new." "A connection between the activities of Crypto AG and NSA is pure invention, obviously construed to discredit Crypto AG," the statement said. It shrewdly hinted that our article might be disinformation fed to us by the NSA, which would benefit if countries stopped using unbreakable Crypto AG machines and turned to less secure cipher equipment. But no one at Crypto AG ever complained to us or to our bosses at the *Sun* about the story. And the company's statement, I was relieved to see, made no mention whatsoever of Nora Mackebee.

24

Shipbreaking

Will Englund

I was to cover the waterfront. It was John Carroll's idea, and he was the editor, so that meant it was a good idea. Nobody seemed to have a firm notion as to what this beat would actually entail. The only thing we all understood was that it was not to be about the shipping news, since we already had a reporter on the business staff who covered that. One editor thought I should be uncovering corruption on the docks. Another thought I would be writing about fisheries. Much later, I got the impression that Carroll himself had long-distance sailboat racing in mind. But his larger idea was that a paper the size of the *Sun* needed to establish a few themes where it could really shine, and since Baltimore is a port on the Chesapeake, water made sense. He was smart enough not to get too specific.

It was the late summer of 1995. I was returning to Baltimore after four years in the Moscow bureau. One golden September evening, I joined a boat tour of the harbor, led by the maritime historian Donald Shomette, that was to focus on the various wrecks scattered about the city's long shoreline. My plan was to write a feature about a generally unknown part of Baltimore history, and at the same time to get better acquainted with my new territory.

After following the shore along the Fells Point and Canton waterfront, we turned south and then west. We cleared Fort McHenry and came up into the Middle Branch. Shomette lectured about the ghosts of Maryland Drydock, and privateers, graceful old steamboats. Some distance away across the water, just in front of the bridge which carries the Harbor Tunnel Throughway, and next to the Toyota pier, sat the still, flat-gray bulk of an aircraft carrier.

"What the heck is that?" I asked.

"That? Oh, that's the *Coral Sea*," Shomette replied. "Guy was going to cut it up for scrap, but he ran into all kinds of problems. I think he went bankrupt."

"Oh," I replied.

And we returned to what seemed more interesting topics, such as the last pirate attack on the Chesapeake by a band of French sailors who, once captured and brought back to Baltimore, charmed their way to freedom.

Three months later, right around Christmas, I got word that an ocean-going Chinese tug had arrived in Baltimore to tow the *Coral Sea* to India, where it could be scrapped more cheaply. I dropped by the yard where it was tied up, had a conversation with Kerry Ellis, who owned it, and wrote a bittersweet little story about a project that had seemed to hold promise, but failed, and now this worthy old ship was heading to foreign shores on its final, sad voyage.

The next day I got a phone call from a man who wouldn't identify himself. This was to be the only reliance on an anonymous source during the entire two-year course of the story I was at that moment innocently embarking on. "There's more going on there," he said. "Check with the Environmental Protection Agency. And check with the State Department."

A little digging turned up a raft of EPA citations for violations connected to disposal of PCBs, or polychlorinated biphenyls. PCBs were widely used in electrical insulators and in fire retardant materials, until it was discovered they were also carcinogenic. I had written about them a decade or so earlier, in a story that focused on the railroad yards in East Baltimore, so I knew something about the subject. I knew they were ubiquitous in heavy machinery from the 1950s and 1960s, and difficult to dispose of. I knew they weren't as horribly deadly as some made them out to be, but they're nasty enough. And the *Coral Sea* was contaminated with them inside and out.

It is against the law to ship PCBs abroad for disposal. This is how the State Department got involved—to export the *Coral Sea* for scrapping would require a waiver, based on the fiction that on the trip to India it would be a ship under way, and a not a big piece of floating garbage. It never did get that waiver, in the end, and it stayed in Baltimore.

I began casting the net a bit further, and learned that the Navy had a consistently bad record when it came to getting rid of its old ships. The procedure was to sell the ship to a yard—a shipbreaker's yard—and the new owner would try to make a profit from the scrap he could sell. But all the old ships, loaded not only with PCBs, but asbestos and other contaminants, had environmental problems, and the yards had appalling safety problems. The yards' profits came at the expense of their workers. This was the bottom rung of the maritime industry—all you needed was a pier, some cutting equipment, and a supply of cheap labor. Yet the profit margins were thin, and with environmental and safety violations and the citations that came with them—and the often dodgy financing behind every project—there was a constant stream of troubles, and a lot of partially dismantled ships which the Navy didn't want to know about.

I kept pecking away at this while working on other stories. That winter had a protracted cold spell, and the Chesapeake became pretty icebound. I went down to Crisfield to hitch a ride on a Coast Guard icebreaker to Tangier Island, but the boat left before I got there, and I had to spend the night. I bought a toothbrush at Walmart, and expensed it, and, sure enough, a month later, the accounting department asked me to justify the $1.57 I had spent.

I was about to spend a whole lot more of the *Sun's* money.

At the end of March 1996, I had my story ready to go. It was a good, solid, newsy survey of the Navy's problems, and it led the paper one Sunday. The next day, John Carroll called me into his office, along with a passel of editors.

"Why didn't anybody tell me about this story?" he asked.

That was a difficult question to answer, since it had been on the budget all week long and discussed in news meetings over which he had presided.

We mumbled a bit.

Well, he wanted more. He was sorry this had run. It might tip somebody else off. He saw great possibilities, but it would mean going to shipbreakers around the country, detailing the abuses, and, most of all, persuading workers to talk. At his request, I wrote a memo laying out the dimensions of the problem and what it would take to tackle it.

Carroll saw prize possibilities: that was obvious. He very much wanted the *Sun* to win big prizes, and thereby attract talented people, and win more prizes. This had been the key to the success of the *Philadelphia Inquirer* a decade earlier, when Carroll had been an editor there, and now he wanted to replicate it in Baltimore. Naturally, longtime *Sun* people grumbled about this, on the grounds that it is tawdry to chase prizes, when the main strength of the *Sun* was diligent coverage of the city and state. Newspapers don't win Pulitzers for having thorough statehouse reporting, but that's where the *Sun* stood out. To me a prize sounded all right.

About two days into the project, I was back in Carroll's office. He was giving me a partner. This was too big for one reporter. Sure, I thought, maybe. I was going to be paired with Gary Cohn, who up to that point I hadn't even spoken to. He was one of a squadron of reporters and editors recruited from Philadelphia by Carroll and his new managing editor, Bill Marimow. A few of those who made the move south were less than tactful in assessing the *Sun's* weaknesses and in predicting how much better they were

Figure 24.1.   Will Englund receives a hug from his wife Kathy Lally after winning the Pulitzer Prize for investigative reporting; left to right: Englund, Lally, Rebecca Corbett, editor of the series, Gary Cohn (co-winner).

going to make it. Most were perfectly amiable—Gary certainly was; he never said a disparaging word about the paper. But of course, those of us who had been at the *Sun* before this influx, who had always seen ourselves as the ones who were going to remake the paper, one of these days, resented all Philadelphians, equally and unreasonably. What really stung was that the complaints of the more outspoken newcomers were sometimes on the money.

I didn't, in any case, have much choice at this point. The paper was going to do something big, and I was going to be a part of it. And so was Gary.

He was great at documents, I was told. As we were to learn over the next eighteen months, with the exception of Ellis's bankruptcy case, which took up several yards of file space in the federal courthouse, there were no documents to speak of related to shipbreaking. The navy had turned an absolute blind eye to its problems. There were no files, no records. So Gary and I set out together to see with our own eyes and hear with our own ears what was going on.

Two men stood out among the operators in the business. One was Andrew Levy, a lawyer in New York who handled the contracts and finance, and the other was Richard Jaross, a strangely compelling man who had big dreams for shipbreaking and nowhere near the attention to detail to make them come true.

They had been behind the *Coral Sea* fiasco. They had a project in Wilmington, North Carolina, with a couple of old navy destroyers that was going badly. They had a partnership in Brownsville, Texas, which was equally beset with problems. Gary went to Wilmington. I took Brownsville.

Brownsville is near the mouth of the Rio Grande, at the southernmost tip of Texas. It's a flat, dull place, in one of the poorest counties in America. I don't speak Spanish, and I knew from my years in Moscow that it was important to find the right kind of translator. The workers we were interested in were Mexican.

I asked around a bit, and eventually found David Elizondo, who was the perfect man for the job. An organizer for the longshoremen's union, he took an immediate interest in the project. The workers in the breakers' yards were at the very bottom of the labor hierarchy in Brownsville, and I suspect Elizondo wanted to learn what he could with an eye toward organizing them in the future. No matter. He knew the port, and he knew the culture.

Day after day, we made the rounds in the *colonias*—the unincorporated settlements—that surround Brownsville. Here, away from nosy inspectors as well as normal municipal services, Mexican migrants who might not have had a legal justification for being in the United States lived in rundown houses or trailers in general obscurity.

It occurred to me that if I had known perfect, college Spanish, I would have gotten nowhere with the story. Doors would have been slammed in my face. But David, Texas-born—a *Tejano*—was a big man who gained the respect of the workers. And he vouched for me. Slowly, very slowly, we began to get stories of ghastly injuries and horrifying shortcuts with the hazardous wastes that abounded on every ship. The workers couldn't complain to anyone in authority—they'd probably be booted back to Mexico—but eventually they opened up to this stranger from the north with his notebook open, and his fierce and profane colleague.

Texas law, I discovered, was on my side. At that time, the state had a totally inadequate workers' compensation system, so when Raul Mendoza was killed from a fall, his wife sued the yard—and that put the case on the record (unlike a worker's compensation case), and gave me both her name and the name of her lawyer, who had learned a thing or two about the circumstances of his death.

All in all, I made five trips to Brownsville, usually for a week at a time. I got a little bit fond of the place. I spent an evening at a restaurant where a very lively *quinceañera*—the Mexican celebration of a girl's fifteenth birthday—was taking place. Mariachi bands enlivened the bars. Matamoros, in

Mexico, was a short walk away and perfectly safe, back in those days. One Saturday, when I had run out of things to do, I drove around a corner in Brownsville and came upon an elephant. It was the star attraction of a traveling circus from Mexico, patiently waiting in the parking lot of a store that sold cowboy boots.

In time, I was joined on these trips by Perry Thorsvik, a *Sun* photographer who had an outstanding talent for catching the most vital images. He was a Navy vet—he had served on an aircraft carrier—and was a terrific source of insight and lore about his old service. He was also skeptical of some of our early conclusions, which forced us to rethink and rereport, all of which was a great help.

Besides Brownsville, I visited sites in San Francisco, Quonset Point, Rhode Island, and Richmond.

Together, Gary and I interviewed Andrew Levy over lunch in New York, and Richard Jaross at the yard in Wilmington. Jaross told us he only wished he could get a contract cutting up nuclear subs. "I'd be like a kid with a new toy," he exclaimed.

But we had launched on this project just as the handful of American yards were grinding to a halt under community pressure in some cases and outright bankruptcy in others. The Navy had had to take back two half-dismantled destroyers from the Rhode Island project. We learned that the Maritime Administration, which owned two fleets of mothballed merchant vessels that it was eager to get rid of, was scheming to bypass the US yards altogether and sell its vessels to shipbreakers in India, where labor was far cheaper, equipment was negligible, and regulatory oversight was slim. The Maritime Administration was trying to get the Navy to go in with it on the scheme.

That meant we had to go to India to see for ourselves. Gary made a trip to London, where a lot of these deals were put together, and made a valuable contact there with a broker whose cousin in India ran one of the breakers' yards. We began scouting for a fixer, and found Sharmila Shandra, an astute former magazine journalist in New Delhi. She made a scouting trip for us to a place called Alang in India's northwesternmost state of Gujarat, and came away with such good material and such good contacts that we knew it was the place for us. The workers there were all from the other side of India, from the poorest states, and spoke Hindi rather than the local Gujarati language. They were, in other words, perfect fodder for exploitation, much like the Mexicans in Baltimore and Brownsville.

In the spring of 1997, Gary, Perry, and I flew to Mumbai, and then onward to Bhavnagar, in Gujarat, where Sharmila met us. She cut a striking figure—about six feet tall, always dressed in a bright yellow sari, striding about even in the shipbreaking yards like a woman to be taken seriously. The workers all deferred to her, respected her. She's a Brahmin, which might have had something to do with it. The owners of the yards were entirely cordial; I think they felt no harm could come to them from a couple of American journalists.

The yards stretched along six miles or so of the beach at Alang. It was a perfect spot—the beach has a very gentle slope, and the tides there run about twelve feet. So there was no need for piers: they just ran the ships full speed toward the beach, and jammed them up onto the sand, always at high tide, ideally with a full moon so the tide would be at its peak. Then the workers would swarm aboard and pretty much take the ship apart with their bare hands. At any one time, dozens of ships lay grounded along the miles of strand, bows all facing inland, in various states of deconstruction. The sand was littered with discarded scraps of metal, drenched with oil, and mounded with human excrement. On average, about one worker died every day at Alang. Some men died when they fell from a ship; others when they were hit by a chunk of metal dropped from high above them; and others still by the explosions that occurred whenever someone with a cutting torch cut into a pipe full of accumulated gases. We watched a funeral cremation on the beach (of a worker who had actually died of illness). It took place at low tide, so the incoming flood would wash his ashes away.

One night we were invited to witness a beaching. It was surprisingly cool, and the workers had gathered around barrels where they stoked fires. Out to sea, in the deepest black, we saw the light of a ship. It turned toward us, and then, just at 3 am, when the tide was highest, began its final sprint. The lights came closer, then suddenly the outlines of a dark ship against the dark sea and sky became discernible. It grew larger and larger, and it seemed nothing could stop it. Now we could see the white foam at its bow. Then, up and up, slowing, it rose onto the sand and sighed to a halt. It was a Russian freighter, the *Nikolai Pogodin*, named for a Stalinist playwright who extolled the virtues of work. After the ship's crew clambered down onto the beach, the breakers went aboard. Half an hour later came back word that they had found, improbably, a case of vodka on board. In Gujarat, which is a dry state, this caused huge rejoicing.

In Bhavnagar one day, we went to talk to a lawyer about his many personal injury cases against the owners. Some of them had been in the courts more than twenty years without resolution. In fact, he had obtained a judgment on none of them. His office was on the second floor, up an impossibly steep staircase—so steep it had a rope, knotted at intervals, hanging down to give the climbers something to grab on the way up. The lawyer got out his files, each one thick with paperwork, each tied with a faded piece of red tape. He chewed betel nuts all the while as we sat there, leaning over every few minutes to spit out the open window onto the passersby below.

In India, I had my greatest athletic feat. The four of us and a driver were on our way to the state capital, Ahmedabad, in an old Indian car called an Ambassador. The suitcases were tied on top, and from my seat by the rear right door, I could just see the edge of Sharmila's. We bounced along, and I saw her suitcase leap higher with each jolt. Finally, we hit an epochal pothole, and the suitcase went flying off. I stuck my arm out the open window and, to my own astonishment, caught the thing in mid-flight. Sharmila seemed to accept that as her due.

We flew home in April, made a last round of visits to the American yards. Then it was time to write. Rebecca Corbett was our editor, and she brought a meticulous eye for every word. Day after day, I'd sit there barking at Gary to get me some quotes, or some facts, or some description, and I'd turn it over to Rebecca and she'd comb through it. It was an exacting process. September came, and John Carroll wasn't satisfied with the opening of the first story. (There were three stories altogether.) One day he told me to sit down and just bat out eleven ledes. One of them had to work. Why eleven? I don't know. In the end we didn't go with any of them. But we did find a way to get started. Here it is:

> Raul Mendoza knew that scrapping ships was dangerous, knew about the smoke and the fumes and the accidents. He'd worked in Baltimore, where asbestos clouded the air, and North Carolina, where oil spilled into a river, and California, where workers were told to lie to government inspectors.
>
> But he needed a job. So, on Dec. 22, 1995, in Brownsville, Texas, he climbed into the hold of the USS *Yukon*, an old Navy tanker. Working in total darkness without safety equipment, he walked across a girder. Then came the scream.
>
> Mendoza had fallen 30 feet into a tank, straddling a cross beam in a blow that split his pelvis. He flipped off the beam and landed on his chest. He was pleading for help. Untrained in shipboard emergencies, rescuers took three hours to extract him. By Christmas Eve, he was dead.
>
> Raul Mendoza is just one of the casualties of a little-known industry called shipbreaking. Spurred by the Navy's sell-off of obsolete warships at the end of the Cold War, the business has grown up overnight in some of America's most economically depressed ports. And almost everywhere the industry has arrived, harm to human health and the environment has followed.

The series ran over three days in December 1997. We had to write quick followups demonstrating that we were getting results, because that's how you win prizes. We did get results: the US government suspended its program, then recast it so that breakers were paid by the taxpayer to do the work, and the government got the proceeds from the scrap. US ships were not exported to India. And we did get prizes.

In the years that followed, I found that the new system didn't work so well either. The Navy didn't care to spend serious money on decommissioned ships, and the Maritime Administration was annoyed because it would still have preferred to send ships to India. Amazingly, to me, Andrew Levy and Richard Jaross resurfaced as key players in the business.

In India, I'm told, the series caused enough of a stir that the government imposed some safety regulations, and began staffing the medical clinics that had been empty and locked when we visited. The death rate was cut 90 percent from the four hundred a year who were killed when we visited; that meant that every year, 360 people survived who would have died if not for our series. That was the most gratifying thing about it.

25

Tribune

The Rupture

Sandy Banisky

The new millennium began with the *Sun* newsroom focused on one big, cheerful change: moving from the fifth floor to a state-of-the-digital-art space on the second floor: new furniture; new computers on every desk; new Internet connections; a clean, modern style for one of the nation's top news operations.

The year 2000 would be big. As it turned out, the move was the least of it. By the time the newsroom had actually packed up and moved three floors down that spring, the *Sun* had a new owner: Tribune. A few weeks later, it had a new editor. And more profoundly, its new corporate chiefs had made clear their primary interest in newspapers: profits.

Profits. Shareholders. Journalists at the *Sun* already were trying to cope with all the changes that technology was forcing onto the way we gathered and published news. Now, all of a sudden, we were being told that our job was not just to keep readers informed, but investors happy. Tribune stressed this corporate philosophy. It fueled resentment, and over time the resentment many felt hardened into hostility.

And though daily news operations felt pretty much the same for many months, giant shifts were happening within the building on Calvert Street, within the business of journalism, and throughout American culture.

Soon, newspaper customers around the country would consider it quaint to wait until dawn to open the front door and retrieve a rolled-up publication that had been tossed onto the doorstep in the dark—as quaint as waiting for the milkman to leave glass bottles on the porch. Why read the news once a day when you could read constantly updated coverage on line?

But in 2000, the digital shift in news delivery seemed something that wouldn't bother us for a while. The *Sun* was Maryland's largest newsroom, the state's dominant news operation. Job applications from journalists around the country flooded the editor's office. Times Mirror, the *Sun's* owner since 1986, had the money to pay for a first-class operation and a justified reputation for fine journalism.

Everything seemed to be thrumming along smoothly, solidly, much as it always had. But our position was precarious. More people were turning to the Internet, not newspaper ads, to find jobs. Buyers were going online to hunt for houses and cars. People with puppies to sell or antiques to auction were finding bigger audiences on websites than in newspaper pages. Readers were looking elsewhere for their news just as advertisers were looking elsewhere for customers.

With the pace of change accelerating, the *Sun* was not going to be allowed to find its own way of dealing with the new model. The paper's future would no longer be in the hands of executives in Baltimore and Los Angeles.

On a Monday morning in March 2000, *Sun* employees awakened to the surprise news that Times Mirror had been sold to the Tribune Company, owner of the *Chicago Tribune.*

BEFORE TRIBUNE

For fourteen years, Times Mirror had been a benevolent corporate parent. Some Los Angeles types had moved to Baltimore to head a few *Sun* business departments. But Times Mirror's touch in the newsroom was light.

It could afford to be. The business model worked beautifully. Advertising—from multipage department store spreads to dozens of columns of classifieds—paid decent salaries and benefits and returned plenty of revenues to the corporate offices.

Michael E. Waller, the *Sun's* publisher since 1997, was a change from the serious, somewhat distant businessmen who had come before him. Waller had spent about forty years as a copy editor and editor, and he loved newsrooms. He wandered through daily, and knew everyone's name and everyone's job.

He wanted to hear what was going on. If someone was ailing, he'd ask how he could help. He wanted to schmooze and he wanted to discuss news coverage. He had a habit of talking out of the side of his mouth, like some 1930s Hollywood tough guy. His observations were sometimes hilarious, often profane. He didn't visit just to talk to the editors. He would stand shoulder to shoulder with a reporter, his arms folded across his chest, and carry on a conversation as he surveyed the newsroom.

The *Sun's* editor, John S. Carroll, was ambitious. He wanted authoritative daily coverage as well as imaginative long-term stories—the kind that would win national awards and bring the *Sun* more attention. He hired staffers who he believed would further his plans, which meant that many veterans who were at the paper when Carroll arrived in 1991 were challenged to prove they might actually have talent.

(Carroll's push for prizes was the source of newsroom tension, with some of us disdaining the editor's passion for big awards. We wanted colleagues who were in the newsroom for the work itself, not for prizes. At least one of Carroll's hires was so focused on attention that, at best, he was guilty of arranging facts in his stories selectively to create the punchiest tale he could. At worst, he flat-out made things up. Even when confronted by veteran reporters worried that his guy was harming the *Sun*, Carroll stood by him and was angered by staff skepticism.)

Carroll hired big names. He also recruited people who he thought were interesting, though they had never worked at a newspaper. He began a two-year internship program, which allowed him to bring on new talent without officially expanding the number of permanent positions on the payroll.

In Carroll's last year at the paper, 2000, the *Sun's* sprawling newsroom was still expanding. It numbered more than four hundred reporters, editors, photographers, graphic artists, clerks, research librarians, and technicians. The place was joyfully noisy—phones ringing, reporters shouting across the room or huddling in efforts at conversation, photographers peering at negatives on light boards, editors rushing into meetings, then circulating around reporters' desks for updates on daily stories.

Activity. Always, activity. From Calvert Street metro editors managed satellite bureaus in five suburban counties, plus a bureau in the State House. A correspondent in Frederick covered Western Maryland, another in Easton covered the Eastern Shore. Business writers handled finance, real estate, government dealings, as well as the national economy.

The *Sun* also had a Washington bureau of more than a dozen reporters, columnists, and editors. The foreign desk in Baltimore ran the overseas bureaus—five in 2000, down from eight in 1995. The features desk put out sections every day, plus travel, food, health, and entertainment sections weekly. The sports desk covered the Orioles and Ravens as well as horseracing, high school sports, and college teams. The paper sent a squad of reporters, columnists, photographers, and editors to every Olympics.

The paper had pulled back a little, closing its bureaus in New York and California, but the paper's national correspondent still reported from around the country. And when major stories broke—the school shooting at Columbine High School, the Oklahoma City bombing, a plane crash, a big trial—teams of local reporters were sent as well.

Sun staffers were used to hearing complaints from the public about coverage. The comments fell into a couple of categories: the news columns, readers charged, were too liberal or too conservative, in the pocket of some elected official, or completely unfair to him or her.

But the fact that so many people complained about the paper at some level reflected the depth of its readership. The *Sun* guided the community conversation. Television newscasts were filled with recaps of stories published in that morning's editions. Radio morning shows read rewrites of *Sun* coverage.

The *Sun* may have been owned by a company from Los Angeles, but the editors in Baltimore were in charge of the *Baltimore Sun's* reporting.

Being part of the Times Mirror operation had benefits. Times Mirror ran a national wire service, sending stories from its newspapers to its clients across the country. That meant *Sun* reporters' and photographers' work appeared on front pages from Boston to Los Angeles.

From California, Times Mirror ran a program called MetPro, which recruited the best young minority journalists, gave them two years' training in Los Angeles, then placed those reporters and photographers in Times Mirror newsrooms around the country. Some of the *Sun's* most talented young journalists were MetPro alumni.

Beyond that, and the words "Times Mirror" in small print on business cards, most *Sun* reporters, editors, and photographers did their jobs without ever giving a thought to the corporate chiefs in Los Angeles. The flagship shared journalism values with other news organizations in the chain. In the *Sun* newsroom, reporters and editors felt Los Angeles mostly, blessedly, left Baltimore alone.

TRIBUNE TAKES CHARGE

But in the spring of 2000, Tribune made clear it ran its business differently. Men from Chicago arrived to explain to assemblies of *Sun* employees that Tribune executives were in business to benefit shareholders, then readers. The Baltimore staff noted that shareholders were mentioned first. This, as far as anyone could tell, had never happened before in the paper's 163 years.

Years later, the newsroom reaction to the Tribune's shareholders-first pronouncement sounds shockingly naïve. But here it is: we were appalled. Of course we knew we worked for a business. Of course we understood that revenues paid our salaries and allowed us to have expense accounts.

But we in the newsroom saw ourselves as detached from business considerations. Our mission, enshrined in the First Amendment, was to be watchdogs of government and others in authority. Our mission was to be fair, independent, and protected from the influence of powerful interests that might seek to rein us in. This is, after all, what the founder, A. S. Abell, had promised from the outset in 1837.

Hardworking people in other parts of the building handled the money side of things. *Sun* journalists could not remember—outside of a warning not to fly first class—ever having a boss tell them to consider business interests as they went about their work. We were proud of the fact that if unhappy advertisers called and complained to the publisher we never heard about it.

We believed the wall between business and news had to be inviolate. But in some of journalism's corporate offices, that belief was fading. Eventually, even within Times Mirror, executives had begun suggesting that the wall come down—or at least become a little porous—to allow the industry to cope with new times. Tribune officials had stronger feelings. They believed that, with the business changing quickly, the newsroom and business could no longer afford what they considered the luxury of separation.

NEW STYLE, NEW VOCABULARY

The Chicago executives offered some reassurances: they said they respected the *Sun*. They said they had no plans to close the paper's foreign bureaus. They said the Washington bureau was in no danger of losing staff. They said *Sun* reporters would contribute to the Tribune news service.

But they made it clear there would be changes. They saw a more centralized and disciplined future for their newsrooms. They even used a different vocabulary. What Baltimore reporters called "stories" the Chicago bosses called "content"—a "platform-neutral" term that covered all forms of news stories, whether print, video, photos, or graphics, from a newspaper or a television station.

"Editors" eventually were called "heads of content." The top editing position was renamed "director of content."

And there was much talk of "synergy." Reporters would no longer be limited by their old job description. Think of the economies! A Tribune newspaper reporter might stand up and report a news story on a Tribune television station. A television reporter might team with a newspaper reporter on a project that would run in print. Reporters at Tribune newspapers and television stations from Chicago to Los Angeles to Fort Lauderdale would be working together to provide "content" to all Tribune news properties.

Journalists would contribute across "reporting platforms"—television, print, web, no matter. This was the future, Tribune executives said, and it was, they averred, a financially sound one. Tribune would provide more content to its various news operations using fewer people than under previous models.

THE EDITOR MOVES ON

John Carroll had begun his reporting career at the *Sun* in 1966, had reported from Vietnam, and had won a Nieman Fellowship. He had left the paper in 1973 for an editing job at the *Philadelphia Inquirer*, then became editor of the *Lexington* (Kentucky) *Herald Leader*, where he led his newsroom to a Pulitzer Prize.

When he returned to the *Sun* as editor in 1991, he said he expected to finish his career in Baltimore. Over the years, he raised the *Sun's* profile, reinforcing its reputation as a destination paper—a place a reporter could expect to spend his career doing top-flight work.

But in the spring of 2000, after weeks of rumors that he was leaving to run the Nieman Fellowship program in Cambridge, Massachusetts, Carroll told the newsroom he was moving to Los Angeles to become editor of the *Los Angeles Times*.

He was succeeded by his managing editor, William K. Marimow. Marimow had won two Pulitzer Prizes for reporting at the *Inquirer*, and he told everyone he remained a reporter at heart. (He kept copies of his reporting projects in his desk drawer to use as examples for his staff.)

By the time he became the *Sun's* editor, he had worked in Baltimore for several years. But his conversations almost daily still included references to Philadelphia—his experiences, his sources, his life at the *Inquirer*.

Marimow's elevation reassured the newsroom. He chose the newsroom veteran Anthony F. Barbieri Jr. as managing editor. He ran the paper in much the style of Carroll, giving the staff a sense of continuity.

He hired young reporters who were eager to come work in Baltimore. Some aspired to the Washington bureau or one of the *Sun's* overseas operations. But many wanted to dig into the workings of the city and state, to investigate how business and government were serving Marylanders.

NATIONAL AWARDS

Under Marimow, *Sun* reporters and editors continued to win national attention. Diana Sugg won a Pulitzer Prize for beat reporting in 2003, and *Sun* reporters were Pulitzer finalists in 2002, 2003 (in two categories), and in 2004.

In local reporting, *Sun* investigations had impact. One example: after an investigation by a *Sun* team led by Michael Dresser, the former head of the University System of Maryland's Board of Regents who was also a money manager for the state employees' pension system, was convicted in federal court of fraud in dealing with state pension funds and went to prison.

In the newsroom, the run of big, powerful news stories felt great. But on the business side, the news was not as happy.

The movement of readers from newspapers to news websites gained momentum daily. The *Sun's* web report was a stunted affair, an unimaginative site that was updated sporadically if at all, and featured *Sun* stories that already had been in print. It was, like many other newspaper sites around the country back then, trying to figure out what to offer online.

Readership studies of the day showed that readers came to the site between eight and nine o'clock in the morning when people arrived at work and sat down at their computers, then spiked at lunchtime, then saw a late-afternoon rise, just before workers went home.

The website wasn't organized to post breaking news. In 2003, when Hurricane Isabel was forecast to hit Maryland overnight, web editors said they would delay their usual 10 pm sign-off and stay until 11 pm—not much help when waters would be rising all night. *Sun* reporters, photographers, and editors worked hours past deadline into the morning—some reporters and photographers in rowboats—but they had no place to file their stories. The last print edition had closed by 2 am, and the website wouldn't spring back to life until dawn.

Readers looking for the latest news couldn't turn to the *Sun*. The readers' dependence on the local newsroom was fraying.

MARIMOW IS DISMISSED

Early on a Tuesday morning, January 6, 2004, Marimow and his managing editor, Tony Barbieri, left their offices and walked upstairs to the publisher's office. I was deputy managing editor for metro—later I became deputy managing editor for news, charged with developing stories for the front page—and I knew my boss's behavior was unusual. Other staffers who closely followed Marimow's routine—which did not include Tuesday morning visits with the publisher—knew something was up.

And within thirty minutes, Marimow was calling editors into his office one by one and calmly telling them that he was no longer the editor of the *Sun*.

The publisher, Denise Palmer, who had succeeded Mike Waller, had spent her career at Tribune, beginning as a corporate auditor. Her last post before the *Sun* was as head of a cable news station in Chicago that Tribune owned. She arrived in Baltimore in 2002 as financial pressures were building.

Firing Marimow was the highest profile action she'd taken in her sixteen months on the job. And when pressed for a reason, she told a *Sun* reporter, "It is about personality, fit, style." That was as specific as she got.

Marimow acknowledged he could be stubborn. His firing came amid talk that Chicago wanted layoffs and other cuts to keep revenues on track. Marimow had consented to trim the budget by letting vacancies go unfilled. But in newsroom conversations, Marimow had said he could not justify firing employees when the company he worked for was making money but simply wanted to make more. "Immoral," is what he said.

Neither he nor Palmer would publicly discuss the reasons that led to his firing.

Marimow remained in his office that day as shocked reporters wandered in and out. He read e-mails, took phone calls, and projected serenity. As he sat in his office that afternoon, he watched the newsroom staff stream past his door to assemble one floor down to meet his replacement.

Timothy A. Franklin, who had worked at the *Chicago Tribune* before he became editor of the *Orlando Sentinel*, another Tribune paper, had flown in to address his new colleagues. The crowd was not entirely welcoming. Some were proposing protests on Marimow's behalf.

Franklin, who had spent most of his career in the Tribune family, brought a reputation as an aggressive newsman who liked hardworking reporters and energetic coverage. Reporters in Orlando adored him. But he was not of the *Sun*.

In his years at the *Sun*, Franklin pushed for coverage that was consistent with the paper's reputation. When a player for the Baltimore Ravens was mentioned in a federal court file in Atlanta, Franklin sent a team of reporters and a photographer to tell the tale of how an old criminal drug case would send an elite athlete to prison. When Pope John Paul II died, Franklin—mindful that Baltimore was the first See of the Catholic Church in America—sent a reporting team to Rome and published a special section.

About a dozen *Sun* journalists trekked to New Orleans and provided dramatic coverage of the devastation caused by Hurricane Katrina.

Locally, *Sun* reporters continued dogging public officials. Mayor Sheila Dixon was convicted of embezzlement and removed from office after investigations by the *Sun* City Hall reporter Doug Donovan.

Maryland's US attorney, Thomas DiBiagio, was reprimanded by his Washington bosses after Stephanie Hanes reported he had commanded his staff to produce "front-page" corruption indictments by Election Day.

And David Nitkin enraged Governor Robert L. Ehrlich Jr. with stories that investigated a state plan to sell a tract of state land to a politically connected developer who would receive tax benefits.

But Franklin would preside over many painful losses as the lurching Tribune Company demanded the *Sun* make cuts.

Chicago never understood what the *Sun* was. It chose not to understand that readers, even those who groused about *Sun* coverage, were at some level proud of their paper.

When Robert Blau, who succeeded Barbieri, arrived in Baltimore in November 2004, he said he was amazed to see the *Sun's* role in the community. Morning radio commentators were either praising or castigating the *Sun*, he said. On evening radio shows, sports fans were arguing about stories in the paper's sport section.

The *Sun*, he said, was in the region's DNA in a way he hadn't seen in other cities.

But this seemed to be lost on the executives in Chicago. They lumped Baltimore in with a group of other papers and managed them from a distance: Hartford, Allentown, Newport News, Fort Lauderdale. The fact that those papers and those cities had little in common wasn't important. The fact that Baltimore had a Washington bureau and foreign operations that readers relied on wasn't important either.

Consolidation was good. Synergy was good.

In 2005, Tribune shut down *Sun* bureaus in Beijing and London. The little good news was that three other bureaus would remain open. That lasted until the following July, when Tribune announced their closing.

The *Sun's* foreign coverage would now come from reporters for the *Chicago Tribune* and the *Los Angeles Times*. The change would mean better coordination of coverage, Tribune said, and save money as well. Tribune did not mention what impact the closings would have on *Sun* subscribers.

In Baltimore, reporters were in despair. Franklin promised to send *Sun* reporters overseas for selected reporting projects. But times had changed, he said in a *Sun* story on the closings. "We're competing in a different environment than we were five, ten years ago," he said. "International news is more of a commodity than ever because of the Internet."

Chicago ordered more economies. To save on newsprint the *Sun* cut some sections and combined others. To save on the cost of wire services, Tribune discontinued the *Sun's* use of the *New York Times* news service. *Sun* readers instead would be offered stories written by Tribune Company reporters.

Rounds of layoffs began. Veterans left. Talented newcomers fled. Vacancies in suburban offices went unfilled; those bureaus, which once had staffs of about a dozen, now were down to three or four people. The metro staff was reorganized to try to cover gaps in coverage, then was reorganized again as more layoffs meant even fewer reporters and editors.

Staffing was cut at the Washington bureau, so long the source of pride. Tribune did not see why Baltimore readers needed their own source of Washington news—despite the fact that thousands of readers commuted to Washington, or worked for the federal government, or that the *Sun* had had its own reporters in Washington since 1837. Quickly, many of the remaining Washington reporters offered their resignations. Eventually, the remaining few reporters were folded into a consolidated Tribune Company bureau.

But all that didn't stanch the drop in revenues. Tribune had a new strategy—actually, a successive series of strategies—none of which bolstered readership or ad sales.

For one stretch, Chicago's directive to its papers in Baltimore's category was local news. The theory went like this: readers could find foreign and national news anywhere—on television, on a variety of websites. But local news was the province of local papers. That's something readers would pay for, and advertisers would pay to reach those readers.

Generations of readers had relied on the *Sun* for foreign and national news as well as local coverage. Chicago, however, was convinced it was right. Local news belonged on front pages. News from the rest of the world—save for the very biggest events—belonged inside the paper.

So men in Chicago began monitoring the *Sun's* front page and taking charge of what readers in Baltimore would see. Each month, an editor in Chicago would send Baltimore's top editor a report that detailed how many local stories, how many foreign and national stories, and how many feature or trend stories had appeared on page 1 of the *Sun*.

Local was good. Anything else needed to be justified. If the US Supreme Court issued a major ruling, could that story run on 1A? Maybe, if editors could find a way to explain the direct impact in Maryland at the top of the story. If they did not, they risked having the story counted against them in the next monthly report.

The editors who won praise at Tribune papers around the country were those who followed Chicago's orders and produced colorful front pages filled with stories from the hometown, embellished with outsized illustrations. One example: a Florida front page that featured a giant bottle of red nail polish spilling down the center of the news columns, with an ominous headline asking about the safety of *your* nail salon.

Editors in Baltimore resisted. They made some changes but were intent on keeping the *Sun* looking like the *Sun*.

The *Sun's* connection with its readers was fraying more quickly. Print subscribers did not renew. Why bother paying for a shrunken product? No longer did the *Sun* provide original stories from Washington or from foreign bureaus. With cuts in staff, it no longer could offer comprehensive coverage of the region. Readers learned to go to other online news operations for their news.

In Chicago, the Tribune Company was struggling for revenues. In 2007, it sold itself to Sam Zell, a Chicago investor who wore a leather jacket and rode a motorcycle and desperately wanted to be viewed as cool. He paid $8.2 billion for the Tribune Company. The following year, the company declared bankruptcy.

At the *Sun*, the buyouts continued. I left the paper in July 2008 to begin teaching at the Philip Merrill College of Journalism at the University of Maryland, College Park. Blau left the paper in September 2008, and joined Bloomberg News as editor of reporting projects. Franklin left in December 2008 to run a sports reporting center at Indiana University, his alma mater. After a stint at Bloomberg News in Washington, he was named president of the Poynter Institute.

Franklin was succeeded by Monty Cook, whom Franklin had brought up from Orlando in 2004 to be a deputy managing editor in charge of the copy desk, graphics, design, and production.

In April 2009, under the direction of publisher Timothy Ryan and Cook, the *Sun* fired more than sixty people, including its reader representative and the head of its editorial pages. The newsroom had expected layoffs, but the depth of these cuts was shocking.

Staff members would later say they watched for hours as reporters, editors, photographers, and graphic artists—newcomers and veterans—were called one by one into the editors' offices to be fired.

Security guards were posted at the entrance to the company parking garage. Some staff members were escorted from the building moments after hearing their fate. Their colleagues clapped in sad tribute as fired journalists made their way out of the newsroom, carrying personal belongings.

A few days later, in *Real Clear Sports*, the *Sun* sports columnist David Steele told his story. He wrote that the entire *Sun* staff had been on edge for days amid grim rumors that mass firings were imminent. The night before, some veteran sports editors had been let go and said farewells via e-mail.

But Steele said he went to work as usual and took his seat in the press box at Camden Yards, preparing to write his regular column on the Orioles game.

His routine began to unravel. He heard that another columnist was assigned to write for the next day's paper—a confusion that Steele wanted an editor to straighten out so that Steele could get to work. And then Steele's cell phone rang. He said he went into a hallway to take a call from an editor who told him he was sorry but Steele's job was gone. When Steele went to tell the game photographer Elizabeth Malby, he found she had gotten a call, too.

Chicago kept pushing to combine tasks and save money. Tribune began formatting several of the *Sun's* inside pages and sending them digitally to Baltimore every day. That meant editors in Chicago decided which stories readers of the *Sun* and its sister papers would see, how prominently those stories would be displayed, and what their headlines would say.

The *Sun* remained the biggest newsroom in the state. Its reporters continued to do distinguished work on a smaller scale. The *Sun's* first female editor, Mary Corey, oversaw an expansion of online news and pushed for original stories. After Corey's death from breast cancer in 2013, Trif Alatzas became editor and hired reporters for a new investigative team to supplement daily reporting of local governments, the State House, and the police.

Just before the race riots of April 2015, the Sun did solid reporting on the sad state of race relations in the city. During the disturbances, the paper's coverage was broad, energetic, and deep. Its reporters were first with reliable reporting on Twitter, Facebook, and online. National news outlets, including the television networks, relied heavily on the *Sun*. For its efforts, the paper went on to place as a finalist in two categories—breaking news and editorial writing—in the 2016 Pulitzer Prize awards.

But that level of coverage is harder for the *Sun* to sustain now. The newsroom that once numbered just over four hundred has been cut by 80 percent.

• 26 •

A View from the Boardroom

W. Shepherdson Abell

When I joined the board of directors of the A. S. Abell Company—the owner of the *Baltimore Sun*—in 1975, the last thing I wanted was for the paper to be sold. And that, I am sure, was the prevailing view on the board.

Most of the other directors were Baltimoreans and shared a keen sense of the importance of the *Sun* to the Baltimore and Maryland communities, and pride in its national reputation and influence. Gary Black, a Baltimorean, was chairman of the board. His son, Gary Jr., was a member of company management. Harrison Garrett was a respected financier in the city; his son Rob was a banker in New York, but had been born and raised in Baltimore. William E. McGuirk Jr. was CEO of Mercantile Safe Deposit & Trust Company, then the premier trust company in Maryland. William F. Schmick Jr. was president of the company, as his father had been before him. Donald H. Patterson was general manager and soon to become president—as *his* father had been before the Schmicks, father and son. My own father had grown up in the Washington area, as had I, but we had deep roots in Baltimore. My great-great grandfather—whose middle name I carried—was Arunah Shepherdson Abell, one of the three founders of the *Sun* in 1837, and the one among the three who ended up owning the paper and passing it on at his death to his three sons, Walter, Edwin, and my great-grandfather, George W. Abell.

George's son Charles S. Abell—my grandfather—had been vice president and general manager of the company. He was presiding over a board meeting in 1910 when he brought up the final item on the agenda: "Is there any new business?" Yes, he was told, there was. A controlling interest in the company had been sold to a syndicate headed by Charles H. Grasty, a competing newspaperman, and including members of the Garrett, Black, White,

261

Figure 26.1. Arunah S. Abell, middle, with two associates in Philadelphia 1836, one year before Abell established the *Sun* as a penny paper. On the left, Azariah H. Simmons; to the right, William M. Swain. The three men established the *Philadelphia Public Ledger* in 1836.

and Keyser families, all among the leading citizens of Baltimore. How did that happen?

Part of the reason was a falling out among Abell family members. Relations between my grandfather and Walter W. Abell, his cousin, were strained. Another important factor was the role of John J. Nelligan of the

Safe Deposit and Trust Co., a board member who acted as trustee for a large number of family shares. Grasty had first approached Nelligan, whom he found receptive. Nelligan apparently had little trouble bringing along Walter Abell, who was trustee for another block of family shares. With control of a majority of stock, they concluded the deal with Grasty. Within two years, Charles Abell had left the company, and no member of my family was to be associated with the papers for over thirty years.

Unlike most members of the Abell family, my grandfather held on to all of his common stock in the company and declined to exchange it for preferred stock or more lucrative bonds. But it was not until after World War II that a representative of the Abell family—my father—was invited back onto the board of directors. And eventually, to my deep satisfaction, I was asked to become a director, too. I had no real newspaper credentials; I worked as a gofer for the reporters and editors at the 1964 national conventions, and I had done some reporting from a rather tame Baltimore police station another summer. But I loved newspapers and was thrilled to be on the board. My wife had been a reporter for the *Hartford Times*, and we both consumed news voraciously. I read the Sunpapers closely—it was easy in those days to obtain daily delivery in the Washington suburbs, where you could also readily find the *Sun* and even the *Evening Sun* in street boxes. I arranged to receive clips marked to show who had written the editorials, and I enjoyed visiting the newsroom and complimenting the authors of articles and editorials. (But like all the other directors, I never thought of pressing any view of my own. That simply was not done at the *Sun*.) I was proud of the massive investment in the Washington bureau and the numerous foreign bureaus, and recalled with satisfaction that the *Sun* had been said to be the first newspaper Lyndon Johnson read each morning at the White House. My four years working in the State House in Annapolis as an aide to a lieutenant governor and a governor had shown me how respected both the *Sun* and the *Evening Sun* were for their thorough reporting and relentless digging. I wanted to be part of the enterprise that produced that kind of journalism.

The story of the sale of the paper in 1910, unsurprisingly, became an important part of the oral history handed down in my family, and not just for the rupture between my grandfather and his cousin Walter. As a trust and estates lawyer, I became particularly interested in the manner in which the company stock had then been held—large blocks of shares controlled by trustees—and the fiduciary responsibilities that entailed.

In 1975 (when I joined the board) and thereafter, a major part of the company's stock was held in trust (somewhat similar to the situation in 1910). A trustee was obligated to act in accordance with the financial interests of both the immediate and the future beneficiaries of the trust. Those interests would include *current income*: How substantial were the dividends in comparison with the value of the stock? Then came *liquidity*: How easy was it to sell the investment? Finally, the trustees were obliged to try to *diversify* their investments. For a trust that was invested heavily in A. S. Abell Company stock, there was little or no diversification. If the company encountered heavy financial weather, and reduced or eliminated the dividend, the trustees would have few options.

A trustee could not take into account the benefits to Baltimore and the other "stakeholders" beyond the financial interests of shareholders. Nor could he be bound by what he thought was good for the newspaper or its employees. If a trustee concluded that the sale of the paper would bring an immediate increase in income to the current beneficiaries and would provide liquidity to the investment and an opportunity to diversify—thereby benefiting both present and future beneficiaries—he would have little choice but to agree to sell. Even if current beneficiaries of the trust happened to be opposed to a sale, trustees needed to consider the interests of future beneficiaries.

I said above that the last thing I wanted was for the papers to be sold. Actually, that was the next-to-last thing. The *last* thing, in my view, was for the paper to be sold in a bidding war that resulted in a sale to a buyer who was interested solely in financial gain.

Moreover, I thought if a bidding war were to develop, the trustees would be practically forced to accept the highest bidder, regardless of the impact on the quality of the papers and the welfare of the community. All of this, to my way of thinking, posed a continuing background threat, invisible to most observers, to the operation of the newspapers and the business of the company. There had been an informal offer from Newhouse to buy the company in the 1960s, but it was rebuffed by management. A substantial and serious offer, reflecting the real value of the company—if it were to come—could not be dealt with so summarily. Yet in my discussions with other board members, especially my contemporaries Gary Black Jr. and Rob Garrett, I can recall no mention of selling the company.

So, although I can't speak for any other board members, I know that my father and I had every intention in 1975 of keeping the company in private hands, if at all possible. And I believed that it was possible. I also believed that most, if not all, of the other directors at the time felt the same. But the financial picture of the company was mediocre at best. For that, some blamed the large (even lavish) expenditures on bureaus in Washington and abroad—the same practices which distinguished the *Sun* in the history of American journalism and also helped to make it so attractive to write for, as seen in the other chapters of this book. The rest of us hoped that we could make the company more profitable without compromising the quality of its products. That was the next challenge.

A series of board discussions, accompanied by reports from a New York consultant, led us to reorganize the company's management and select a new publisher who would serve as CEO of the newspaper division. After considering several candidates, one of them Steven Muller, then president of the Johns Hopkins University, the board settled in 1981 on John R. (Reg) Murphy, editor-publisher of the *San Francisco Examiner*. He was an experienced newspaperman with some interesting ideas about maintaining and extending the quality and reach of the papers, while raising profits. And so it proved to be.

When the company was sold five years later, some observers said that Reg Murphy had been brought in for the purpose of fattening profits to make the company a more attractive target for prospective buyers. It is possible that some directors had that in mind; but most, I am confident, did not. I met from time to time with the younger members of the board, and our hope was to continue local ownership with improved profitability *and* quality. It seemed to me, in fact, that increasing profits—and raising the dividend— might make it less likely that shareholders, even trustees, would be interested in selling. And so annual dividends rose from $23 in 1982 to $26.50, then $29, then $39 in 1985, and a rate of $50 in 1986. This reflected an increase in profits from $1.5 million in 1981 to nearly $21 million in 1985.

At the same time, the directors believed that the quality of the papers had improved. Writers for both the *Sun* and the *Evening Sun* won Pulitzer Prizes in 1985. Television did well, while the acquisition of radio stations— new territory for the company—was not productive; directors joked that the typical purchase price for a station was nine times losses. The company disposed of its radio holdings.

On the whole, the future looked very rosy when, in April 1986, representatives of the Times Mirror Company approached Reg Murphy with an offer of $550 million for the company, including TV holdings. The board was advised of the offer at once.

Thus did the possibility that had loomed in the background become real and immediate. The board of directors—from which my father, Harrison Garrett, Bill Schmick, and Gary Black Sr. had retired—had added Osborn Elliott, dean of the Columbia School of Journalism, and George Bunting, CEO of Noxell, one of the major businesses in the Baltimore area.

The nature of the existing ownership of the company's stock was crucial. By my estimate, between 40 and 50 percent of the stock was held in trust. Another 19 percent was held by the A. S. Abell Company Foundation, which had received the vast majority of Harry C. Black's stock when he died in 1956; he had been chairman of the board since 1930. The trustees of the foundation—all drawn from the board of directors of the company—were bound by a somewhat different set of fiduciary duties than the trustees of private trusts, but their prime concern had to be the interests of the foundation's possible charitable and educational grant recipients, which would be greatly enhanced if a sale went through.

Some of the directors knew a good bit about the Times Mirror Company, and the rest of us learned as much as we could as quickly as we could. It was controlled by the Chandler family, and owned the *Los Angeles Times*, *Newsday*, and a half-dozen other papers. The *Los Angeles Times* had become one of the top newspapers in the country (and certainly the fattest, with its enviable combination of extensive coverage and massive advertising). It had won fourteen Pulitzer Prizes since 1942. The company had poured money (later estimated to be $100 million) into *Newsday* in an effort to offer a second high-quality paper to the New York market. It had broadcast, cable, book, and magazine holdings. With revenues of $3 billion, it seemed to have the financial base to take a long-term view, and the Chandlers seemingly had a firm grip on the company and a strong commitment to quality journalism.

In short, it seemed that if the Sunpapers were to be sold, Times Mirror was as good a buyer as could be found, from the perspective of encouraging and supporting quality journalism.

I can't recall the details of my discussions with other directors, but I can say what my thinking was at the time. (As a director, I tried to put out of my mind the fact that my siblings and I had been able to purchase shares from our cousin's estate a decade earlier at an attractive price, and hence a sale would make each of us financially established for life.) In general, it might be said that we had (in theory at least) four options: (1) we could reject the offer and refuse to take it to the shareholders; (2) we could accept the offer, perhaps after demanding a higher price; (3) we could test the marketplace for possible higher offers; or (4) we could delay the process to see if a local group could come together to keep ownership local.

The fourth option, attractive on the surface, seemed to me to be illusory. It was by no means certain that any local group that could put together an offer would be committed to long-term, patient investment in quality journalism. The Times Mirror offer was such a full price that it was hard to believe that local interests would be able to match it. Financing would be essential, but this was 1986, and the prime rate was 8.5 percent. Word would inevitably get out and create the chance that other national bidders would make an offer. In effect, the fourth option merged into the third. And the prospect that the papers would simply pass into the hands of the highest bidder alarmed me more than anything else.

As a group, the directors were keenly interested in the welfare of the city and in the highest standards of journalism. There was little appetite for the loss of local ownership. A couple of directors initially resisted any thought of a sale. Rob Garrett, Oz Elliott, George Bunting, Gary Black Jr., and I were cool to it at the outset. But as discussions went on, and the realities of the alternatives came more into focus, the board decided to pursue negotiations with Times Mirror—not without a considerable sense of regret. Directors, and particularly those from families that had been invested in the company for generations, had to put personal feeling aside. Bill McGuirk, the Mercantile bank executive who joined the board in 1966 and became chairman in 1983, was strongly in favor of the deal and was active on the sidelines. McGuirk was the first board chairman who was not a member of one of the controlling families. His bank, as a trustee, controlled just over 40 percent of Abell Company stock.

Once the board decided to continue talks with Times Mirror, McGuirk flew to Los Angeles. Our thought was that if the price could be substantially increased, not only would our shareholders benefit, but we might regard the bid as a premium price, and thus allay any misgivings that shareholders might have about not having tested the market further. In the event, Bill McGuirk negotiated an increase to $600 million.

Things moved quickly. The initial offer had been made on May 12. The revised offer was approved unanimously by the board of directors on May 28, and announcement of the sale was made that afternoon. In a matter of a little over two weeks, a tradition of local ownership that had lasted close to a century and a half had melted away. Ratification by the shareholders on June 12 was a foregone conclusion.

The aftermath of the sale has been described elsewhere in these pages. Reg Murphy, who had received stock options as part of his compensation package, was rewarded with $14.5 million. Bill McGuirk was paid $500,000 for his part in increasing the purchase price by $50 million. The biggest winner was the A. S. Abell Company Foundation, which owned over 19 percent of the company. After the close of the merger, its net worth on October 31 had jumped to $112 million. The sale enabled its transformation from a small foundation focused largely on local arts, hospitals, and private schools to the largest foundation (and, as it turned out, the most proactive and imaginative) in Maryland.

Reading the paper following the sale, my sense was that a high level of quality was maintained for a number of years. None of us could have foreseen that just fourteen years later, after a well-publicized falling out among Chandler family members, the Times Mirror Company would be sold to the Tribune Company, which became the second-largest newspaper owner in the country. And then the Tribune Company was itself sold to real estate magnate Sam Zell, who had no evident interest in quality journalism, but a paramount interest in making a buck. He was in bankruptcy a year later, and a massive squeeze on the resources available to (and demanded from) the *Sun* continued. Our worst fears of 1986 had come to pass.

The end result is, of course, nothing like what any of the directors envisioned (or any observers predicted at the time). Baltimore is far from the only city that has suffered from a decline in journalism in recent decades. From what I know, the *Sun* is still superior to the papers of most other comparable cities. But it has turned out to be, nonetheless, a sad story. I see no other city where the fall has been so dramatic, from such great heights.

I am not thinking merely of journalism for journalism's sake. All of the directors, management, reporters, and editors associated with the Sunpapers in their prime believed in the vital role of the press in informing the citizenry. As more experienced observers than I have noted, the consolidation of newspaper ownership within conglomerates and the incessant demand for high and immediate profits, all in the context of the Internet, have increasingly placed that role in jeopardy. The citizens of Baltimore and Maryland are the real losers.

· 27 ·

What Will Become of Newspapers?

John S. Carroll

John S. Carroll, who edited three newspapers—the *Baltimore Sun*, the *Los Angeles Times*, and the *Lexington Herald-Leader*—had planned to contribute two chapters to this book, one on his reporting from Vietnam for the *Sun* in 1968 and a second on the advantages of family-owned over corporate newspapers. He died on June 14, 2015, of a rare neurological disorder.

Carroll was editor of the *Sun* from 1991 to 2000, when the paper won two Pulitzer Prizes. Afterwards, at the *Times*, he directed a reportorial staff which won thirteen Pulitzers before he quit in 2005 in a dispute over severe cutbacks that Tribune, the paper's corporate parent, insisted on making.

Carroll believed that investing in the newspaper would eventually produce higher profits and that cutting costs, while temporarily improving the bottom line, would erode the quality of a paper and might someday destroy it.

He thought America's best newspapers were those owned by families "who value the quality of their papers above short-term financial performance," as he told Ken Auletta of the *New Yorker* not long after he left the *Times*. As for his differences with Tribune executives, Carroll said, "On the surface, it's about cuts. But it's also about aspirations for the paper, and for journalism itself. It is test case No. 1 of whether a newspaper chain can produce a first-rate newspaper. It may be that it is simply structurally impossible."

Expanding on those thoughts—which are conclusively relevant to our book—Carroll addressed the American Society of Newspaper Editors on April 16, 2006. Excerpts of his speech follow, provided by Harvard's Shorenstein Center on Media, Politics and Public Policy.

269

Like many of you, I've been worrying lately. What will become of us? More important, what will become of our newspapers? More important still, what will become of the kind of public-service journalism that newspapers produce? And, vastly more important than all that: What will the public know—and what will the public not know—if our poorly understood, and often unappreciated, craft perishes in the Darwinian jungle?

Quite a few of the people we hear from these days—the talk-show hosts, the bloggers, the political operatives, the marketers, the flacks of all sorts—dream wistful dreams of a world without newspapers. What power they would have! How blissfully simple their lives would be! And, it could actually happen. Let's imagine. . . . If, at some point in America's newspaper-free future, the police decide that the guilt or innocence of murder suspects can be determined perfectly well by beating them until somebody confesses, who will sound the alarm, as the *Philadelphia Inquirer* did in 1977? Or, if those federal scientists who tell our doctors what drugs and what dosages are best for us are secretly allowed to take salaries and stock options from drug companies, how will we know it, if the *Los Angeles Times* is not there to tell us, as it did in 2003? Or, if some future president secretly decides to nullify the law and spy on American citizens without warrants, who—if the *New York Times* falls by the wayside—will sound the warning?

More routinely, who will make the checks at City Hall? Who, in cities and towns across America, will go down to the courthouse every day, or to the police station? Who will inspect the tens of thousands of politicians who seek to govern? Who—amid America's great din of flackery and cant—will tell us in plain language what's actually going on? Since I left the *Los Angeles Times*, I've been thinking about our craft and about the commerce that sustains it. . . . I don't have the big picture yet. But I do have some important parts of it. Consider this, then, an interim report.

The economic rules that govern the newspaper business have changed. We all know this. The old business model is defunct. Under the old model, owners got rich and newsrooms became juggernauts. That golden age is over.

With the advent of the web, our rotary presses, those massive machines that once conferred near monopolies on their owners, are looking more and more like the last steam engine. Young readers are going online and not coming back. Circulation revenues are dwindling. The equivalent of circulation revenues on the web is negligible. Circulation itself is falling. Ad revenues are weak and web-based competitors are stealing our advertisers. Some of these competitors are even helping themselves to our stories and our photographs, which we have produced at great expense.

Then there's a more subtle problem, a crisis of the soul. Every journalist believes that he or she works, ultimately, for the reader—not for the editor, or for the publisher, or for the corporation, or for those opaque financial institutions that hold the stock. We all know journalists who have lost their jobs on principle. They have refused to kill important stories, or to write glowingly about politicians or advertisers who don't deserve it. They have done this because their first loyalty is to the reader. Whole newsrooms, on occasion, have taken the same principled stand.

What lent overwhelming moral force to their cause was the flagrant betrayal of the reader. We work, however, within large organizations that hold a different view of duty. Our corporate superiors are sometimes genuinely perplexed to find people in their midst who do not feel beholden, first and foremost, to the shareholder. What makes these people tick?, they wonder. The job of any employee, as they see it, is to produce a good financial result, not to indulge in some dreamy form of do-gooding at company expense.

The conflict between those who serve the reader and those who serve the shareholder might seem a bit abstract, but it's important. It affects the way we see ourselves as editors, and the way we behave. It inhibits us when we ought to be bold.

How long has it been since an editor was so rash as to cite public service in justifying a budget? You might as well ask to be branded with a scarlet N, for naïve. Our corporate superiors regard our beliefs as quaint, wasteful, and increasingly tiresome. Even outside the corporation we have lost stature. We might see ourselves as public servants, but does the public see us that way? To some, these words may seem overly harsh. But it is important that we understand our position clearly, without illusion, because we have a mission ahead of us, and we need to be rigorously clear-headed.

Our mission is more daunting than that of our predecessors. It is not merely to produce good stories. It is not merely to save our newspapers. It is—and this may sound grandiose—to save journalism itself. It is to ensure the existence, long into the future, of a large, independent, principled, questioning, deep-digging cadre of journalists in America, regardless of what happens to our newspapers. You and I know it won't be easy. I'd like to pull out a few samples. I offer them in the form of five questions, each of which I will attempt to answer.

Question No. 1: Are newspaper editors really necessary? It will not surprise you to hear that there is a backlash these days against people who presume to be gatekeepers. That, of course, means us. We're all familiar by now with the vocabulary of the argument. Paternalism, as we know, is dead and should never have existed in the first place. Disintermediated news is news without intermediation, which is to say, news that's not selected by editors. And, finally, markets are capable of making better decisions about news than editors.

We're getting this from two sides. First, there are the web people, who have ingeniously figured out how to decide what's important by tabulating the collective wisdom of online readers. How galling for us—to be replaced by an algorithm. Second, we're getting it from our own corporate leaders, who believe in market research. Why not just edit by referendum?, they wonder. Why not just ask people what they want and give it to them?

I am happy to respond to this critique. You don't need to look any further to see where editing by referendum takes you. It takes you to tabloid-land, to Angelina Jolie, to Brad Pitt, to the lurid murder of the week, to campaigns to save Christmas from imaginary enemies, to mass-produced political vituperation, to a whole cornucopia of sexual indiscretions. . . .

The question here is whether a newspaper ought to lead or to follow. Should a newspaper actually stand for anything? Or should it be a transparent vessel for the truisms and vulgarities of the age? My view is that America already has enough cheesy consumer products. And let me add a corollary: I think a newspaper should be willing, on certain occasions, to offend even its most loyal readers. Back in the 1980s, the *Lexington Herald-Leader* offended an entire state by disclosing widespread cheating in the University of Kentucky basketball program. Seemingly, that was a mistake. Angry citizens boycotted the paper's advertising and circulation. A bomb scare emptied the building. Someone fired a rifle shot into the pressroom. The electronic media mounted months of abuse, including a talk show whose topic was, and I quote, "How Can We Destroy the Newspaper?" But the newspaper was not destroyed—far from it. In circulation and in profits, the *Herald-Leader* flourished during the 1980s as never before or since. That's because, over the long haul, people don't buy the newspaper because it serves them pabulum, or because they think the editor is a nice guy. They buy it because it tells them significant things they don't already know.

In marketing, the idea is to manage the number of complaints down to zero. That's fine if you're making toasters, but a newspaper that gets no complaints is a dead newspaper. So, to Question No. 1—are newspaper editors really necessary—the answer is: yes, absolutely.

Question No. 2: If newspapers disappear, should the public care? Never have the American people been more lavishly supplied with news. Yahoo, Google, and a whole galaxy of websites—not to mention radio, television, newspapers, podcasts, cellphones, and Blackberries—bombard us with journalism. But where does it come from? Well, some news announces itself—a tsunami, for example. The rest of it is dug up by reporters.

When I was a young reporter at the *Baltimore Sun*, I viewed my job as turning over rocks. Usually there was nothing under a given rock, so I'd move on to the next rock. It was humble work, but every now and then it would produce something worthwhile. I remember, for example, visiting a potential source again and again for months without getting a thing. Then, one day, he gave me a tip. The resulting story saved hundreds of thousands of Maryland citizens from a 26 percent increase in their health insurance rates. This kind of reporting is unglamorous, inefficient, and expensive—and in America it is done almost entirely by newspapers. In my reporting days, I almost never saw radio or television reporters turning over rocks.

Newspapers became the nation's rock-turners because they made enough money to employ large staffs. Go to just about any city or town in America, and you'll find that the newspaper has more reporters than all other media combined. This is our role: newspapers dig up the news. Others repackage it.

The blogs, noisy as they are, have virtually no reporters. They may be keen critics, or assiduous fact checkers, but do they add materially to the nation's supply of original reporting? No, they don't. I wish I could tell you precisely how much of America's news originates in newspapers, but apparently there's been no definitive study.

So, instead, I've been asking smart people to make estimates. So far, nobody has given me a figure lower than 80 percent. If, then, in the worst case, newspapers fade away, and if nobody else steps forward to provide a new army of rock-turners, what will the American public know in the future? What stories will go untold? What issues unraised? What will serious-minded people have to talk about? The answer to Question No. 2, then, is: yes, the public should care if newspapers disappear.

Question No. 3: What is the strategy of the newspaper industry? It was heartening when McClatchy emerged victorious in the bidding for Knight Ridder. McClatchy's CEO, Gary Pruitt, bases much of his strategy on good journalism and on optimism about the electronic future. This is a plan we can all understand. Whether it will actually work under the new economics of our business is not known. We should all be lighting candles for McClatchy. We should all be lighting candles for the families that still own newspapers.

In difficult times, they have persisted in upholding traditions of journalistic excellence. Many of these papers, such as the *New York Times*, and most others have created electronic editions, which are crucial to the long-term survival of newspaper journalism. Revenue from those editions is growing at an impressive rate, but the absolute numbers are still small. These are strategies for building, strategies that preserve journalism as the core of the business. They fall into the category of investment strategies.

Now let's turn to another kind of strategy, the opposite of an investment strategy. It is called a harvest strategy. I first heard the phrase "harvest strategy" in the 1990s, when it was briefly mentioned in a board meeting at the *Baltimore Sun*. I was the *Sun's* editor then, and merely hearing those two words gave me the willies. I suspected they meant milking a declining business for all the cash it can produce until it dies.

Much later I looked up "harvest strategy" in a business textbook, and my suspicion was right. The idea of liquidating the *Baltimore Sun* in this way was unthinkable to me. This was the paper of Mencken. This was the paper that got the story when Samuel F. B. Morse sent his historic telegram. By the way, you won't believe this: the *Sun* got that story but somehow managed to miss the quote that would ring through the ages: "What hath God wrought?" Like all newspapers, the *Sun* was fallible, but it was also the voice of a city, and of a state, published daily since 1837. How could anyone even think of "harvesting" it? For the record, I am unaware of any formal decision to harvest the *Sun* or any other paper. Further, I've been advised by those who know more about finance than I do that a frustrated owner would do better these days by selling a paper than by running it into the ground. And yet, symptoms of harvest are staring us in the face. They include a low rate of investment, fewer employees, fewer readers, falling stock prices, and, most especially, high profit margins.

In 2005, our troubled industry reported operating margins averaging 19.3 percent. That's double the average enjoyed by Fortune 500 companies. These high profits were achieved by relentless cost-cutting, which is rendering newspapers less valuable to their readers each year, and less able to compete. Many of you have had the unhappy task of laying off or buying out your newsroom colleagues. This is tough duty—especially when there's no inspirational reason for doing it. It would help if there were some clear strategy for a brighter future.

To a journalist, merely hitting some short-term profit target does not make it all seem worthwhile. I'm still hoping that newspapers, like certain troubled industries before them, will succeed in finding a new business model. This is a matter of urgency. Each year that we fail, our army of rock-turners will shrink. Without them, there will be no reason to read newspapers. So, in response to Question No. 3—What is the strategy of the newspaper industry?—the answer is that there are two strategies, and they are at war with each other: There's the investment strategy, which optimistically builds something for the future. Then there's the pessimistic harvest strategy, which, either deliberately or by default, drains all the available cash from a business before it collapses.

Question No. 4: What do current owners want from their newspapers? There was a time, some of you may recall, when owners were identifiable human beings. We've all heard colleagues say, "All this would never have happened if Jack Knight—or Otis Chandler, or Barry Bingham—still owned the place." Unfortunately, the old owners are gone. If they did return, they'd be amazed at what's happened—and not just to their newspapers.

They'd be amazed at what's happened to the very idea of ownership. Who are the owners today? Have you ever actually met one? In order to track down the owners, you've got to knock on doors at such places as Private Capital Management of Naples, Florida, or Ariel Capital Management of Chicago, or Southeastern Asset Management of Memphis.

If you succeed in getting past the receptionist, you'll find a scene not unlike a newsroom—people talking on phones or tapping away at computers. These are highly motivated people—intelligent people working in a disciplined fashion. Much of their work, unlike ours, is mathematical. The most accomplished of the math people are known as "quants." Like journalists, these fund managers are seekers, trying to find out things before their competitors do. They monitor hundreds, perhaps thousands, of companies—franchise companies that create Tex-Mex restaurants, perhaps, or mining interests in Bolivia, or chains of nursing homes in the South; and, among all these, companies that operate newspapers. All are given equal consideration; everything depends on the numbers. Until recently, the ongoing conversation between the fund managers and our corporate leaders has been conducted out of public earshot. I'm told that contact has been frequent and that there is only one real subject: profits.

Lately, however, the funds have become more open in expressing themselves. Bruce Sherman, of Private Capital Management, publicly demanded that Knight Ridder be sold—and it was. More recently, Morgan Stanley has been trying to torpedo the two-tier stock structure at the *New York Times,* which would bring an end to generations of family leadership at America's foremost paper.

Gone is the notion that a newspaper should lead, that it has an obligation to its community, that it is beholden to the public. The apparent frustration at the funds hints at future instability in ownership—perhaps even the unraveling of a process that started forty years ago. That process began when local owners sold their papers to corporations. For a time, the corporations seemed to be in command. Business was good, and many of the papers grew, both financially and journalistically. Then, as business got tougher, power began to migrate from the corporations to the funds. We are now in a post-corporate phase of ownership. Over the same forty years, we have seen a narrowing of the purpose of the newspaper in the eyes of its owner. Under the old local owners, a newspaper's capacity for making money was only part of its value. Today, it is everything.

With the shrinking of the newspaper's social purpose, we have seen a shrinking of the newspaper journalist. It has happened slowly and subtly, but, if you stand back, as I have lately, it's all too clear. The old, local owners were far from perfect. Some of them were good, most were mediocre, and

Figure 27.1.   John. S. Carroll, editor of the *Sun*, 1991–2000.

some were downright evil. But, forty years later, local ownership is looking better every day.

It is tempting to find a goat here, to single out some individual and heap blame on him or her for the decline of our business. That might be cathartic, but the problem is bigger than that. It is structural. Most of the people in the corporations, and most of the people in the funds, are doing their jobs by the book. Restoring a balance between financial performance and public duty is probably impossible under this form of ownership. So, in response to Question No. 4—What do the current owners want from their newspapers?—the answer could not be simpler: money. That's it.

Question No. 5: Will we see other forms of ownership? With newspapers losing their luster in the financial world, big changes are likely. Some could be good, some could be bad. Here's one of the good ones. I have edited newspapers in three cities—Lexington, Baltimore, and Los Angeles—and in all three cities I'm seeing a new phenomenon: local people seeking to buy the paper back from the corporations. I've spoken with several of them. These are serious people—sophisticated people with real money.

Figure 27.2.   John S. Carroll reporting for the *Sun* in Vietnam, 1968.

Unlike corporate owners, these people talk about the importance of the paper to the community. They talk about restoring its pride. They talk about investing in journalism, especially in local coverage. They see the newspaper as a fallen angel, and they say they'd be willing to accept a lower financial return, which would allow the paper to breathe again. Yes, it seems too much to hope for.

One obstacle, I'm told, is capital gains taxes. If a corporation sells a newspaper for cash, it will probably have to pay a lot of the money to the government. If, on the other hand, the corporation sells to another corporation in a stock swap or merger, those taxes are largely deferred. In this way, the deck is stacked against the local buyer. So to Question No. 5—Will we ever see new forms of ownership?—the answer is: almost certainly yes. Will they be better, or worse? Nobody knows.

We journalists have a set of values, at the center of which is the reader, or the public.

But does the public believe that? It is important for us to understand, in clear English, what, exactly, a journalist is, and what a journalist is not. It is important for us to live by those beliefs, too, and to condemn those who use the trappings of journalism to engage in marketing or propaganda. And, finally, it is important for us to explain to the public why journalism—real journalism, practiced in good faith—is absolutely essential to a self-governing nation. This is a cause that is larger than us and larger than our newspapers. It gives meaning to our labors in a difficult time.

Index

About the Contributors

W. Shepherdson Abell is the great-great-grandson of Arunah S. Abell, the principal founder of the *Baltimore Sun*. He served on the board of the A. S. Abell Company, the *Sun's* parent company, from 1975 to 1986. A graduate of Boston College, Harvard University, and Georgetown University Law Center, Abell is a lawyer in private practice in Chevy Chase, Maryland. He is a trustee of the Abell Foundation in Baltimore and adjunct professor at the Georgetown University Law Center.

Russell Baker is the winner of the 1979 George Polk Award for Commentary, the 1979 Pulitzer Prize for Distinguished Commentary, and the 1983 Pulitzer Prize for Biography for his book *Growing Up*. He served as a longtime columnist for the *New York Times*, writing the syndicated column "Observer," and hosted the PBS show *Masterpiece Theatre*. He also wrote a sequel to *Growing Up* called *The Good Times* (1989). Baker began his career in 1947 at the *Baltimore Sun*, going on to join the Washington bureau of the *Times* in 1954, covering national politics, in particular Congress and the White House.

Sandy Banisky spent thirty-eight years at the *Sun*, beginning as a copy editor right after graduating from Boston University. She worked as a features reporter before moving to the metro desk, where she covered City Hall and the State House. Then national correspondent, she covered stories including the Oklahoma City bombing and the trial of the bomber Timothy McVeigh. Banisky was successively national editor, deputy managing editor for metro, and deputy managing editor for news. She is now the Abell Professor in Baltimore Journalism at the Philip Merrill College of Journalism at the University of Maryland, College Park. She has a law degree from the University of Baltimore and passed the Maryland bar.

293

Tony Barbieri started at the *Sun* in 1968 as a copy boy and retired in 2004 as managing editor. He was a reporter on the metro staff, in the Washington bureau, and for nearly ten years correspondent in Moscow and Tokyo. He returned to the Baltimore newsroom in 1988 to become city editor and held a variety of editorial positions until he was named managing editor in 2000. After leaving the *Sun*, he taught journalism at the University of Maryland, and since 2007 has been the Larry and Ellen Foster Professor of Writing and Editing at Penn State University.

Stephens Broening was Associated Press correspondent in Paris, Moscow, and Lisbon from 1965 to 1976 before joining the *Sun* as assistant city editor in 1976. In 1978, he was named the paper's first Op-Ed page editor, a post he held until 1985 when he was assigned to the *Sun*'s Washington bureau as diplomatic correspondent. In 1990, Broening joined the *International Herald-Tribune* in Paris as a news editor, responsible for the IHT's coverage of the Americas and Asia. He returned to Baltimore in 1996 and for ten years was a visiting scholar in history at Johns Hopkins University.

John S. Carroll, who died June 14, 2015, was a reporter for the *Sun* on the local staff and in Vietnam, the Middle East, and Washington (1966–1972). After serving as metropolitan editor of the *Philadelphia Inquirer* and editor of *The Lexington Herald-Leader*, Carroll returned to the *Sun* as editor in 1991 until 2000. He went on to become editor of the *Los Angeles Times* (2000–2005). During his time in Los Angeles, the *Times* won thirteen Pulitzer prizes. He was Knight Visiting Lecturer at Harvard's Kennedy School of Government and chairman of the News Literacy Project, which gives students critical tools for working in journalism in the digital age.

Muriel Dobbin was a reporter for the *Sun* from 1960 to 1987. A native of Scotland who first worked as a police reporter at seventeen, Dobbin was hired as a feature writer on the *Sunday Sun*. In 1963, she joined the paper's Washington bureau as its first female reporter. She covered the funeral of John F. Kennedy, and the Johnson, Nixon, and Ford White Houses. She also covered the Watergate scandal and later became the West Coast correspondent for the *Sun*, based in San Francisco. She later worked for the *U.S. News & World Report* and McClatchy Newspapers. She has written four novels.

Jerelyn Eddings was an editorial writer and columnist for the *Sun* before being named the paper's bureau chief in South Africa (1990–1994). Eddings then joined *U.S. News & World Report*, where she served as Atlanta bureau chief and chief congressional correspondent (1994–1997). Following that, she was director of the Freedom Forum's Africa media center in Johannesburg (1997–2002). She is a senior program director for the International Center for Journalists in Washington, responsible for supervising and implementing global programs, with special focus on Africa. Eddings won a Nieman Fellowship in 1984.

Will Englund worked at the *Sun* from 1977 to 2008. Along the way, he covered City Hall and education for the metro desk, did two four-year stints in Moscow with his wife, Kathy Lally (1991–1995 and 1997–2001), and spent nearly two years on an investigative series on the environmental and safety hazards of shipbreaking which won a Pulitzer Prize in 1998. He was an editorial writer and then the deputy to the editorial page editor. After another four years in Moscow for the *Washington Post*, he returned to the United States in 2014 and is now an editor on the *Post*'s foreign desk.

Dan Fesperman, author of ten novels, worked for the *Sun* and *Evening Sun* for more than twenty years, reporting from the Maryland State House, Washington, Berlin, the Balkans, the Middle East, and Afghanistan. His travels as a writer have taken him to more than thirty countries and three war zones. His novels include *Lie in the Dark*, *The Warlord's Son*, *The Arms Maker of Berlin*, and *The Letter Writer*.

Ernest B. Furgurson served as a correspondent for the *Sun* in Moscow and Vietnam, as a columnist, and was chief of the newspaper's large Washington bureau from 1975 to 1987. He covered the Cuban Missile Crisis during his Moscow stint (1961–1964), and the Vietnam War in 1965 and 1966. Furgurson is the author of four histories of the Civil War, *Chancellorsville, 1863*; *Not War but Murder: Cold Harbor, 1864*; *Ashes of Glory: Richmond at War*; and *Ashes of Glory: Washington in the Civil War*, and biographies of General William Westmoreland and Senator Jesse Helms.

Frederic B. Hill was a reporter and foreign correspondent for the *Sun*, including tours as bureau chief in London and Paris, covering Europe and southern Africa, before becoming an editorial writer for the *Evening Sun*. He was foreign affairs director for Senator Charles McC. Mathias Jr. (R., Maryland) in 1985 and 1986. He then established the State Department's Office of Special Programs. The office conducted policy planning exercises (war games) and roundtable discussions on security, political, economic, and global issues for state and key national security agencies from 1986 to 2006. He is the author of *Ships, Swindlers, and Scalded Hogs*, about the rise and fall of a mid-nineteenth-century Maine shipyard.

Tom Horton, a *Sun* reporter from 1972 to 1987 and columnist in later years, is a leading writer on environmental issues and author of several award-winning books on Chesapeake Bay and conservation issues. A former staff member of the Chesapeake Bay Foundation, Horton is the author of *Bay Country*, *An Island Out of Time*, and (with photographer David Harp) *Water's Way: Life Along the Chesapeake*. He is professor of practice at Salisbury University's Environmental Studies Department, and writes a regular column, "Chesapeake Born," for the monthly *Bay Journal*.

Arnold R. Isaacs was a reporter, foreign and Washington correspondent, and editor for the *Sun* from 1962 to 1981. Isaacs was the *Sun's* Latin America correspondent from 1966 to 1969, and after three years in Washington, he reported from Asia from 1972 to 1978. During that time, he witnessed the US withdrawal from Vietnam, the continuing wars in Vietnam and Cambodia, and the final defeat in Cambodia and South Vietnam in 1975. He also reported on the death of Mao Zedong, the beginning of China's post-Mao transformation, and many other events throughout Southeast and South Asia. Isaacs is the author of two books relating to the Vietnam War: *Without Honor: Defeat in Vietnam and Cambodia* and *Vietnam Shadows: The War, Its Ghosts, and Its Legacy*.

Kevin Kallaugher (KAL) is the international award-winning editorial cartoonist for the *Baltimore Sun* and the *Economist* magazine of London. KAL has created over 8,000 cartoons and 140 magazine covers in his thirty-seven-year career, published six collections of his work, and exhibited in a dozen countries. A former artist-in-residence at the University of Maryland Baltimore County, he has toured the United States with Second City improv comedy troupe. *The World Encyclopedia of Cartoons* said in 1999: "Commanding a masterful style, Kallaugher stands among the premier caricaturists of the century."

Kathy Lally was an editor, reporter, and foreign correspondent for the *Sun* from 1975 to 2004. She was the *Sun's* first woman assistant managing editor, supervising features. She shared an assignment as Moscow correspondent with her husband, Will Englund, from 1991 to 1995 and 1997 to 2001, and returned to Russia in 2010 for a four-year stint as the *Washington Post's* Moscow bureau chief. She is now an editor at the *Post*.

Gilbert A. Lewthwaite was a reporter and foreign correspondent for the *Sun* from 1971 until his retirement in 2001. A native of the United Kingdom, he worked for the *Daily Mail* in London, Moscow, and Rome from 1960 to

1971. He then joined the *Sun* as a reporter in Baltimore before becoming a national political, White House, economics, and defense correspondent based in Washington, and chief of the *Sun's* bureaus in Paris, London, and South Africa. He was named Journalist of the Year by the *Times-Mirror* (1996) and the following year was nominated for a Pulitzer Prize for a three-part series on slavery in Sudan.

Laura Lippman worked at the *Evening Sun* and the *Sun* from 1989 to 2001 covering social services, the state legislature, features, and Baltimore County. During that time, she wrote seven novels and has written another fourteen works of fiction since leaving the paper. A critically acclaimed best-selling author and multiple award winner, she has been called "one of our best novelists, period" by the *Washington Post*. Her work is published in more than twenty languages, and her 2003 novel *Every Secret Thing*—the first book written after leaving the *Sun*—was the basis for a 2015 feature film produced by Frances McDormand. Her most recent novels include *After I'm Gone* and *Hush Hush*, both *New York Times* best sellers. She is married to David Simon.

Steven M. Luxenberg worked at the *Sun* for eleven years, from 1974 to 1985. He served as a reporter, city editor, and then metro editor, supervising the local news staff and its coverage throughout Maryland. Since leaving the *Sun*, he has worked at the *Washington Post*. As an assistant managing editor in charge of special projects, Luxenberg oversaw the *Post's* investigative staff. Then for nine years he was editor of the *Post's* Outlook section, a Sunday section featuring commentary and opinion. His first book, *Annie's Ghosts: A Journey into a Family Secret*, a non-fiction exploration of a secret in his own family, was published in 2009. He is working on a second book, also non-fiction.

Antero Pietila, a native of Finland, worked at the *Sun* for thirty-five years as a local reporter, correspondent in South Africa and the Soviet Union, and as a member of the editorial board. He is the author of *Not in My Neighborhood: How Bigotry Shaped a Great American City*, a study of how ethnicity, race, and class changed Baltimore. With Dr. Stacy Spaulding, he coauthored an e-book, *Race Goes To War: Ollie Stewart and the Reporting of Black Correspondents in World War II*. He is working on a book about Johns Hopkins, the man, and how the Johns Hopkins medical institutions affected East Baltimore neighborhoods.

Barry Rascovar spent thirty-two years at the *Sun* focusing on government and politics. He covered City Hall, the State House, and worked in Washington as an editor and reporter. In 1979, he was named deputy editorial page editor. A recipient of the Associated Press Mark Twain Prize for editorial writing, he left the *Sun* in 2001 and continued his column in the Gazette newspapers. His opinion pieces now appear on his blog, politicalmaryland.com, and in the *Community Times* of Reisterstown. He is the author of *The Great Game of Maryland Politics* and *Marylanders of the Century*.

Robert Ruby was a reporter, foreign correspondent, and editor at the *Sun* from 1978 to 2006. He served as the paper's Paris correspondent and then Middle East correspondent. He became deputy foreign editor and then, in 2001, foreign editor, a position he held until leaving the paper. He now works for a human rights organization. He is the author of the non-fiction books *Jericho: Dreams, Ruins and Phantoms* and *The Unknown Shore*.

Scott Shane has covered national security in the Washington bureau of the *New York Times* since 2004, reporting on terrorism, the debate over torture, the use of drones for targeted killing, recruiting by the so-called Islamic State, and other topics. From 1983 to 2004, he was a reporter for the *Sun*, covering courts and medicine, serving as Moscow correspondent, and writing series of stories on guns, a drug corner, juvenile crime, the National Security Agency, and a public health project in Nepal. He is the author of *Dismantling Utopia: How Information Ended the Soviet Union*, and *Objective Troy: A Terrorist, A President, and the Rise of the Drone*, which focuses on American imam and Al Qaeda plotter Anwar al-Awlaki and his killing by drone on orders of President Obama.

David Simon, who worked on the *Sun's* metro desk from 1982 to 1995, is a Baltimore-based writer and television producer. He has published two works of narrative non-fiction, *Homicide: A Year on the Killing Streets* and *The Corner: A Year in an Inner-City Neighborhood*. The former work became the basis for the NBC drama series, *Homicide*; the latter resulted in an HBO miniseries. Simon has produced five dramatic miniseries for HBO, including *The Wire*, *Treme*, *Generation Kill*, and *Show Me a Hero*. The recipient of a MacArthur Foundation grant, Simon has received two Emmy and four Peabody awards for his television work. He lives in Baltimore with his wife, Laura Lippman, an author and fellow *Sun* veteran.

C. Fraser Smith was a reporter, editorial writer, and columnist for the *Sun* for twenty-six years (1977–2003). Smith served for many years as the *Sun's* chief political reporter in Maryland. He is the author of a biography of William Donald Schaefer, former Baltimore mayor and Maryland governor, a book on civil rights in Maryland, *Here Lies Jim Crow*, and a book on University of Maryland basketball, *Lenny, Lefty, and the Chancellor*. He is senior news analyst for radio station WYPR in Baltimore.

Joseph R. L. Sterne was editor of the editorial page of the *Sun* from 1972 to 1997, the longest tenure of any *Sun* editorial page editor. Sterne, who joined the paper in 1953, also served as the newspaper's bureau chief in Bonn and London, a roving correspondent in sub-Saharan Africa, and as a correspondent in the Washington bureau. He is the author of *Combat Correspondents: The Baltimore Sun in World War II* (2009).

Robert Timberg covered City Hall and state politics for the *Evening Sun* (1973–1981) and reported on Congress and the White House for the *Sun* (1981–1988). He later served as deputy chief of the paper's Washington bureau (1994–2005). A graduate of the US Naval Academy and veteran of the Vietnam War, Timberg was awarded a Nieman Fellowship at Harvard and the Aldo Beckman Award for coverage of the Reagan presidency. He then was editor-in-chief of *Proceedings*, the flagship magazine of the US Naval Institute. Timberg is the author of *The Nightingale's Song*, an account of the lives of his fellow Naval Academy graduates John McCain, James Webb, Robert McFarlane, John Poindexter, and Oliver North. Other books include *State of Grace: A Memoir of Twilight Time* and *Blue-Eyed Boy: A Memoir*.

Made in the USA
San Bernardino, CA
21 April 2020